nine miles

two winters of anti-road protest

Jim Hindle

Underhill Books

Published by Underhill Books, 2006

Printed and bound by CPI Antony Rowe Ltd, Eastbourne

ISBN 0-9552737-0-6
978-0-955273704

www.ninemiles.co.uk

Thanks to El and Tony for encouragement when I needed it, to Sonya and Merrick for their excellent and much needed editing, to Percy for keeping me on the right track when it counted, to Tim for lending me his computer when mine blew up, to Andy for retrieving the early chapters from the blown up computer and his general invaluable computer support, to John for the cover, to the other Jim for the website, to my parents for their patience and to Rose who saw it all coming, but never let on.

To everyone who was part of it. May your fires never grow cold.

Introduction

Too many people are forgetting.
Too many never knew in the first place.

This book tells the story of my involvement in Britain's direct action movement of the mid nineteen nineties. I began with the intention of painting as broad a picture as possible, even painting myself out of it as much as I could. But it gradually became clear that this was not only impossible, but would also be disingenuous and ultimately misleading. The protests I've described gave rise to a range of experiences as diverse as the many people they attracted. This can only ever be my account of my time but, just as there was great unity of purpose and belief among the disparity, I hope everyone who was there will find a story here that they can recognise, something that rings true with their own experience.

As for everyone else, I just hope this book is fit to tell the story of how it was to be involved in what turned out to be the height of an intense period of action, primarily against new road developments. People were throwing everything down on the line, putting in everything they had, and usually a few things they thought that had which they didn't.

I haven't gone into as much detail as I could about the issues around roads – I know that's been done in great detail in enough other places. Suffice to say that we inhaled the arguments, breathed them every moment, rolled them off to anyone willing to listen, or at least within earshot. But towards the end, this became a kind of inescapable duty, and that weariness remains. For many of us, the way we looked at the world became gradually less incisive and theory driven and more keyed in to subtler dynamics. It had a lot to do with living in the woods. The theories were still important, but secondary now to a wider world view that encompassed everything anyway. I hope my omissions in this respect come as a relief and not as a cause for exasperation.

We need to get back to the spirit that drove the times I've described. It defined the course things took, it helped lead most of us there in the first place, and it gave us the strength to put everything on the line in answering its call. The point was; everything was on the line whether we liked it or not. It still is. And when each of us had read enough reports and seen too many places lost, this was the knowledge that informed our actions.

It is my hope that this book will communicate these inspirations so that, despite many difficulties and complications, we can all meet the times ahead with a deeper sense of our responsibilities and a greater faith in our power to bring about change.

Brighton, 2006

I

Snelsmore

Expect Delays

I don't know how long I'd been asleep for, but when I woke up, I was fifty foot up in an oak. A clear, bright sun had come up through the tree line, covering everything with a fine golden light. It was already late autumn and the leaves were pretty much all down. From here, the effect of the leaves on the ground was stunning, like a vast cloth of copper running all over.

Dawn had come in under a heavy blanket of mist, which had already burned off. But steam was still rising up from the wet earth, the ground erupting with the sound of water writhing in the new warmth. I was in an oak on the edge of an area of older trees, which overlooked a small valley full of coppice; hazel and blackthorn and elder interspersed. This lower storey was visible now as a network of fine hemispheres, all lit brilliantly with the early morning sun. And because of the mild weather, the hazel had recently flowered into tubular catkins. They hung in their thousands, like a cascade of green fire. My breath poured out in white clouds.

It had been my first night in a tree and I'd slept in a hammock. Between one thing and another, I'd had the distinct feeling of being on a boat. Drifting off, I could feel the movement of the tree in the wind, a circular roll around the main mast of the trunk. And it was impossible not to be aware of the distance between my back and the forest floor. In the middle of the night, I'd been woken by the sound of creatures scuffling in the leaf litter beneath me.

I'd kept my sleeping bag half unzipped so I could stay 'clipped on'; the umbilical cow's tail of my climbing harness winding out and securing me to a separate loop of rope tied to a branch. Sleeping in your harness isn't much fun though, so the next day I pulled up two sheets of corrugated iron and wedged them against the framework of the treehouse to form a safe, windproof corner. The house was still the barest of frames; two levels of four-by-two timber lashed in a rectangle around the trunk. Two plywood boards helped form the floor, with a blue plastic tarp for the roof.

A man called Ed lived in the next tree along, connected by a rope walkway. Ed had red dreadlocks and a little methylated stove. Just after dawn, he'd start banging a tin pan with a spoon and I'd clamber over for tea and muesli. Getting up at dawn wasn't so bad as it was pushing November and the nights were getting long. But the muesli always tasted of meths.

Ed was from Swansea and in his thirties, work happy, never quite still, his restlessness and passion spilling out of him even while he talked; a rational animation considering the force of his love for the woods and wild places and his fears of an increasingly carcinogenic country. A quick and skilful carpenter, in the space of a week he'd built himself an impressive miniature chalet, nicely floorboarded with planks from old pallets and walled with tongue and groove reclaimed from a skip. I hadn't done much carpentry before and by the time Ed was putting in his finishing touches - a raised bed and a felted roof - I was still getting to grips with hitting the nails straight.

We were the only two in the trees. Beyond Ed's chalet, a third platform was under construction in an oak that formed a triangle with ours. At the moment, this consisted of little more then a few lashed beams and a long rope walkway, which was tied off above Ed's roof - a good place to sit and accessible by clambering out of a window in his back wall. The window was formed by a fork in the trunk. Sticking your head through, you looked down on a stream which cut a deep bank in the soft clay. The force of this would ebb and flow with the amount of rain and was often the last thing I heard before falling asleep.

I had arrived in the woods a few weeks earlier, but the things that had led me there had been brewing for some time. Perhaps it was when a friend introduced me to smoking pot, sat in his car at the top of the road, drum and bass and smoke billowing around me in equal densities, me trying not to green out, and then the rushes to my head as the waves of psychotropia kicked in.

It might have been the girl I met, our growing dreadlocks in the spring, simultaneously, the trancey tapes she gave me, full of different worlds. The festivals that summer might have had something to do with it all, as did the long walks to meet her in various parts of the country, where my whole world became a place of willows by riversides, rushing in the summertime, urgent with whatever wind there was. I dreamt of the places I camped; places of starlight and willows and women playing funny looking instruments in meadows in the moon.

On my very first night out by myself, walking towards Lincolnshire where my girlfriend waited on the last days of term, I slept on the edge of the woods at the top of a hill, curling quite comfortably among the roots of a spreading old oak. The sun woke me up; a beautiful, strong and quickly ascending dawn and life was suddenly full of footpaths and places I'd never set foot in which all felt like home when I got there. There seemed some trinity; her, me, these places I found myself in, where every leaf and hedge was intimate.

But another beginning had come one morning years before, when a finely presented A4 wallet had been dropped through my family's door, detailing the 'improvements' proposed for our local trunk road. There was a photo on the front of the nature reserve up the hill from us; a high point looking out to the coast and the surrounding downland. Outlined in glossy colours in the fold-out wallet, the alternatives were laid out; different routes for the same road, both cutting even further into the Downs. We lived on the edge of town and I'd always imagined that edge as a fixed one.

It wasn't just one; roads in general were beginning to do my head in. I had been increasingly breaking the gravity of the South East, catching trains and lifts around the country and spending my fair share of time in passenger seats. I was getting tired of climbing out of a car after three hours with no notion of where I was, or the distance travelled, or the places I'd passed through. I knew where we'd fetched up in the obvious sense, I knew how to read a map. But it felt like something basic and important was getting lost along the way.

Driving west one weekend, looking out of the window, spectacular scenery rolled past and it completely failed to stir or move me. Fine as it was, it had become nothing more than a backdrop and might as well have been pasted on or blue-screened. Outside our little shell, everything had become two-dimensional. The road sucked us along as though there was some vacuum to be filled, or an appointment in Cardiff with the edge of the world. A world that, sat in the passenger seat, watching myself turn slowly to cardboard, it was easy to believe was thoroughly flat.

Spending time on motorways changes the way you look at things, they stretch your senses thin, mangle them flat. As in other realms, time runs differently here. Journeys that once took a week or more are now compacted into a matter of hours. Back seat Mint Imperials describe perfect arcs in the air as they're thrown from palm to throat, though the manoeuvre is in fact more complex than that; they're also in flight at ninety miles an hour. Nobody travelling here is in any one place for more than a moment, floating in a limbo between one point and another, neither here nor there. And as much as the impact of the landscape is watered down, the impact of the road is proportionately massive on the places it passes through.

In the popular imagination, the premise that new roads led to more traffic was only beginning to surface and still wasn't taken seriously by many (unfortunately, it often still isn't). But, for those who'd been paying attention to serious research, it was old news and dismay was turning to disbelief as the roads programme rolled on unchecked. In county magazines everywhere, men in tweeds were being captured momentarily, leaning on gates, looking out on meadows, rare breeds. Compulsory Purchase Orders sat hunched on the barbed wire next to them, invisible but grinning like grim reapers, flexing white knuckles at the promises to fight.

It became impossible not to notice the numbers of new roads appearing. They were everywhere: a tarmac pandemic. Wherever you went, there were cones on the road, stretching out for miles on end, usually with no work visible inside the closed lane. A government 'cones hotline' had been set up, presumably just for a laugh. Perhaps it was all an elaborate ruse to make the roads seem more congested then they already were. The Tory road building programme was in full stride, and set to get bigger.

With every journey I took, there was more construction work, more Highways Agency billboards; one scheme or another or another one further along. Lines of empty brown swung out from the verges, tailed off behind some other fresh embankments, or pieces of hill. Convoys of flatloaded construction machinery were becoming a common sight; huge yellow earthmovers covered in clay and bulging with endowments for pounding, grabbing, cutting, scraping and covering up. They'd shake their way along the through roads, thundering from one pummelling to the next.

Every road was billed as a special case; the unique answer for that area's traffic problems, a product of hard and individually tailored thought. The fact that they all joined up, that they were in fact 'motorways by stealth', was not overly advertised. It was said to be the biggest programme of new roads since the Romans. Looked at together with the European Roads Network then being developed and which these formed a part of, perhaps that was true. Except the Romans didn't generally obliterate whole hillsides. Though, as with the Romans, 'divide and rule' was once again a common strategy. Thoughtfully providing a choice of routes would invariably reduce an area to counter campaigning and infighting nimbys. 'No road' was never a choice that they offered. As the heat rose that summer, it began to feel as though the entire country was being torn apart. It didn't occur to me, at first, that there was something I could do about it.

Hyde Park

Things moved quickly with the autumn; I'd been wading all summer into a steadily rising tide. My eyes had been opened to many things since the spring, not least the counter culture that had been flourishing, unawares to me, for years. By September, the undercurrents around had taken hold and I was itching to learn more, to see some things myself. Once I realised this, the chance came along almost immediately: a Scottish woman accosted me in Brighton's Lanes, giving me a leaflet about a new squat and telling me to get down there if I wanted to help. It had been set up as part of a campaign against a new law coming in – the Criminal Justice Bill. They'd squatted the old law courts. Now, what had become a desolate building was being turned into a hub of Brighton's alternative community.

I'd got wind of the new Bill recently, though the full magnitude of it was still sinking in. It targeted the sort of people the Tories would rather be neither seen nor heard; squatters, free party goers, travellers, gypsies, hunt sabs and road protesters. And there was no knowing where it would end; it took away the right to silence and classified illegal gatherings as any group over eleven people, besides plenty of other worrying clauses. Many people didn't see it as too much of a threat; these would be discretionary powers and they found it hard to imagine a Parliamentary government misusing them. That sort of thing simply couldn't happen here. But if you caught a glimpse of Michael Howard zealously expounding Law and Order at the party conference, spittled glee spraying up over the promenade, you'd have good reason to sweat. And for those in the black book, for those who knew how to lead the life they wanted and who cared enough to put their neck on the line for the sake of (or despite) a country going rapidly down the pan, then the Bill was seriously bad news.

For many at the Courthouse squat, it wasn't just an academic or socially conscientious concern; their way of life was directly and immediately under attack.

That was really why the CJB was raising so much opposition; you didn't need to be a bona fide traveller to feel the threat. Free parties and free festivals were a part of life for so many people; they were places where you could be yourself and where people acted out of their own motivation and free will. More importantly, they were places where you felt you belonged, where people looked out for each other, treating strangers like the family they were. It was a culture that could only have developed outside the narrows of Tory Britain.

So many others were about to let juicy portions of their own franchisement get whisked away without a thought of complaint. But to us, it was only a greater example of everything there was to fight against in the prevailing culture. And now, amid promises of locking away younger children for longer, a pale hearted, wraith faced cabinet were poised to pour water on our unsettling signs of life. A generation of lawn mowers were being stirred up again against the perils of the world beyond their hedge. To cope with the expected influx of the newly outlawed, the government had recently bought a prison ship from New York and were planning to dock it off Weymouth, presumably to reassure the pensioners on holiday.

A few weeks after my first visit to the Courthouse, there was a dub gig up at the university. To help get the point across, it got burst in on by people dressed up as riot police. Before the music started, they'd shown a film about the Battle of the Beanfield where, ten years earlier, the Wiltshire police had moved in to shatter a travelling

18

convoy. They did this by not only smashing up every vehicle they could, but also waiting outside people's doors and beating the living crap out of them when they emerged, regardless of whether they were male or female and even if they happened to be heavily pregnant. A shocked BBC correspondent sent an outraged, bewildered bulletin back to London, complete with footage of burning buses, screaming children and people getting their faces repeatedly beaten against car doors. Before it went on air, the tape vanished.

From the other side of a wide roadway, the Royal Pavilion faced the Courthouse, which had half tucked itself behind a block of old buildings. A patch of wasteground opened up the rest of the Courthouse to the road. "Seek and ye shall find..." said the flyer. I arrived by a side street and was surprised to see the onion domes of the Pavilion peering across at the doorway. An unofficial welcoming party was sat on the steps; two men with cans of beer laughing at a concrete post on the edge of the wasteground. It was about ten foot away and someone had painted it pink. "Yeah, and soon everything you look at's going to be pink. Though this is where we're starting. Slowly like, so no one notices until it's too late." They laughed in the way of conspirators who've had their fair share of acid.

It was a grand building; gothic windows bordered by narrow, marble columns, capped with sandstone slabs that stood out from the red brick. A steep pitched, gabled roof. A big place. All in all, a fine and suitably imposing Victorian public building. Being a public building meant it had wide front steps, which was just as well for the two sat there as it meant they weren't in the way too badly, so no one was telling them to move. Inside, the grandeur was of the decaying variety. Tiled floors and marble archways lurked with a shadow of institutionalism down unlit hallways. Pieces of ceramic tile were coming loose under broken, emulsified radiator pipes as wide as your arm. The building had stood empty for years and you smelt it as you walked around, leeching off the stone and plaster. But coupled with this was a frenetic activity underfoot everywhere. The place hadn't opened to the world at large yet – it was intended as a kind of forum and exhibition space – but already it was scuttling with itinerants patching the place up: plumbers shuffling down the steps to the basement and men shouting down from hatches in the ceiling, wires hanging down all over the shop.

Various people were busy along the corridors, sawing plywood and decorating, offering tools up from dodgy old step-ladders. The Scottish woman who gave me the flyer in the first place seemed to be quartermaster for a stupidly impressive tool store; marker pen outlines of saws and hammers decked the walls like collective amnesia, indicating work and many hands. There was a wild, contagious enthusiasm here and I mooched around, trying to look purposeful and like I knew what was going on, though I must have been wild eyed. Nonetheless, I was taken aback by how welcoming people were and in general, everyone seemed more than pleased to have someone keen around. There were a fair few people coming and going, so anyone who knew how not to get in the way was already doing well. And I knew at least that much.

As with any other squat, the fulcrum of its existence rested with a photocopied A4 piece of paper stuck on every entrance. Known as a 'Section Six', they stated squatter's rights, warning of the risk of prosecution if anyone entered the property by violence. Squats could only be evicted after a court summons for possession, and that took time.

The squat was due to open officially in a few days and I ended up helping by cleaning some windows. I couldn't clean windows very well but I was the only one around willing to stand twenty foot up a ladder. And the windows really were very dirty indeed. Filthy in fact. When I left that evening the Special Brew conspirators were still sat on the steps. They were laughing at the Pavilion, which had turned pink with the sunset.

In the weeks after first stumbling on the Courthouse, and as college started again, I found myself visiting the place as much as I could. In between odd jobs and chewing the cud, which had suddenly begun to take a lot of chewing, I spent time looking at the display boards and the various breeds of agit-prop that was appearing along the walls. 'Become an Urban Shaman! TM' one flyer invited, complete with a picture of a stylised aboriginal figure – all wild hair and bendy limbs, briefcase in one hand and looking at his watch. '…no more messy, impractical desires to change the world! Why bother attacking the roots of the dis-sease when you can alleviate it's symptoms?' Everything verged on the bewildering.

From time to time, with everything seeming so new, there were moments when my perspective widened out suddenly in a way that was almost overwhelming. Walking home in the evenings to the last train and the trees by the Pavilion were full of starlings; an urgent crowd in the dusk. I was being plagued by the most incredible sunsets and tonight was no exception; purple fire scouring the sky, opening it all up. Maybe I was smoking too much, but it felt as though I was beginning to see how full everything around me was. And the more I saw, the less I had the measure of it. I couldn't help but stand listening for a while, looking up at the trees.

Back in the Courthouse again and the smell of damp and sawdust got under my skin, became the smell of freedom. But there was an edge to it too, which helped to explain the mild manicness of the work going on. The squat should have been safe enough for the time being - there'd be legal manoeuvrings before any eviction. But in the political climate, it was hard to say just what was in store, or where it might have begun.

In the big room in the Courthouse someone had hung a huge banner. It took pride of place and quoted the piece by the Lutheran pastor and concentration camp survivor, Martin Niemoller:

> "First they came for the Communists, but I was
> not a Communist, so I didn't speak up;
> Then they came for the Jews, but I was not a
> Jew, so I didn't speak up;
> Then they came for the trade unionists, but I
> wasn't a trade unionist, so I didn't speak up;
> Then they came for the Catholics, but I wasn't
> a Catholic, so I didn't speak up;
> And then they came for me, and there was
> nobody left to speak for me."

Only, as I remember, they'd replaced 'Communists' with 'Travellers and Gypsies.'

Deeper into the building, past the big cold rooms and through the broad hallways, the corridors twisted round and opened up into a large central space; cheerful with bright paint and day-glo plywood boards. It had been set up as a café during the day and people sat around drinking tea, talking about getting their trucks over to Spain where it was safer, or staying here and putting up a fight. Besides the crew of characters for whom the squat was as good as home, there were all sorts of types around. Students and young hippies looking eager or uncertain, the more conventionally dressed lefties - their features bitten by the snarling dog of dissent. Of course, there'd never come a day when I myself would look similarly tired and embittered by the state of the country. Elsewhere, the quietly sympathetic or generally curious were drifting around in twos and threes, reading the literature, ready to float off at the drop of a hat.

Events were being organised for most evenings; films and talks and debates, the café tables getting shunted away and the whole hall getting crowded out. Everyone was trying to work out the best way to tackle the coming law; there was some split about how far to take things and where the best tack lay. Many were putting their faith in spreading awareness through the media, an apparent coup being a mass appearance on Kilroy. Unlikely to send housewives and the elderly out on the streets perhaps, but hopefully responsible for livening up countless daytime pot smokers. It was a fervent time. I sat listening to everyone's observations and arguments, rubbing my neck once in a while to make sure my head hadn't exploded.

The Bill had become a major issue already and there was something on the news about it most nights. At college, to general bemusement, I'd become a suspect agent provocateur, putting up anti CJB posters around the place. "Deeds not Words," read the slogan, which probably didn't endear me to many tutors. To me, though, it seemed a well chosen distillation of the way I was coming to view things, particularly in a college environment. As Gerrard Winstanley, the Seventeenth Century radical said:

> *"Yet my mind was not at rest, because nothing*
> *was acted, and thought run in me, that words*

and writings were all nothing, and must die, for
action is the life of all, and if thou does not act,
thou dost nothing."

I was frequently met with suspicion or hostility by other students, not so much for the content of the posters, but because something photocopied and put up for no other reason than my own convictions was automatically assumed to be dubious; a suspicion borne of cynicism for cynicism's sake. If any ulterior motives were immediately apparent then it probably would have been more acceptable. The reasoning seemed to be; any action that seemingly doesn't boil down to some kind of self-interest must be based on some kind of belief. And acting from some sense of right or wrong, or even belief in a cause, as many students these days will tell you, is the most dangerous and suspect activity around. Far better to pseudo philosophically step back and let the professionals take care of it.

And for many, a piece of literature handed to you in person immediately lacks any real legitimacy, possesses none of the brands of authenticity that we're trained to look for. What is only, after all, just another opinion, becomes a piece of 'propaganda'. If exactly the same argument is reproduced in a national paper or appears on the curriculum in your Contentious Studies course, then that's obviously different.

All the activity was leading up to a one big focal point – one last march in London before the CJB was due to be passed. The amount of opposition was now so widespread and so strong that it almost seemed possible that the Bill might be overturned. Unfortunately this was in fact pretty unlikely: Tony Blair was keen to show that Labour weren't soft on Law and Order and ordered his party not to oppose the Bill. For everyone else who saw (and cared about) the implications of the law, despair was compounding into defiance. Defiance wears many faces, some of which are easier to demonise than others. Those in charge of policing the coming march were very aware of this, and were no doubt seeking to ensure we'd behave exactly as they wanted.

I got myself on a coach going up from Brighton and was soon stood in the bright sun on the Embankment, underneath the nose of a sphinx. There was a strange mix of apprehension and jubilation and everyone around me was hoping the day would go off peacefully. Scots Queen of the Tools and a few other women were dressed up and doing rituals with facepaint and bindis; a kind of glamorous warpaint. But with sunglasses too, since they were from Brighton and not Glastonbury. My girlfriend had come down from Lincolnshire with some friends and I managed to run off with them before I got covered in glitter too. Besides, I had my own face paints; chalk and blackberries that I got from the top of the road, held in little metal beakers. If you mixed them in your palm with a bit of spit, they formed a paste in various shades of white and purple. I was quite proud of them but everyone else seemed strangely wary.

Stood in the crowd now, waiting for the march to get going, we were jostling shoulders with students in German army coats, middle aged men with packs of provisions, the clean cut, the odd and the multitudinous shades of the generally outlandish. Someone was dropping pocket-sized flyers from a narrow bridge above our heads, spinning down like tickertape from between the tall buildings. "Keep it Fluffy" was their main message; "Keep it fluffy, keep it right, remember this is a peaceful fight." Two terms had been coined on the protest scene in recent times:

the 'Spiky', i.e. the violent, aggressive or merely alarmingly provocative that you never generally saw until you ran into them in the papers, and 'the Fluffy' who, where bulldozers were concerned for instance, would get in the way with the best will in the world.

There was suddenly a surge of noise and expectancy in the crowd, everyone was blowing whistles and drumming, and we began to shunt off in our rusty couplings. Whitehall trudged by over the course of a few hours and we chanted and waved our placards at it until it went away entirely. By the time the rally point, Hyde Park, rolled up, the atmosphere had relaxed considerably. Pre-rolled spliffs had emerged from various tins and pockets along the way and when a cycle-powered sound system came snaking through the crowd, everyone started dancing and bouncing along after it. In the park, there was more than an hour of speeches from a large stage. After a period of attentiveness I found somewhere to sit and have a laugh with my mates, get stoned and generally act daft. Under the circumstances it seemed the only sensible thing to do; it was a sunny afternoon, the amount of people in the park and the hosts of strange characters made a spectacle worth taking in.

By the time the speakers on stage had diminished to complete obscurity, it had grown noticeable how quickly people were thinning out. It was a bit strange, because the crowd had been so huge not so long ago and it'd be a while yet until people's coaches were due to leave. Whereas before we were sat in the middle of a heaving throng, now there was just a thinly scattered crowd sat around the immediate area of the stage, with a clear view across to the edges of the park. It was all a little disquieting but it still came as a shock when a girl burst on stage, grabbed a mike and started rabbiting excitedly. At first we thought she was having a bit of a laugh or was off her head, but it was soon clear that she was, in fact, a very together character. She was pretty wound up but we soon got the drift that she was asking us to head towards Speaker's Corner where something was kicking off. No wonder it had got so thin on the ground: there'd been a riot going on.

It turned out that hundreds of people had never made it into the park, they'd been following a couple of mobile sound systems, fat ones mounted on trucks this time, which the police had stopped from entering the park. Unwilling to back down, the crowd had kept on dancing and the systems had carried on pumping out music. Police had appeared in riot gear and soon after that someone let off a CS gas canister, affecting nine policemen. This was the first time someone besides the police had used CS gas in Britain. Oddly enough, some police had been seen donning gas marks before the canister was actually thrown.

A friend later told me that all this was partly a result of an incident earlier in the day, that was started when a crowd of people started dancing around a police riot van. They were all pretty good natured, though the police obviously didn't see it that way, especially when the van started to get a bit of a rocking and people started dancing on the roof. Feeling surrounded and freaked out, the police reversed into the crowd in an effort to get away, running over a woman in the process, who was then stuck under the van with a broken arm. A fire engine was called to get her free, but was stopped by the weight of the crowd. Though it was probable that most people had no idea why the fire engine had been brought in, and might even have seen it as an attempt to break up the party, the ensuing tension set the tone for the rest of the day, though many of us had been totally unaware of any trouble brewing.

Back behind the stage, the outburst from the girl was initially met with a stunned silence. Then, after a moment or two, people started to move en masse towards Speaker's Corner. We made a move that way and ended up near some railings, still in the park and way to the back of the huge crowd that had gathered in the Corner. There was nothing obvious going on besides a general hum of human voices but, along with my friends, I was none too keen to wade into the crowd; at least we could see what was going on from here. Between us and the main park railings was a wide gravel walk. It was packed with people so we didn't really have much idea what was going on out on the road.

After a while, there was a huge cheer; the soundsystems had been let through off to our left, the other side of us from the main crowd. There was a stream, a column of people accompanying them and the noise and the cheering and the bright dancing figures was a bizarre contrast from the crowd in the Corner, simmering darkly with apprehension and indignation. There'd been some kind of confrontation before the soundsystems were let through and now this quickly re-ignited itself. The shouting and noise from the crowd swept up sharply by several pitches and the general heaving became more agitated. A troop of mounted police charged the crowd, which fragmented and scattered, people pouring away in panic. After this second charge, the mounted police brought themselves to an orderly halt and a large part of the crowd rushed back in at them. Plenty of others were still flooding out backwards, seemingly totally bewildered by the attack, wheeling round when they reached open ground to see whether they were safe. The police horses were being showered with missiles, mostly thin ply stakes from the little placards people had been carrying, but I could also see a few clods of earth flying through the air, mud flaking off in spirals. They couldn't control their horses under it and the riders themselves were shrinking back in their saddles, so they wheeled round and retreated to the police lines, a huge cheer going up at their heels.

People were coming over from the rest of the park now, even as others were trying to get away from the trouble. It might have seemed like eagerness for a fight, but there was more of a sense of people looking out for their own. It wasn't clear why the police were charging and the people here weren't the kind who'd stand by and watch while any number of their mates might be getting smeared across the park for no good reason. Legal observers and stewards were sprinting in to the thick of it.

I stood by and watched, disbelieving and on edge, ready to run. The police horses charged again, the crowd shattered and then swarmed back in, forcing another retreat. People were emerging from the back with blood pouring down their faces by this stage, being helped out by their friends. Behind them, drums were beating and someone was waving a big black anarchy flag. The air at the front of the crowd was thick with the whippy placard poles, you could hear them bouncing off the police's armour, though it could also have been the sound of police shields making contact with people's limbs and skulls. Defiance had been stirred up into a face of dark rage. I was looking into a black cloud.

Eventually, the charges and counter attacks came to an end when the police retreated into Park Lane. This seemed like a good time to try and get to our coaches and we set off down the edge of the park towards where they were meant to be waiting for us. The trouble was, police had blocked off the exits along this side of the park and may have even stopped the coaches from getting in to the pick up point.

I don't know how, but we managed to find a gap in the fence in the vicinity of some coaches. It might have been just big enough to slip through, or it may have been near a gate and much bigger than that. The police were on one side of it though and there were a load of people on the other, faces up against the fence hurling abuse and angry

29

pleas to stop at the coppers. It was dangerous out on the street and I was vaguely aware that there were scuffles going on not so far away from us, individuals caught out and getting dragged off, or getting a pummelling there and then. I didn't pay too much attention to that though, all I could see was the momentary lull and an avenue of escape to the other side of the road and the coaches.

I slipped out into the street in front of a line of police, hand in hand with my girlfriend. A sergeant in plain uniform tried to stop us and for a moment he seemed like the only sane one here. A bunch of black clad riot police were on our left, bobbing up and down and champing at the bit. To our right was a wall of snarling faces behind the railings, the nearest shouting at us for talking to a copper. At that moment, I didn't have much time for any of them either.

I was determined to get across the road and the sergeant, with plenty of other things to worry about, left us to it. We kept our heads down, scuttling over debris and around the broken lights of a traffic island. Heads swimming, we got behind the wall of coaches and it didn't take too long to find the one going back to Lincolnshire. It wasn't exactly safe here – people sprinting past from trouble nearby - but, on my own now, it seemed a shame not to see some more of what was going on.

I managed to get back into the park easily enough and found myself stood by a bonfire as it got dark. The crowds had thinned out massively but chanting was rising up from all around the eastern edges of the Park. A police helicopter started to sweep low over the park with a spot-light, maybe thirty feet from the ground. It was fixed up with a P.A. system telling us to leave the park or face the consequences. Someone by the fire was wearing an American World War II helmet, looking somehow hopefully expectant.

It was definitely time to go, so I loped off in the direction of the coaches and managed to find the bus to Brighton, making it in the end with a sprint. People who knew me were pleased to see me back, worried I'd got caught up in everything, and the coach left soon after. If I'd stayed on in the park, I would have found it hard to avoid the trouble that the night finished with. The nearest tube stations had been closed and most roads out of the area had been blocked by lines of riot police. Many of those remaining in the park ended up bolting through a gap in the tightening police lines, running up Oxford Street against oncoming traffic. Making the bus involved more luck than I realised at the time.

Back in college and, besides a flurry of initial curiosity and concern, very little seemed to have changed. The newspaper reports seemed to have been written by people who weren't there, which helped back up the general easy cynicism. Almost as much as the riot itself, I was shaken by the media coverage and how little resemblance it bore to what I saw during the day. To read the reports, you'd think everyone who'd come on the march were a mob just out for a fight with the cops. There was very little about the Bill we'd been opposing, the coverage just seemed to back up the need to legislate against such blatant trouble makers. Riots are very useful things, if you want to discredit a movement, though pitched battles have their purposes too, if you have a particular aim in mind, like blockading a target, or surrounding a delegation. There was no such objective at Hyde Park though, and the scenes that had developed, where many people had perceived they were being surrounded by the police, served the government very well, whether or not they'd been orchestrated.

My doubts about the authenticity of press coverage had been growing recently, but now it suddenly felt as though a slab of old meat had fallen clean away, leaving the grim white truth glaring back at me.

At home my brothers settled down to their routine of gas fire, Neighbours and wrestling the dog. The sun was slipping through the branches of a copper beech right outside the window, hurrying towards another glamorous extinction. Up on the hill and out on a ridge past the woods, I sat on a stile and weighed things up. I couldn't see myself carrying on with college, the way things were going, couldn't see myself studying with so much going on in the country. But what, exactly, should I do instead? Where was the place I belonged in all this? The sun had gone down, the October wind was getting up and everything was fading to brown and grey. A few feet to my right, backdropped by the vanishing Weald, a wooden path sign was coming loose in its post. It rocked back and forth in the wind, no longer sure of itself, or the way ahead.

Penwood

"Just go down to Penwood, you'll see the people there, you can't miss it." It was a Saturday night and I'd ended up at some kind of gig at the Courthouse. Everyone was sat on the floor, crowded into one of the big rooms at the front. There was a bit of a wait before the act started and I'd got talking to a traveller girl behind me with thick black dreads. We were having a smoke; Dylan the Rabbit took prominence on a banner behind the girl's head, toking on a big carrot. She'd just come down from Newbury with her dogs and a picture of harmonious woodland life was taking root behind my eyes. Above Dylan's ears, stenciled in big letters, hung the question; "What is the Way?"

When the act started I realised I'd seen it before at a festival; it was a piece of moralistic pyschedelic theatre - one of us in that room had already sold out, apparently - but was a satisfyingly bizarre show so I was glad to see it again. Listening to the girl, it sounded as though the wood was already carpeted with protesters. My thoughts of joining the protests were becoming steadily more serious. The answer to everything sat at the feet of the rabbit; "Just Go."

Arriving in Penwood, it was clear at once that things weren't going to be as easy as I'd hoped. I'd taken a train up from my hometown, chatting to a train guard as we set off under the promising blue of an autumnal morning. I had an old army rucksack, jeans that I'd split to show the red and white striped trousers underneath and an old para camouflage smock on long term loan from my dad, who wasn't one to stand in the way when I clearly felt so strongly about something.

I had broken the news to my mum as we sat watching a documentary about traveller sites. "I hope you don't go off and do something like that," she mentioned, not really aware of the way things were going. It seemed a natural point to set her straight. As the news sunk in, we watched a man covered in oil slide under his truck in a sea of thick mud.

Penwood was three miles or so south of Newbury town centre, a railway embankment forming the wood's northern boundary, a brick tunnel forming the entrance itself. The tunnel sat right in the middle of the northern edge, so as soon as I was through it, I was already in the thick of things. It wasn't an overly sunny day and the pines cast a heavy shade. The road rolled itself out ahead of me, straight as you like, broken up along the way by bands of pale light. I could see down it for maybe half a mile before it lost itself in shadows and mist. Newbury's a low-lying area, sitting between the Lambourn Downs and the North Downs and the countryside here is covered with rivers and streams. The autumn rains had been around for a while already and the mists needed little provocation to make an appearance. I had no idea whereabouts in the woods the camp was. Great Penwood was over three miles square.

It was around noon and I was confident I'd find the camp before it got dark. There was a carpark right by the tunnel, though besides a couple of dog haired estates, there was no sign of anyone. I climbed over the forestry pine fence and stuck my rucksack out of sight under a rhododendron bush, ominously treading in some dog shit as I did so. The ground was a thick clay and orangely acidic with all the pines. There was enough deciduous foliage to add a thickening layer of blackening leaves to the brew underground. The ground was sopping and stuck to me without enticement. Loving mud.

That afternoon, roaming the forestry tracks that swung round disorientatingly, slightly thrown by my pooey boot, I succeeded in discovering a whole village in the middle of the wood – Penwood Village. It didn't look like a particularly friendly place, council houses founded on scowls, so I didn't hang around. Later, I saw some surveyors with theodolytes at a road junction but had no idea whether they had anything to do with the road so I sloped off again, thinking I'd mention it at the camp when I arrived. I passed one or two dog walkers, probably the drivers of the dog wagons, though didn't ask them for directions, thinking it'd be unlikely they'd be able to help. For all I knew, the camp might have been a highly clandestine set up and I was beginning to feel a little conspicuous wandering around like this, as if I was blowing their cover.

The whole afternoon, I didn't find a trace of any hippies or any camp. Several hours after arriving, I was sat on a storm felled trunk and had only just begun to get the most tenuous of bearings. The sky had cleared and I was now, just about, outside the boundary of the woods. The fallen tree was a wide oak and formed a jetty out over a bed of brambles from the trees at the edge of a road. I'd walked out to the start of the crown and was sat letting my feet dry in the sun, socks steaming on a branch. It was a pleasant view; the crown of the tree hung out over a meadow, long grass grown white, the sun doing tricks in the clouds with oranges and pinks after some rain. But it took an effort to dispel the feeling of uncertainty taking hold. I tried to side step it, and pretended not to notice when it stopped and sat down by my side.

It was ridiculous sitting here. Coming up here, even walking up on this oak was a fine little stunt, but where was it taking me? It was a bridge that led nowhere, besides the crown of a tree and a view I couldn't touch. The sky, the water in the air everywhere, the bark under my feet and the autumnal trees were all beautiful and I knew that this was all part of why I was here. But I felt suddenly very alone, that this new road was taking me beyond everyone I'd known. There were a couple of houses backing on to a corner of the meadow where people would be getting back from work and school around now. The houses were suddenly different to look at; I wasn't out here on a walk or some camping trip, this was now where I lived, with the sky and the wet. I scrawled the start of a letter to my family. I ought to have been worrying about my boots, which were already letting in water.

I managed to find my way back to the car park as the dark began to settle in. There was a camper van on the other side of the road with a few shadowy figures huddled by the side door. It was hard not to be shadowy - the night falling unusually quickly under these trees. But this was the most promising thing that'd happened all day and I sidled up to the van. After a little wariness as I emerged from the halflight, it turned out these people were involved with the protest. They'd been out looking for trees marked for felling. Their tactic was to spread confusion into the heart of the chainsaw crew by disguising the original mark with a piece of cloth or ribbon and... marking all the trees around it for felling too. Terrifying.

They were friendly enough though and, as I shared a spliff with them, they told me how Penwood was once part of the New Forest and one of the King's hunting grounds. There were stories of Norman ghosts roaming around here and, casting my eyes around in the gathering gloom, it was easy to see why. Two figures came crunching out of the dark but turned out to be reassuringly mortal; the others had been waiting for them to get back from some recce or other.

The tunnel of the long straight road was the most luminous thing now and stood to its side, underneath the main canopy, we were sinking into pitch blackness. A wind was picking up along the road and I wasn't too upset when everyone began to move. They were a little confused by my questions about the camp, though someone then mentioned some kind of site on one edge of the woods and I was soon I getting a lift in an auxiliary car.

Whatever sense of local geography I'd managed to build up was completely obliterated by the ensuing journey. We had to take a tortuous route around the whole area and down a dual carriageway, trees torpedoing past in another rainstorm. The man who was kindly giving me the lift didn't hold an optimistic view about things. They'll never stop the road he told me, I won't stop the road, they're really just wasting their time. It was black and wet outside and the windscreen wipers looked despondent in the face of the downpour. I was tired and hungry, and now also fuzzy headed with the spliff and did not attempt to lighten his mood. Before being dropped off, I heard him spell out his vision for the future of the world and of humankind. Unsurprisingly, it was as bleak as it was emphatic.

The rain was stopping as I got out and, under the open sky again, there was still enough light to get my bearings. I was stood on a concrete drive opening out onto a massive hard standing. The woods were silhouetted against the sky ahead of me and to the left was a swathe of felled pine in the process of being sorted and stacked. I could just make out the outlines of a caravan and a truck, and started towards them, beginning to wish I'd just pitched my tent near the car park. I'd have been settling in to my sleeping bag and book with a full belly by now, though in a way I was glad not to be spending the night alone in these woods. Smoke was rising up from a chimney stack in the caravan roof and dogs started bloodcurdling as I got near, two or three trotting to bark and snarl close up.

Once past the dogs, I knocked on the caravan door and after a while a gruff voice called out,
"Who is it?" Feeling like an idiot and not knowing what else to say, I asked if this was the Newbury Bypass protest. The door swung open on a broken hinge and a man in his forties with a flat cap and stubbly beard stared blankly back at me. He got my measure pretty quickly and his face livened up, crumpling into a gappy grin.
"Naaah, this isn't it boy, but come in and have some cider anyway. You don't want to be out in this rain." He introduced himself as Johny Star, a name quickly explained when he took off his cap. On his forehead, tattoed in blue ink a bit bigger than a fifty pence piece, sat a fine Star of David. Inside, heaped round a two bar gas bottle fire, we shared cheap chemical cider while he told me stories about begging and lucky breaks. Most seemed to involve his two whippets, who were now making themselves useful as part of the sofa, squirming around under our backs. A fair amount of the stories also involved altruistic rich men, bags of chips, local ladies and the county magistrates, some of which he was on first name terms with.

Later that evening, we were sat smoking and drinking in the back of the neighbouring truck. I was sat on the floor - near the door and opposite a burner - my back propped against the wall. At the other end from the door, on the Luton above the cab, were a couple sat on a bed; a swarthy bloke in his thirties who seemed benign though he didn't say much, and a woman in leather trousers with close cropped hair, tugging on her lip ring with her teeth. She was recovering from a recent ordeal where she got discharged from Basingstoke nick in the middle of the night and, with no money, started to walk back. It was a long way and she ended up crashing out in a hayrick sometime before dawn. She said she'd done her feet in. I didn't ask why she was in Basingstoke nick in the first place but Johny Star told her she was a bad girl and she laughed. Johny Star was missing some teeth. Swarthy bloke got the burner going and soon it was warm enough to keep the back open. "There she is..." said the woman; a full moon was rising low over the treeline, and we all turned our heads in appreciation.

I thought of the last full moon; I'd just started back at college and everyone in art class was acting a bit loopy. That evening I climbed up the hill to the fringe of the woods. The trees were oldest and thickest here, marked out deep in blue from the bright silver grass; a moonbath. I waded around in it feeling larger than life before surrendering to the urge to stand on my head. Harvest moon. The woman said it was a Hunter's Moon now. Black bits of cloud were haring after each other across the sky and she looked past them and in at us, beautiful and hungry, piercing us with strange calls and questions. It was a welcome sight - the only familiar face here. Everything had stood itself on its head since the last full moon and I wondered where I'd be by the time the next one rolled up. None of these people had heard of the camp.

I was woken early by Johny Star clambering over my head. He was keen to get going for an honest day's begging and was busy clearing his lungs and rooting through stuff under a tarp outside. Two lads from Somerset had turned up during the night and I'd been sharing the outer room with one of them, his mate opting for the main room with the carpet and the dogs. It was cold in the outer room, caravan panels disintegrating on all sides. It hadn't been light long and the door by my head was hanging open from its one good hinge. There was frost on the ground and I didn't feel too good from the cheap cider.

Reassuringly, the lads had come up for the protest too, though like me they'd got no idea where the camp was. They'd got the details of a campaign office though and we set off to find it in their beaten up Escort. They weren't much older than me and their hair was clipped short enough to make me wonder if they weren't squaddies on leave. They had a gauntness to them too which was somehow reminiscent of the potato famine. They told me they had to get back to their flat in a few days because someone else was looking after their dog, which I imagined to be large and black. They were friendly and earnest and easy to get on with.

We found the office on a quiet street of redbrick Victorian terraces, all with strange and dandy corrugated iron porches that I've never seen the like of before or since. A green truck was parked up across the street as a kind of announcement. It was a converted Green Goddess army fire engine and was known, as you'd expect, as 'The Green Goddess'. It was all somehow satisfying and I'd run into her intermittently for here on in, parked up in side streets, her occupants brewing up tea and wearing medieval green jackets. It was a predictable thing to believe, but I couldn't escape the strange feeling that she'd somehow been waiting for me.

Inside the office, the mood was disjointed; people were sat on a sofa bed in the living room, smoking, dogs running round at their feet. It wasn't a far cry from the world of Johny Star. Emanating from upstairs was a simultaneous aura of organisation and hostility to the downstairs world. I sat around and chatted for a while, the Somerset lads having already left to look at some stuff they saw in a skip on the way here. They didn't appear too interested in anything going on at the office and their motives were beginning to seem slightly ulterior. I think they said something about scrap metal, but there didn't seem much point in trying to pin them down.

I took a seat on a crumpling armchair while I got to know the characters around me a bit more. A man in his thirties was sat on the bed, and seemed to be at the dense centre of the living room's gravity. His hair was shaved so that only a few rat tail dreads were left at the back and he seemed to find a lot to laugh about, as though he was nursing his own private joke. Though he was gregarious enough, his grin was a bit sharp and there was something weird about his eyes.

Someone saw the tin whistle sticking out of my jacket and started haranging me to play a tune. Once it'd been said, the sofa crew clearly wouldn't be happy until I'd played them something. Halfway through a Scots reel, a black haired man came down from the office and told me that my whistle playing sounded very nice but could I please stop it because they were trying to use the phone. He talked to me with a forceful quietness in a foreign accent that was impossible to place. It was the first time someone from upstairs seemed to notice I was there.

There were as many dogs as people. Seemingly, there were now only two types of dogs in the world; black and sleek ones like juvenile Dobermans and ragged-furred, wild-eyed mongrels. A notice next to my head proclaimed;

IS YOUR DOG BORED?
SHITTING ON PEOPLE'S FLOORS?
WHY NOT GO AND LIVE IN THE WOODS?
YOUR DOG WILL BE HAPPIER TOO.

I couldn't see much point in my hanging around here; the office bods seemed to need peace and quiet more than help, and I didn't want to contribute further to the general malaise. I got myself a bit of watery soup from the cold kitchen and, just as I was thinking about walking back to the woods, the Somerset lads turned up and I chipped off again in their Escort. It would have made sense to ask someone from upstairs as to the camps whereabouts but I'd already contented myself with a seemingly adequate description from someone on the sofa. It was getting dark when we arrived back on site, so the search would have to wait until morning.

Johny Star wanted a bit of a quieter night tonight so the lads parked their car just inside the tree line and crashed out on a mattress crammed into the back. Though it'd been a wet day, and the skies didn't look favourable, I decided to try out my rubberised army poncho as a groundsheet. The lads reckoned I was being a bit ambitious here, but it looked like enough of squash in their car as it was. With the bottom of my sleeping bag in a binliner, I slipped into a dark sleep of wet leaf mould, stormy trees and, soon enough, heavy rain. I wrapped myself in the poncho and vowed not to do it again.

Dawn found me damp but generally dry, if a little under rested. My boots hadn't come through the night so well; they'd been soaked. They were Doc Martens; I was quite proud of them and had decorated them with various pictograms, but they were obviously not made for being out in all weathers, and my feet had been wet for a while now.

As I rolled my stuff up, the lads - who were parked about twenty feet away and already up and about - got a visit from a stout looking, middle-aged man in a green waistcoat and a tweed hat. In a very short space of time, the man was shouting at them, amazed at their impertinence, and making it very clear that they'd best be leaving. The lads didn't seem particularly fazed by this, which infuriated the tweed man further. After a final outburst of indignant authority, he stormed back into the woods, apparently without noticing me.

It was enough for the lads to decide to make an early move back home. They couldn't be bothered with any more hassle, and it wasn't as though anything was happening with the campaign that was worth sticking around for. I grabbed the rest of my stuff from under Johny Star's caravan and walked into the woods to see if I couldn't find the camp again.

I wasn't far in, walking along the green belt of a forestry track when I ran into the tweed man. There was a sudden moment of mutual disbelieve and dismay. He stopped short in stunned silence and his face went a darker shade of red. After a second or two, he erupted,
"There's another one! I don't believe it! Don't you people understand this is private property?" I looked at him blankly as he stormed past, swearing, to make sure the lads were moving off. A little further on, I waded into a cutting full of orange bracken, bright in the sun that was now showing its face. A safe distance in, I sat down for a rest and a think about this first encounter of hostility. I was a bit surprised about the strength of his reaction; didn't he know they were about to build a road here? Wasn't he a bit more concerned about that? It wasn't as though this was someone's back garden. It was a bit bloody big if it was.

When it looked like he wasn't coming back this way, I found a good spot to pitch my tent, keeping an ear out at the same time. After the experience of the first day, I didn't want to be setting it up in the dark. Just in case I *didn't* find the camp, that was. When I was done, I made sure the tent wasn't visible from the track, propping a pile of bracken against it to be on the safe side. I climbed inside to celebrate with a nap, which was well needed after the night in the rain.

After waking up, I rummaged around in my rucksack for a late breakfast. Besides a Pot Noodle I had stashed, there was cheese and stale bread; if you swigged a bit of water while you chewed it, it was pretty good. Things appeared to be looking up; it was a beautiful spot, the sky was blue and, for the moment, I didn't have anyone too interesting to contend with.

Climbing the tree lined embankment that rose at the other end of the cutting, I looked back towards my tent, distinguished only by a mound of bracken. Beyond this mass of rusting foliage, broken by the grey stumps of trees, was the green belt of the grass on the track. Beyond that and another cut that was still full of timber, was a swathe of more trees, blue in the damp air and the distance. The air was full of birds darting out from the dense flanks of pine to either side, gliding across the gap or arching down to hop among the crumbling pine stubs. There was no noise besides the small birds and a pheasant far away to the south. I could feel a stillness settling in.

A footpath ran along the embankment and I stormed along it, massively confident again. Deciduous trees lined the path to either side, mad with the height of autumn; small yellow birch leaves drifting down transparently, red field maple and every colour in between. This was more like it. The embankment path provided a highway along the northern end of the wood. Free from the winding machinery tracks, I began to get my bearings, though everything was trees.

I'd been wandering through the woods for several hours when I saw an indistinct grey blur off to my right. I'd left and then returned to the embankment, and could now just make out the weird, amorphous shape through the leafless lower branches of the pines below. I walked down and found it was a tarp, strung up above a firepit, which was grey and empty. Some kind of shelter was lurking nearby. As I squatted down next to the ashes, a dreadlocked woman appeared out of nowhere in a barbour jacket, holding a frying pan. She was faintly surprised by the appearance of a total stranger at her fire, but not overly troubled. "Dr Livingstone I presume" she said, lighting the fire with a series of quick movements. "Feeling hungry?" She fried me an egg and offered me some sliced bread. I thought it was breakfast, but then I realised it was getting dark.

This still wasn't the camp, more of a private settlement. I'd only just finished my egg butty when a couple of other girls turned up and I was getting dragged off to something in town. A public meeting had been organised about the road. It was in a school on the southern edge of town, so we'd not got as far to walk as we might have had. As we emerged from the firepit, I realised it wasn't dark at all, just the tarp casting it's shadow. Combined with the density of the pines, living there must have been like being in a perpetual soup of twilight.

We came to the bridge I arrived in the woods under and slipped down to it by a muddy path. Watching the day-glo beads of the girl infront, swinging bright in a very real twilight now, it occurred to me that all of us had dreads. It was a handy, instant sign that you were on a kind of similar level; it was probably why barbour coat woman wasn't too phased to find me sitting in her kitchen. All these women had also shaved the sides of their heads, which must have made me the hippy. The dreads I'd started growing in the spring were just knitting together properly now. I was still getting used to the narrow eyed, distrusting looks in the high streets.

Down in the tunnel under the bridge, someone had painted 'NO ROAD' in big letters on the red bricks. The tunnel was about twenty feet long and there was no pavement. One of the girls told me how a mate of hers was walking through here at night and almost got run down by local lads in a pickup truck, deliberately driving up close to the side. She had had to sprint to get out and off the road. 'Hippy baiting' was already offering an alternative field sport for the local rednecks.

We walked out to shaggy fields and a wet sky. It was dark by the time we got to the school and the stars had come out. Nobody tried to run us over.

Cadbury Castle

Back at the office, there was one ray of hope; a geezer called Len who was up for finding the camp in Penwood. He had short, brownish dreads and red combats and seemed a wandering soul, like drifting was an art form and he was well on the way to being a master already. After walking most of the day, we sat down by a lakeside, where I took the chance to start drying my socks, hanging them from a young tree as the sun cast bright sparks from the water. Though the grass around us had been mown quite recently, we didn't think much about it until two middle aged men in green body-warmers appeared from behind a bush and informed us, in disbelieving tones, we were on a private estate. We beat a semi-dignified retreat, spouting off about the injustice of laws of trespass, laying down denouncements like covering fire. Didn't the land belong to each and every one of us, if it belonged to anyone at all?

As it grew dark, we found a strange, dome shaped shelter of canvas and wood, lurking in the pines just off the track, only just visible, as though it didn't want to be discovered. We reasoned it must belong to someone on the protest, and that they were unlikely to mind our sleeping there for the night. All the same, it was hard to feel totally welcome, and we wondered just who might be coming home at anytime. The shelter itself felt somehow alive in a way I couldn't quite place but which made me a little uneasy.

Having run out of water and being less than totally sorted, we did separate missions to a nearby spring we'd found earlier. With all the pines, it was pitch black, black in a way I'd never experienced before. Even the water was black. I got lost on the way back, getting snagged in invisible branches as I wandered off the path, sure the shelter was somewhere dead ahead. When I finally found it, we crashed out early, not wanting to burn too many candles. This was a first taste of the long hours of dark of the winter.

The next day we found a nature reserve within the woods, where conifers gave way to a lake bounded on all sides with deciduous riots of autumn. The trees rose up, rich limbed, the intensity of the colours like bright jewels in a cave. We found a small bridge over a weir, the roaring of the water and the beauty of the scene removing all thought as we stood there, so it didn't seem to matter that we hadn't found the camp, or were hungry, or had no way of knowing what waited ahead.

But by the next morning we were feeling a little wild eyed from wandering in a woodland that only seemed to get bigger the more time you spent there. We made our way out to the nearest main road, where there was a garage that sold milk and chocolate and rubbery pasties. Len mentioned a party on a hillfort in the West Country and suddenly my horizons opened up; I didn't need to sign on till next week and, for the first time in my life, there was nothing to stop me going wherever I wanted.

We set off from the office a day or two later, walking up to the nearest junction of the M4, a few miles north of town. It was my first time hitching and despite the hardship of the walk up the main road and a steady developing rain, it was no bad experience. In two easy lifts in the dark, both from affable couples, we'd made it down the rest of the M4 and down the M5 as far as our turning, where we camped on a hill half a mile from the road.

We were woken at dawn by a herd of rough tongued cows trying to eat my tent. Emerging, we could see across the Bristol Channel, past plains and hills of sunwashed fields to half shrouded mountains and the promise of more

48

rain. Len fended the cows off as I packed up the tent, which had leaked in the night, leaving our hips icy and wet. It was enough for Len and he headed back down to the junction, to catch up with friends further south.

I spent the rest of the day in the rain, half walking, half hitching along semi deserted Somerset roads, snaking black tarmaced under a sky like a duvet. My army poncho stopped just above my knees; everything below was soon a dripping testament to the realities of Autumn.

In Glastonbury I climbed the Tor where the rain eased away but the clouds gave no view. Retreating down the hill, I drank tea in a mock indoor village, scribbling letters on dampening paper as a stage managed stream ran through the middle of the floor. Somehow the stream was still mesmerising, though perhaps it was partly the effect of a day in the rain. In a stall, a postcard showed a girl with pink dreadlocks playing a flute infront of a yellow coated security guard. Outside, travellers had parked their van in a lane and were bottling spring water as it emerged from a bank. They were barefoot with copper and cloth fixed around their ankles and were smiling at the serenity that seemed to permeate everything here. Across the way, people had left offerings where more water ran down a wall of bare stone; necklaces and coins and dreadlocks tied to a tree intermingled in an atmosphere of charged reverence. There was a pleasant, gentle buzzing in my head, as though the stream was running through there too.

Walking through the outskirts of town as it grew dark, a man with dreads and a waistcoat called a dog into a house as I passed by. The lights in the windows were welcoming and I could see and smell a fire on the go. Out here though the rain was creeping back in and I felt the old feeling of my life being outside of walls now, removed from all everyday measures of homeliness. I slept the other side of a dry-stone wall a few miles down the road. The tent leaked again and one uneaten custard cream dissolved in the course of the night, making everything smell skanky.

I arrived at the hill late the next day, the road sloping up in a long, straight line from the nearest village, a woman announcing my proximity as she appeared behind me on a pannier laden bike. Within minutes a van stopped and we piled in the back for a lift the rest of the way.

The party was a celebration of Hallowe'en; *Samhain*, the death of the old year and the start of the new. It was being 'hosted' by the people who'd lived on Twyford Down several years before and who'd seen in the wave of anti-road campaigns that were still growing ever larger. By this time, they were touring the West Country in a convoy of handcarts and horse wagons, plotting a course from one hillfort to another.

Our present towns and villages were for the most part laid down by the Saxon settlers, who liked their lowland farms. A fondness for life on the high hills shows a kinship with an older spirit.

It felt like a homecoming in many ways, arriving at Cadbury. The summit of the hill was uncannily flat, as though someone had sliced the top clean off. It looked deserted when we first got up there, but in a dip near the ramparts we found the camp. Suitably enough, the clouds parted at the same moment to show a rain washed dusk; pink and orange and beautiful.

Figures stood on the ramparts, outlined in their wrappings of blankets and ponchos. Behind them, the Somerset Levels rolled away into the damp clouds, rich with water and the hedges and the new light. A sloping bank rose up from the dip by the ramparts and a long, tunnel-like shelter had been put up in its lee, smoke chugging out from a flue. Small kids were playing around a firepit near the doorway and a tapering banner was catching the wind; a red dragon on white cloth.

There was a big fire later; people playing pipes and mandolins with loads of cider and drumming. The stars had come out. It was an amazing night. I eventually crawled into the shelter as the sky was growing pale with the dawn, and managed to find a clear space amongst the dark shapes already fast asleep. As I lay my head down, the rain came on up again, throwing itself against the tarp.

The next day, I met three people who would change everything. I'd been squatting with some others around the firepit on top of the ridge, watching them fry chapattis - a kind of dough mixture - and looking at the Levels. After chatting a while, I wandered down to look in the shelter, and there they were, sat around the burner. Like me, they'd got soaked during their journey and were taking the chance to dry out their stuff.

The shelter, like the one in Penwood, consisted of tarps thrown over a curving frame of bent hazel poles - a 'bender.' These had been used in certain parts of Scotland once, and also been popular with some of the British based gypsies. They were pretty simple to put together, making them good for travelling with - provided you had something to shift the poles with.

This one had a ridgepole - a fat piece of wood forming a kind of spine along the ceiling. Holes had been drilled along the sides and the ends of the poles had been trimmed down to slot into them. It made for a stronger design; the poles could be shorter and you didn't need so many.

The flue from the burner snaked around the ceiling before finding a means of escape. Not only did this keep more heat in the whole bender, but it was also really good for drying things near. The poles around and above the three were hung thick with steaming clothing. A second door tarp had been left open and I could see a few people squatting round the fire up on the ridge. The watery sunlight fell in through the opening, lighting up the steam from all the damp clothes.

The youngest; a girl no older than me, was sat cross legged, mending something with a needle and thread. Long, thick, black dreadlocks hung down over a poncho of white and brown wool. This was Tami. Two older men sat on her left; Badger with ginger brown hair and the dark haired Moonflower.

Moonflower might have been Finnish, but we never found out for certain, and could as well have been from the Mediterranean or the Middle East. It was truer to say that he inhabited a country of his own, maintaining the borders with a relentless and habitual affection, or realization of mystery. Sat by the burner he was down to a plain black t-shirt and leggings. But there were layers and layers of wool and wraps to go back on before he'd step out in the cold.

I knew them all from the campaign office in Newbury - it'd been Moonflower who'd asked me to stop playing the whistle that time - though this was the first time we actually got talking properly. And the first time, I thought, that I was recognized as someone who might be any use. This was no small thing, because it was nearly the end of half term, and if things hadn't started taking a more promising shape soon, I might have laughed the whole thing off and gone back to college and my folks.

It was ironic, but somehow fitting, that I'd had to travel all this way to properly meet the people I'd been wanting to talk to all along. The three were buzzing with a plan to abandon the office and set up a new camp in some oak woods north of town. Moonflower waxed lyrical;
"It's a misty, boggy place," moon saucered, dark eyes implored me to understand his description,

"streams come out of nowhere and disappear back into nowhere." His hands curved and folded in on themselves for further effect.

He'd a very strange lilt to his voice, had Moonflower. He'd spent time all over Europe and had cultivated a theatrical blend of Scandinavian shaman, Irish storyteller and Hellenic priest. But the mystery was; it was hard not to warm to him. These were no idle postures, and he was more than faintly aware of their apparent ridiculousness. The deepest impression he gave was of a man trying to communicate the most wonderful, subtlest joke. Somebody passed me a pipe and I felt like laughing.

We came down off the hill with the last of the sun. There were plenty of warm farewells for the others, though I was just happy to be there in the first place. And the prospect of the new camp felt like a firm foothold in the whole plan.

The previous evening, one of the first people I'd got talking to was a man with matted black hair and fingernails like talons. He played two recorders at once and laughed like he could easily slit your throat in your sleep. I liked him though and we'd chatted for a long while about walking places. It was still warm in the sun and we were sat with our back to the stone wall of the ramparts, turf curving over the top, socks and blankets laid out to dry all around us. Now, as we left, he shouted after us "stop that road and then come back and join us!" and broke into another murderous cackle. I was meeting more and more people who were larger than life, but life had got larger than they were.

Founding

At the bottom of the hill that Cadbury Castle sat on, the footpath levelled out as it approached a main road. Badger pointed out a tree on our left and we all stopped to look. I was keen to get going, not sharing the other's confidence of making it back to Newbury in a few easy hitches. The others were clearly in no hurry and I had no choice but to stand there with them in what I thought was probably a slightly overblown gesture of appreciation.

Over the fence, stood on it's own in a green meadow, a young birch was throwing itself out to the sky. It's leaves were lit from behind by the autumnal evening sun and were making a graceful descent to the grass, one touching down lightly every other moment in the windless air, like a silent fountain of gold. I'd never seen a tree so clearly before. It was like waking up to women, or discovering drugs. I was suddenly grateful to have been stopped like this and when we carried on down to the road, it seemed stupid to worry about the journey.

I hitched with Moonflower. Despite his being wrapped in a black shawl against the cold, we weren't kept waiting long. When we got back, we were hungry. Someone offered me some flapjack that was lurking on a worktop in the kitchen. It wasn't until my second or third slice that somebody mentioned, or I simply realised, that the currants weren't currants at all. They were mushrooms.

My first taste of magic mushrooms had come the week before, during a party at the office. The Criminal Justice Bill had just become law and people wanted to meet the occasion with the right spirit. Early in the evening someone came out with,

"When freedom is outlawed, only outlaws will be free."

The mushrooms and their brewing up and dishing out had taken pride of place. People talked of their potency by the hundreds. Of all the experiences I was due to taste, this was to prove the wildest, and the most hazardous.

We drank it by the cupful in tea mugs and old glass jars, inhaling the sour, brown brothiness of it first, the spongy heads and stringy stems dancing against our lips. A man known as Wild Ben had appeared about the same time as me from a protest in London. He wore a ragged assortment of charity shop cast offs beneath a shaggy fur trimmed coat; all carried off with a natural shamanic flair. He was clearly living on the extremes of existence and shrieked his ecstasy to the empty kitchen. Which should have been a warning to us all.

I spent most of the trip gazing into the fire – it was the come down I remember more clearly, everyone gathering together to fend off our mutual demons of paranoia and exposed nerves.

We'd picked the mushrooms a few days before, out in a field by Wash Common near the middle of the route. We'd been looking for contractors at work and were on a general wander south of the railway line when we came across the field. Maybe someone who was on the lookout for 'shrooms did an initial recce, but soon the whole half dozen of us were swooping across the rounded slope of the field, hats in hands, hunting down in the damp grass for sporadic outcrops.

It was a good harvest; the weather having been so wet, conditions were perfect. The sun had come out now though and the domed outline of Beacon Hill hung over us from the south, like a benign guardian, a silent and genial patriarch. I wasn't too bothered about the mushrooms but it was good to join in with everyone else, who were clearly over the moon scrabbling around on their hands and knees. It was the first time since arriving in Newbury that I felt a strong kinship with the people around me. The warmth of it took me by surprise and left me smiling. If this was a sign of things to come, then I was definitely on the right road.

Back in the kitchen now, and having polished off nearly half the baking tray, a man I'd met called Gordon offered to lead me away from the office – which would soon descend into it's evening bedlam – and out to the tranquillity of a camp in the woods.

Gordon was a public schoolboy-done-good, having run away to France several years back. What must have once been a Byron-esque or teenage indie mop had dreaded up nicely now, thick and black, and he looked somehow Trojan, with a vaguely aristocratic nose, like his father had been fighting roads before him and his father's father further down the line. On the way out of town he regaled me with stories of his life as a distinguished down and out on the streets of French cities. Thanks to his time in the squats there, he was one of the best cooks around. In every stew he made, he included a whole onion, with just the very middle hollowed out. The rest was left to lurk with all the malice of a well stewed sea mine. It was meant to be the best bit, but the rest of us never quite saw it like that.

When we finally reached the woods, the mushrooms had really begun to kick in. I followed the shaded figure of Gordon under the tree line and along a narrow track. As we went, he told me a story about these woods, about how when he first moved into them there was a rubbish dump nearby and he had nothing but bad dreams and strange feelings off the trees all around him. It was now very dark and the track had grown very narrow and it was taking a disconcerting effort of balance and will to stay on it, as though the darkness on either side was trying to physically drag me away from the path.

Gordon carried on with his story. One day, he told me over his shoulder, he decided to clean up the rubbish. It was a fly tip from a nearby lane and only really consisted of a broken mattress and a scattered assortment of the usual crud – so it was no more than a day's work to clear it up. And after that, the bad dreams stopped and he liked to think that the woods now welcomed him and were grateful.

I liked this story but Gordon was now only the thinnest wisp of grey in front of me and I found it hard not to imagine that the darkness to either side dropped down below us as well and we were walking on a narrow causeway spanning the chasm of the night. Half imagined black shapes started to dance around our feet like silky cats or wisps of something else.

We scrambled down a slope into a hollow, over the mattress in the dark – now the only testament to the previous havoc – and along to the camp itself. Gordon insisted we jump down onto the springy mattress in the pitch dark, just for the crack, but that was what he was like. The camp consisted of a firepit and a homely round bender and Gordon sparked up a good fire in no time at all. The mushrooms were in full torrent now and when I gave myself up to them it felt as though I'd dipped my head under a rushing stream, as though I'd entered the minds of the trees themselves.

It wasn't until the next morning, when I retraced my steps towards town, that I had a good look at the path. It was on top of a crumbling railway embankment, the sides dropping away a foot or so to either side of where we'd been walking, falling precipitously a good twenty feet to the ground. Gordon hadn't mentioned it.

Not long after, we founded the camp at Snelsmore. The idea was to keep it secret initially, to avoid it getting swamped by the disruptive elements that had descended on the office. A further effort at the clandestine was to treat the treehouses we would build as nature enthusiasts' observation platforms. There were some large badger setts near the edge of the woods, which were under immediate threat of 'eviction', having already been surrounded by fences with gates designed to let the badgers out but not in. And once they were out of the way, they were one less obstacle for the road builders.

Badger had spent several days sleeping on his own among the blackthorns, guarding the camping stuff the others had shipped up from the office via Ed's green and white 2CV. Its peel back roof was handy as it meant that things such as timbers salvaged from skips could be thrown in without any major hassle. Badger said he'd had dreams about badgers, milling around him during the night, welcoming him to the woods.

The day I finally made it up to the Common, I was once again following in Gordon's wake. It was a long walk from town, about three miles, and most of that up a main road. Eventually the suburbs thinned out to golf courses and a string of well landed houses lining the road in the woods. The road wound uphill, while long gravel drives slipped off behind names like 'Beech Croft' and 'Donnington Lodge'. This was already the Common; a Special Site of Scientific Interest. SSSI's are supposedly protected under European Law. There were three triple SI's on route.

The Common was a nature reserve, of which the road was due to cut through a southern tip. The land to be lost to the road from the reserve was meant to be compensated by the gift of other land elsewhere. But once it was gone, that was that. Even in ecological terms, and ignoring the effects of the road on the surrounding area, a separate, isolated bit of land that could be used as a reserve wouldn't come close to compensating for the loss of a habitat that was part of a much larger area, whose wildlife had the run of so much undisturbed woodland all around it. The rest of the Snelsmore reserve backed away over the Lambourn Downs in a primordial soup of ferns and birches and moss. It seemed like another country, stretching away further than we could rightfully imagine; half wild and ancient and vast. We only stood at the threshold, and that was already enough.

The Common was also supposed to be the inspiration for the 'Wild Wood' in Wind in the Willows. Kenneth Grahame had lived in Bagnor village; just over the ridge from our camp. Badger and Moonflower talked about this and, later, about a medieval settlement that was meant to have existed here. There'd been a city here, according to the old Badger himself, in the book, but that had disappeared a long time ago. According to an archaeological report, there'd been a medieval settlement, a hamlet or village, near where the camp would be going.

My overriding impression on arriving in the woods was of the long walk, and an empty belly, but this soon changed when I saw the platforms. Work had started several days ago on these – and they already looked impressive. Moonflower was working on the platform that I was to inherit, thirty foot or so up in a broad trunked old oak. It was a huge, straight tree with only a few minor branches jutting out until the place where Moonflower was working – putting in a rectangular base where fat limbs branched off from the main upright trunk. The trunk itself carried on straight up, Moonflower building the framework right around it. I was itching to get up there and help out, but stayed for the time being on the ground, tying on wood to be pulled up and staring at the work above.

A few days later I helped build the first bender – a warm, dry place for everyone to sleep. The whole thing was done in the course of an afternoon, a blue plastic tarp going over the top as the light faded, a burner installed at the far end from the door.

Someone had bought a bale of hay from somewhere and we spread this out over the floor for insulation, with blankets laid on top. I was to share this with Badger, Tami and Moonflower for the next week or two, sleeping head to toe in our sleeping bags. I was impressed with how homely the whole thing was. Privacy in getting changed wasn't too much of a problem because we didn't get changed very often. It was cold and wet, so we didn't need to do more than peel off our outer layers – leaving us to sleep in soft, clean inner layers. The level of dirt on our outer clothes became apparent after a couple of weeks in the woods when we realised it was pointless to wipe our knives on our trousers – it was only getting them more dirty. That was probably the time to start thinking about the laundrette. But I was happy enough to smell of woodsmoke.

After the bender had gone up, much of the next week was spent hauling things through the woods from the nearest road and Ed's car. The weather was wet and the Common was living up to Moonflower's description of misty and boggy, particularly in the quaggy hinterland where the bender was.

When it was really wet, we'd sit in the bender with the burner going. Just sitting for hours on end in the company of a woodburner was new and highly satisfactory, a spliff or two compounding the homeliness, the wood as it burned sending out welcoming sounds of settling down. All our imaginations were fertile with excitement, so there was no lull in the talk, though there were often long monastic silences which I felt completely at ease with, a feeling of deep satisfaction welling up from somewhere at having found such excellent people to be living in the woods with.

Tami was quite possibly the quietest person I'd ever known, but it didn't seem to matter here, it was in fact a positive blessing in somewhere so quiet as this already. And just as the woods seemed full of a language that could only be understood on the other side of the silence, Tami seemed to carry something of equal importance, that talking too much would only have ushered away.

The back of Badger's head was covered in a crop of chestnut hair, which he wore tied back, his front and sides having been shaved in the style of an oriental monk, something like a tonsure in reverse. He was calmly self possessed, seeming content with the whole enterprise we were establishing here, but also as though he was carrying it, on guard at all times for anything laying in wait.

But tempering this, he never took himself or anything else all that seriously, or never appeared to, even if he did. He liked to turn things on their head, catch you out or tie your brain in knots by spoonerising sentences, assumptions falling out from your mind like loose change, your whole way of thinking having been turned upside down. In the evenings, among the many other things discussed, he'd read from a botanical encyclopedia, flicking through pages at random until some germinating stories formed, where stamens and stigma sat side by side with dicotyledons and visions of trifoliate perennials.

Inseparable from Badger was his dog Rose, though if you asked him, Rose was her own dog, not his. She was all black, a bit like a collie but with none of the markings. She seemed gifted with an intelligence far above her species and you wondered sometimes if this was all her masterminded scheme. When she walked with Badger in town, it was always off a lead, her having a good sense for traffic. When a supposedly respectable woman took him up on it one time, he told her that he was only walking from one wood to another and it wasn't his fault that someone had put a town in the way. Rose's reply would have been better, but talking was never her strong point.

Moonflower talked a lot about Finland. In particular, the triple storied wooden churches, that I'd only recently heard about myself and liked the sound of. There were places he'd been in the snow, that could have existed only in the semi fictional world he seemed to inhabit; ice palaces, glass roofed chambers underneath lakes, an entourage of creatures that only he could sense; moomin faces fluting in the forests of the North. When we all had a treehouse, he'd tell me, we could hang the food out the sides, which would naturally refrigerate it. I had a sense of snow filled winter looming, icicles forming feet long from our platforms, the Common somehow joining itself with tracts of Scandinavia.

On a dull, wet afternoon, sat still and stoking up the burner, we were paid a visit by the security guards. It turned out we weren't occupying part of the nature reserve; we were 'over the borders' in the lands of a neighbouring farm. The security were paid to keep an eye on the farm buildings on the end of the ridge between us and Bagnor village.

The sound of the rain muffled everything up and we didn't hear them until they were right outside, a man's voice dispelling our peace instantly and thoroughly before lifting up the door tarp to poke his head inside, looking a little disturbed at the lack of anything more solid to bang on.

Badger and Moonflower went out to talk to them. They were friendly enough but it was quite clear they wanted us out of the woods. The farmer wanted to clear fell the mature oak standards before the Highways Agency compulsorily purchased the land, and our presence there would potentially cost him hundreds, if not thousands of pounds. Oak is highly valued stuff and these were massive, towering trees.

Our only means of defence was a plastic coated Section Six stuck to a tree by the doorway. It was a low doorway and Tami and I stared out at the others' feet as they talked. Although the guards obviously didn't have it in for us, their appearance was still a rude awakening. Another edge had been added to the life we were living, another reassurance had been stripped away and another step taken towards a state of conflict. The security guards' shoes were black and shiny and looked far too clean to be tramping around in the mud.

During the next week we had other visitors. A dull droning from the eastern edge of the woods turned out to be a landrover scanning the undergrowth for wildlife with an infra-red light. Moonflower and myself had ventured out of the warmth and light of the bender to investigate the noise, which sounded less like a four wheeled vehicle than a tank or something altogether more otherworldly. The combined effort of this noise, the weird white and red lights disappearing and reappearing among the spindly silhouetted branches and the hash we'd been smoking was completely unnerving. The bender was moved over the border and onto the relative safety of the nature reserve not long after.

Meanwhile, work was continuing on the tree platforms, even if we'd given up all pretence of being neutral badger observers. Nobody builds badger observatories thirty or fifty feet up. For several days I dutifully lumbered timber over from the roadside and tied it on a line for Moonflower and Gordon to work with.

Nearly all the wood had been salvaged from skips and needed to be cleared of nails; so this was my first lesson of hitting straight with a hammer. I also learned pretty quickly that tying on to the middle of a beam was no good if people were to try hauling it up through a mesh of branches. That way, it would stay horizontal, getting stuck on just about everything. It was tricky enough to find a straight line to lower a rope through in the first place. Tied on the end, a beam would hang down. I made sure of my knots pretty early on too, not much fancying the idea of a beam coming down on my head.

On the third day or so, Moonflower was away in town, so I borrowed his climbing harness and went up myself, shinnying up the climbing rope with prussik loops that gripped the rope for you. One loop was attached to your waist and the other formed a step for your foot. When you trod with your foot you could move the waist loop up, and when you leaned back with the weight on your waist, up would go the loop with your foot in it. James Bond used the same technique with a pair of shoelaces but my bootlaces are always breaking so I'd never try it myself.

I'd been a bit apprehensive at working up in the trees before, but once I made it up I was in my element. I'd been a keen tree climber as a boy and to my relief, found that my years as a lanky teenager hadn't played havoc with my natural reflexes. Later, I had to force myself to remember that not everyone had a natural affinity with heights – for them, climbing around up a tree was a real conquering of fears, whereas I was just having a laugh.

Moonflower eventually left and never came back. We don't know where he went, but by the time he'd gone, the camp was on firm footing. Or at least as firm as could be. He had also left me with the beginnings of a fine, if already highly eccentric treehouse. Which set the tone of things to come.

At some point in the first few weeks, we pooled our giros to buy climbing equipment. I now had my own harness and felt like I was the business. I'd signed on during the early days at the office, being steered through the filling of the form by a gnarled heavy drinker sat on the sofa bed. I didn't much like the idea but it was clear things were operating on a limited budget and I had no money. The last thing I wanted was to be a burden to the campaign.

Someone told me the best thing was to sign on as homeless – 'no fixed abode,' which sounded better in a Scottish accent.

"So, where are you staying?" asked the women behind the desk in the benefits office. She was in her early middle ages with the kind of weary expression you'd expect in her line of work. I wasn't prepared to be quizzed like this and answered with the first thoughts that came into my head, telling her I was sleeping in an alleyway down by the canal, putting in some complaints about the damp for good measure.

The woman, having already got wind of my hitherto promising prospects of a university education - which I alone knew was a complete joke, as I had no idea what I wanted to do with my life – fixed me with a tired, withering look. "You stupid, stupid, stupid boy" she said.

Her words gave voice to an unseen consensus that I felt was creeping up around me; ex tutors and family, family friends and what once were prospective employers, all passing silent judgement on my rashness leaving home, wringing out quiet dismay from their hands, shaking their heads at the loss of my prospects. And while the fight was on to prove the sceptics wrong, it was fair to say I was being led down some pretty strange paths. It seemed rude, for instance, not to hang out for a while with some other young characters from the office, sitting with them and their shaved heads and flouro beads on the steps of the Benefits Agency, while droves of respectable Newbury denizens droned past us, unable to hold back their worst dirty looks.

And it seemed equally rude not to acknowledge or stop and chat to the groups of Newbury's fellowship of street dwellers; from the clinically insane to old boys down on their luck or too fond of their booze. The men on the street were a rough company of beards, army camouflage, overcoats and eyes that never saw enough sleep. Some of them ripped each other off, but most of them banded together, looking out for each other, and each others' dogs. One man used to advance down the High Street, standing in each doorway by turn and whooping his head off, until they gave him some money; a tactic which seemed to work fairly well. But I came across him several times after he'd had his money taken off him by some more slippery, underhand street characters who I only saw him with once and who I was too unsure of myself to confront. This was a world where I was still uncertain of territory and rules and where I was playing everything by instinct and by ear.

Another young lad had some serious problems and I saw him once trying to get some sleep under a bush by a main road. It was the middle of the day in November. He'd tried to find support from the protest but was generally shunned after people realised he was being pushed by the local police for information on people. The police would sort him out with some soup for his trouble, trouble that had grown beyond all scope thanks to their attention.

Walking through town was often a trip into strange company. But seeing my own reflection in the big glass panes could be disconcerting too. There were no mirrors in the woods and so no reminders of how badly you needed a shave and no pointers as to the angle of your hair. My fledgling dreads were finding their feet at last, but stuck out all over the shop. There was no option but to walk tall through it all, larger than life all of a sudden and ready to stare back at all comers.

I now wore a big overcoat of thick grey wool that was seriously needed in the November cold. I'd had a sudden rush of materialism with the arrival of my first giro – more money than I'd ever had in one go in my life. A shop called Strawberry Fields, that hosted a predictable but satisfying array of hippy tat, furnished me with a pleasing ensemble of woollen gear. I wore it all at once in an intricate layer system; t-shirt, shirt, woollen undershirt, woollen tunic-thing that still smelt of sheep, Morrocan top, overcoat. A pair of cotton trousers under my jeans. The overcoat was a step too far in the end and split at the armpits. After the worst of the winter had passed, I reverted back to the camouflage smock.

I found my overcoat in one of Newbury's charity shops. Some towns feel as though they were built solely for the sake of these shops. There's probably a belt that runs from Stratford-on-Avon, through Wiltshire and on to Windsor or thereabouts that houses the heartland of the English charity shop. They were an ideal place to look for blankets; where rounded old ladies fumbled with change and stared back bird eyed and outraged by my hair and my clothes.

On the canal near the back streets that led to the office, there was an amazing antiques shop. The canal here opened out to the width of a large pond, it was near the bridge on the high street and was probably used as a passing point when the waterway carried more traffic. It was a tranquil spot now, full of ducks and people feeding them. Old wooden mill houses towered nearby and a band of mature sycamores stood serenely over the water. It was places like this that kept my head together amid all the madness. I could have done with sitting there more often.

The antiques shop was clapped in whitewashed wood and stood near a funky swing bridge. On my first and only visit I got drawn into an intractable conversation on the bypass and the protest with the woman working there. I was feeling lucid and determined to get my points across: we came close to arguing more than once. The old stuff around us took in our views and I left with a bike and a trumpet. The bike had belonged to the woman's father in law, who had been a proper old country gent in his day. I was ordered to take good care of it, as the family wanted to see it in good hands. The trumpet was from a local hunt. I'd had a romantic idea of blowing a trumpet on a hill ever since I'd seen a picture of an old Celtic battle horn. The woman in the shop saw me off with the disgruntled admission that she supported what I was doing, but was glad it was me up a tree, not her son.

Although the ground camp had been moved, the treehouses were still 'over the border' and at risk of immediate felling from the farmer. The only sure way to prevent this, we felt, was to ensure someone was up in the trees at all times. Badger and Tami were kept busy with looking after the new camp, Gordon had built a bender there too but was off busking in town quite a bit and Ed was more often than not away at his home in Wales, welding burners for the masses. He'd been down at the camp in Penwood and had realised that people here needed stoves if they were going to make it through the winter. He'd made us an iron trivet to cook over the fire with – three legged and topped with three horse shoes joined at each edge. The burner in the communal bender had been his handiwork too, an old gas bottle fitted with a swinging door and grate, a removable plate on the top and an intricate extension on the back where the flue was stuck in. It worked nicely.

Ed was good to have around when he was there, but that was getting less and less. There were a few other characters around, who stood in when I needed a break, but I found myself spending most of the time up in the trees.

For something like the next six weeks I lived a semi hermetic existence up on the platform, coming down once a day to use the shitpit and maybe spending one day a week on the ground. Someone would bring me my dinner across from the ground camp and I'd haul it up in a bucket on the end of a rope. It was always stew.

The threat from the landowner continued with early morning visits in a landrover. This was the caretaker of the land, a farmer – the actual owner was a Japanese businessman, Mr Tonensho, who also owned the extensive nearby golfcourses. The caretaker would turn up with the men from the farm, chainsaws at the ready, hoping to catch us unawares. Once, they even set about clearing some of the smaller trees, seemingly more for the sake of showing they were still in control of the situation than for any physical gain. The caretaker of the land was in fact a fairly receptive man and was sympathetic to our stance and perspective, even if he did keep us on our toes initially.

When the landrover appeared, everyone from the ground camp would gather under my tree to try and negotiate with them. Or just generally get in their way. Usually though, from what I could hear, they largely only succeeded in scrambling the farm workers' brains with a potent combination of hippy logic and tree mythology. I had to admire the audacity of anyone who could stand in front of a chainsaw crew and tell them not to cut any elders because they held a witch inside.

The biggest grievance of the farm workers seemed to be that they were no longer able to come down to the woods in the evening and shoot the stray pheasants. Two of them came on their own one evening to give out, hoping we'd move off, pack in our games once we'd realised the extent of their troubles. We'd ruined their sport, but it was only the first of many changes that were coming in.

The pheasants, for their part, did their best to keep a low profile and only gave themselves away when the sonic boom of a passing concorde threw them into a sudden turmoil. This always happened once a day around twilight, a distant reminder of the other, outer world imprinting its mark upon the woods, a weird temporary inversion in the natural order of things. Every day this piercing cry of confusion ushered in the evening, calling to mind everything that was lost and was due to be lost.

The ridge that separated us from Bagnor Village was echoed by a valley which ran down towards Donnington Castle. This had been built in the Fourteenth Century and was an important Royalist stronghold in the Civil War, commanding the crossroads of the way down from Oxford to the ports and the Great Bath Road from London to the West. It held out against numerous attacks and sieges before being sacked and reduced to ruins in the spring of 1646, after a siege that had lasted the whole winter. Only the eastern gatehouse now survives, two rounded towers rising five stories high.

The valley that mirrored the ridge the castle sat on the end of, also separated the treehouses from the ground camp and in the evenings it would often fill with a fine mist. The two solitary towers of the castle stood silhouetted against the fading colours to the south. I was learning to play the whistle and had a tune called 'Drummond Castle'; a Scots tune which I called 'Donnington Castle' instead. There was a flag flying from the towers sometimes and I would have liked to have had a flag of our own, so anyone stood on the battlements could look down and see there was a new garrison in the area, in the living towers of the old wood and that we had every intention to hold out a long while.

Playing the whistle passed the time well in the evenings, playing for the sake of it and for the sake of everything that was ebbing away around me into the night. Eventually, the swinging orb of a hurricane lamp would appear along the path through the blackthorns, a thin pin-point of light, undulating with the step of the carrier. This would mean food and a shouted conversation up and down the thirty feet that separated me from the ground. From the direction of the camp, I could just about see the chinks of the fire and sound of voices, wood being broken, and the faint, persistent chords of a guitar. It all seemed a long way away.

Under the Beech

The new ground camp, set up across the valley from the treehouses, was just over the boundary of an old earth bank. This bank, and the ditch that mirrored it, was clearly ancient; a rounded curve of earth among the trees. It probably marked the boundary of the woodland hundreds of years before and now it marked the official edge of the nature reserve.

The remains of an old, broken down, barbed wire fence hung straggling along this boundary. Rolling this up and putting it out of the way was one of the first tasks undertaken, besides the building of a communal bender. The fence hadn't just been in poor repair – it was totally dilapidated; the posts were all pulled out from the ground, leaving the barbed wire as a tangled, shin high hazard to any animal or person trying to pass by.

The major feature of the new camp was a huge beech tree that spiralled fantastically up into the sky, a young oak growing out by its hip. The beech took pride of place – the firepit was placed under its branches and the open area in front of it formed a kind of courtyard, along with the doorway of the communal. It was a tower and a hub and shed it's copper leaves all around us with the November storms. It lost none of it's majesty as it laid itself bare, but seemed to spread further and further up into the canopy, underpinning the sky.

Two friends, perhaps the first people to enter these woods with a view to trying to save them, had walked the route of the road the summer just gone. The beech had stood out even then and they'd sat down beneath it, agreeing there should be a camp here. We only heard of this months later, when the new ground camp was well underway, one of our friends rolling up, telling us they'd seen this place before. Things seemed increasingly fated.

At some stage, we knew we'd build a treehouse in the beech. A whole village was taking shape above the ground camp, trees being singled out for habitation, shadow platforms springing up in our imagination.

The new communal bender had been constructed more ambitiously than the first; probably on account of there being a handful more people on site than before. A big burner had been procured from somewhere, with an old cast iron drainpipe rammed in the top as a flue. The idea was that this would provide more heat – the exposed flue acting like an additional radiator – but the drainpipe turned out to be badly clogged and caused it's fair share of troubles, smoking the whole bender out on some occasions and leaving an alto stratum of thick smoke lingering in the rafters for much of the rest of the time. I for one was worried about it toppling over on my head whenever I spent a night in there, which wasn't very often. As it turned out, I had plenty of other reasons not to sleep easily.

The roof of the bender was roomy at the end near the doorway and the burner – with the space to stretch your arms over your head. A raised platform for sleeping on had been formed alongside this, constructed from red plastic bread crates with cardboard laid on top. It stretched away to the murky back regions. A fallen trunk had been incorporated back here and someone had chipped away at the top of this to form a rough table.

During a week when Badger and Tami had gone away and very few others were around, I was trying to sleep on the edge of the bread crates. The only other person on site that night was a girl called Angela, someone who'd been around off and on since we first started the camp. Angela was amiable, half Persian and had been living in a tepee in Germany the winter before. A bit older than me, half

73

doughty, half dizzy with slightly posh tones and an afghan scarf round her neck, she came across like an off kilter war correspondent. She wanted to go travelling among the Mongolian herdsmen. She'd been in Ireland most recently where she'd left a cottage half painted, which was arguably better than not painted at all, depending on your perspective.

She'd just left the bender for a piss and I began to drift off, the sound of the burner chugging contentedly away behind my back. A little further down the track to sleep, some bells started ringing; distantly as though they were underwater or a long way off. They were alarm bells. I could just about hear the sound of the flames growing louder and louder and eventually managed to throw my head back for a glance at the burner.

I was awake instantly. A living wall of bright yellow fire was dancing up the door tarp. I scrambled out of my bag and leapt to pull the door tarp down, my blood pounding in panic. Pulling the tarp away from the hazel framework made the flames flare up even more with the sudden movement and for a moment or two I thought the whole structure would go up. Angela arrived back in time to help me pull the piece of burning canvas clear away from the rest. She'd left a candle in a bottle just inside the door.

We stood looking at the smouldering material. We'd both heard stories of people dying in bender fires – from accidents with candles or burners – and this was far too close to home. Angela was giddy and apologetic and almost half amused. I couldn't believe what had just happened and wanted to shake her by the shoulders. As far as I could see, there wasn't much to laugh about.

Another of Angela's adventures took place on a night I was taking a break from tree sitting. She was due to take my place for the evening and I'd left her in her prussiking gear, loops and all, dangling off a rope below Ed's treehouse. She'd done plenty of prussiking before so I thought it was safe to leave her to it. She certainly seemed happy enough and it would take a good ten minutes for her to reach the top – and I was itching to get to the pub. It had been a long week alone in the treetops.

It was probably stupid to leave someone alone halfway up a tree, but being thin on the ground we tended to do it all the time – so long as whoever it was was a confident climber. In Angela's case, I was maybe too trusting.

I was just climbing onto my bike, ready for a swift descent down the Wantage road, when I heard her crying out from the other side of the valley. By the time I'd climbed up next to her, using a rope ladder, a strong wind had started up, blowing a heavy rain with it. I'd told her, just before I'd left her to it, to remember not to prussik above the branch below the treehouse. Unclipping yourself at the top of a climb meant you had to be able to place all your weight on something solid. In this case, a big branch. She'd prussiked just above the branch and was now stranded, dangling adrift, thirty foot up.

For prussiking, instead of just rope, we used grips that clicked over the climbing rope when the weight was on them. To make everything worse, it turned out that the main grip Angela was attached to had jammed, its teeth locked solid against the rope. By the time we managed to get her unstuck, by passing a loop under her arms from the platform above, hours had gone by and she was losing the feeling in her legs. Afterwards, she lay for a long while on the floor of the treehouse, letting the circulation return. The wind was still blowing and the pubs were all shut. I swore never to use the prussiking grips again.

On the other side of the courtyard from the communal bender, Gordon had put up a structure of his own. It was new, and spartan with it; no blankets were lining the inside of the tarp yet and the hazel branches stood out finely against the clear green backdrop. One morning found the pair of us in there, discussing the merits of treehouses verses ground dwellings. I was growing accustomed to life up in the branches, not least because I felt secure up there – there had been a couple of nights when the security guards from the farm had woken me up, trampling through the leaf litter below me. When I stuck my head over the side of the platform, they shone their torch up in my face, leaving me no choice but to swear at them and go back to sleep. But I was glad of the distance between us. I bought myself a big maglight of my own to shine back at them, to see how they liked it next time. They never came back.

There was more to it than just a sense of security though. There was a strong feeling as you fell asleep that you were being cradled in the arms of an older being. The rest of the time it was like being at sea, each sway and turn of the tree putting you not just in closer touch with the tree itself, but also with the wind. At times it grew hard to tell if the trees were being blown by the wind, or if it was the dancing of the branches that summoned the wind in the first place. Each breath was like the spoken thought of the woods.

Gordon had had a good dream of me and him up in my treehouse, talking and making things right in our heads. Only the treehouse wasn't like my waking treehouse, as its walls were round and formed of woven hazel, small windows looking out on the woodland. Everything in it was close to its natural state, and all the better for it. I could see myself living in a place like that.

For all that, Gordon loved his new home and his proximity to the earth. Among the intermeshed branches of the inside of his roof, you could make out every rune in existence and every letter of the ancient ogham alphabet. If you looked long enough, or in the right way. With Gordon's current Spartan aesthetic, there was literally nothing between us and the ground. This kept you rooted and on a firm footing with the rest of the world. Badger had spoken about this too – during the tree camps at Solsbury Hill, the protest in Bath over the previous summer, people were spending all their time in the trees. For some it was psychologically unearthing, as well as physically.

I had declared a holiday from the trees for the day, someone had gone up to take my place and Gordon was making toast to celebrate. A hot plate on his burner was well up to the job. Besides bread he had also taken it upon himself to toast my socks, which were in need of drying out.

We were smoking and before long had managed to burn a huge hole in sock number two. Gordon's burner was a strange enamelled affair and as I smoked and stared at it, I found myself becoming absorbed in an imaginative ambience of the 1930's, the sensations of distant generations circling round in my head. Grandfathers and grandmothers, austere but warm with it; white haired and knowing and poking the coal. To be sat by a stove on a winter's day was by itself an act of sympathy with my forebears. Until the radiators came in, everyone lived with fire on a daily basis. Whether it was stove or grate or a range in the kitchen, coal or wood, it was a vital part of everyone's life. Every house had its hearth.

Gordon eventually left to go into town and left me to relax in his home. There was no door tarp, or it had been left open, but I was content to stare out at the woodland on the other side of the canvas. I didn't realise how cold it was. I was beginning to think I was growing impervious to the weather, but had forgotten that in the trees, I was constantly moving and at night had an excellent sleeping bag. Down in Gordon's bender, I felt like I could sleep for a week and climbed into a thin sleeping bag to make amends, the burner winding down with a series of cooling taps and cracks behind me.

Outside the door, the wind was stirring in the dry leaves. I noticed, vacantly, that there was still ice on the ground and fancied that I could almost feel it descending. There was something Holy at work in the woods now, a presence gliding among the frost, a soft soled Ice Queen treading her graceful way among the plants, gently kissing them to sleep. She was very close now, I felt that she was coming for me, but I wasn't worried because she was kind and very beautiful and it would be no hardship at all to feel her lips on mine...

Gordon came bustling into this dreamworld and brought me to my senses. It was freezing, the sleeping bag was hopelessly thin and the burner had gone out. It was a mistake I wouldn't make again.

When the ground camp was moved, the communal bender was originally built right in the middle of a footpath. It was rebuilt about ten yards to one side after a week, but before that I was sat in it when I had a strange experience. A friend of ours had come up from town and got us all stupidly stoned with the aid of his pipe. It was a very clever pipe because the head could be screwed on in one of two ways – one forming a pipe, and the other a silver magic mushroom. As it turned out, much later, he was using the pipe to smoke cocaine during the same period, which probably helped account for our seriously affected state.

That evening it was blowing a wet gale and we were all very glad of the cosy heat the burner was providing. When it rains in the woods, it rains twice; the trees giving a second shower as they shed their water. And on that night it was windy enough to feel that the wind and the trees were throwing the wet at us in bucket loads.

I went out into the rain for a piss and was almost immediately put into a panic. Across the valley, and from the direction of the treehouses we had for once left unguarded, came the sound of engines and machinery working. They had caught us well and truly off guard. I shouted through the doorway to the others and we all scrambled out and down into the storm.

When we got to the treehouses there was no machinery in sight, and nothing to be heard besides the crashing of the branches above us and the rain in our ears. Perhaps I'd heard the sound of a golf buggy in the next valley, or a landrover from the farm. It was clear though that nobody else was impressed, even if they did laugh it off and try to make me feel better. I couldn't understand it – it had been no vague noise that I'd heard. It didn't make any sense.

Early the next morning, a large yellow digger arrived. It was possible they'd been biding their time as both Badger and Moonflower had gone off to get climbing supplies. The rest of us stood around feeling hopeless as the digger ploughed up the fenced off badger sett near the base of my tree. It was a tricky situation because this was a procedure that was supposedly in the badgers' best interests. The fence and the one way gates should have ensured that the badgers had all moved out to find another home. This bulldozing would ensure they didn't move back in to the path of danger.

On the other hand, they seemed a little over sure that the badgers had actually moved out – they certainly didn't seem to take any steps to find out before they crushed the whole lot. And what if a gate had been faulty, what if the badgers had burrowed back under the fence? Having seen pictures of artificial setts, it was hard to imagine an animal willingly opting to live in one. They had only clocked the serious amount of badger activity on route that spring. And construction work was due to start sometime in the winter.

The badger relocations were rushed jobs, using the minimal amount of time for a procedure that was ideally carried out over several years. And relocations were a last resort anyway – displacing whole families, forcing them to abandon what were practically ancestral homes, shifting them to areas that might already be overcrowded, upsetting a balance that was generations old. Added to that, badgers are hugely habitual creatures and very reluctant to move to new setts or change paths. It's all far from ideal, though developers might have you believe that they're almost doing the badgers a favour.

Also, the 'relocation' was actively part of the road building scheme – a method by which an endangered species was being moved off route – one less obstacle in the event of an Environmental Impact Assessment. In opposing the road, shouldn't we have been actively stopping the sett's destruction? It was hard to know what to do. EIA's were required under European law but there was still no sign of one taking place. If they'd had one, they might have noticed the badgers a little sooner.

It was a tense and lame morning all at once and one which left everyone's stomachs feeling uneasy. Nobody obstructed the digger in the end, and by the time it left, the sett had been turned completely over and the track leading up to it was a quaggy, churned up mess. Nobody was giving me anymore sidelong glances about my performance the previous night.

Every so often, we'd all troop down to the kitchen of some local supporters – the Stoughtons. They had a big house, not far at all from the camp. When we first arrived we'd visit quite often, sitting in their kitchen with mugs of tea in our hands, wet storms of November battering the woods outside. The Stoughtons were heavily involved in opposing the road, and were trying to fight it in the European Courts. Now and again, they'd fly off to Brussels and come back with weary expressions.

But there was real hope of having the road stopped via Europe. Having no Environmental Impact Assessment was the most obvious reason. But there were directives which had become British law that year, which were meant to safeguard certain rare species, which Newbury had coming out of it's ears. Besides dormice, bats and badgers, there were also kingfishers, hobbies, sparrowhawks and kestrels. Snelsmore itself was home to between four and six pairs of nightjars; sufficiently endangered to be classified as a 'red data' bird. Their presence made the Common eligible to become part of proposed a Special Area of Protection, which should have secured automatic protection for the place under a European habitats directive.

The effect of pollution from the road was likely to damage sensitive heath species further into the Common. And the noise pollution would have a serious effect on the breeding and feeding of songbirds in the area. There was also a barn owl breeding programme less than a mile north of where the road would go. Barn owls like to hunt on the verge of roads and their low level, drifting flight makes them particularly prone to collisions with vehicles.

It was easy in the Stoughton's kitchen, sat in the warmth, chatting about things which seemed both immediate and far removed. There was a feeling of entering into a vast arena, full of the machinations of bureaucracy and powerful states. At the same time, we were in a quiet corner of the woods, tucked away from everywhere, next to a radiator. Jan Stoughton and her niece, H, kept us well stocked with biscuits, which we tried to ignore so as not to eat them all in one go. But we knew that sooner or later we'd have to return to the wetness of the woods, the wild movements of the branches enveloping us again as we stepped outside.

As the word seeped through, other characters drifted up to our camp. The mysterious camp in Penwood was by all accounts struggling for survival and the office had been left to implode under the lodestones of the sofas. For a while, the communal bender became a smoking lounge, if not quite a den of iniquity for any other reason. It was frustrating because I was aware of just how much work was needed to make all three tree platforms habitable, never mind begin to create the tree village that was possible, before clearance work started in earnest. And that might happen sooner than any of us thought. Perhaps as soon as the New Year. The new dwellers of the communal held none of this sense of urgency. Poking my head round the door tarp in the morning, and being met with a sea of glazed faces, was not the most inspiring sight imaginable.

Occasionally though, everyone would pile to the other end of the valley to help in the trees. The other five days of the week would often find me working alone, perhaps with a helper to tie on wood if I was lucky, and that was lonely, boring work for whoever was on the ground.

Badger came to see me one night in my tree. He was getting worried and dismayed at the mounting lethargy in the camp. It went further than not working – it also included not cooking and not getting enough wood, sitting around and complaining instead of making the camp a better place to be. In other words, everything was getting lunched out. Badger and I could see quite clearly the things that needed sorting. Between us, we hatched a plan.

A few days later, Badger put up a cardboard notice that I'd written out, detailing all the things there were to do. But half the problem was one of communication, and this new list didn't help matters much. It certainly made our grievances known, but it only created bad feeling and didn't inspire many people to get up and do anything anyway. I realised, too late, that talking to people face to face and earlier on would have been a far better way to go about things.

Though some people would have only needed a quiet word, others wouldn't have shifted their arses whatever was said. A few people drifted off after the notice, a couple of others moved out of the communal and built themselves a wonky but pretty much habitable teepee and kept themselves to themselves, spending more and more time in town and opting, now and again, to do a spot of begging.

Before the notice, I found myself hanging out with the whole crew, who were concocting a scheme to get money off the NHS. The idea was to pretend they had scabies, which, they reckoned, would have made them eligible for a fund to replace all their clothes. It was a hairbrained nightmare and I found myself getting swept along with it, unable to make them stop, or to simply walk away myself.

Scabies are one of the worst things that can befall you while living outdoors, though you don't need to be outdoors to get them. Tiny mites, virtually invisible to the eye, are transmitted by clothing or bedding or the touch of the already damned. The creatures then burrow, unseen, under your skin. By the time you notice them you're very likely to be soon itching all over, and if you don't get it treated right away, itching like you've never itched before. It won't let you sleep. You give yourself sores. And to treat it you need to wash all your clothes and your bedding, at the same time as dousing yourself in chemicals which make you feel sick, and then repeating the process twenty four hours later. Even then, they can come back, if you haven't been thorough enough, or if people around you have got it and haven't been treated.

To cap it all off, you have to live with the knowledge that hundreds, maybe thousands of little creatures are living in your flesh, multiplying, leaving red runnels near the surface of the skin, on route from one breeding site to the next. And because the incubation period is several weeks, by the time you realise you've got them (and if you've never had it before, that can be quite a while) the chances are everyone around you has got them as well.

Mind you, if you catch it fairly early, it's not too hard to treat, provided you're sorted about it and people around you treat themselves and their stuff as well. Though some people can't handle it at all and react a little hysterically. However you look at it, it is at the very least a major pain in the arse.

The initial itching – and the first visible signs – arrives on the backs of the hands and the webbing and base of the fingers. So the means of faking scabies came in the form of rosehips – the inside of the berries contain minute hairs, which supposedly act as a skin irritant. I'd never had scabies, barely knew what it was, so had to take it at face value as the others told me about their devious scheme.

We took a handful of rosehips off an otherwise bare hedgerow on the edge of town. Taking one or two each, we rubbed the insides over our fingers and hands. If I'd been in any doubt before, by the time we rolled into the doctor's surgery, mob handed, I was sure I shouldn't have had so much faith in those around me. We gathered conspiratorially near the reception desk, still trying to get our stories straight. "You don't need to tell me…" said one of the men from the camp "I've been blagging the government for years." He sounded older and much, much louder than he should have done. When I saw the doctor, he stared back, full of impassive expressions, all knowing in his eyes. He knew that I knew he knew, so it hardly seemed to matter that I told a pack of lies. All the same, I left his office feeling like I'd let the side down, because I hadn't lied with my eyes.

The whole thing left me feeling more than uneasy and I tried to avoid the others after that, whenever I saw them in town.

Skips

Badger and Tami had built a bender of their own; to get a bit of privacy from the communal. Badger had a good eye for symmetry and their bender was properly round, their doorway facing down into the courtyard from the side of the beech. On either side of their doorway, behind the door tarp, stood two upright logs of oak, a foot high. When someone from the communal stumbled in there one night and started pissing on the logs, it felt particularly hurtful, an act of desecration that had been saved up for like compost, or supermarket savers points.

The rest of the time, the bender was a haven. After some time, I began to come down to the camp every evening, only returning to the treehouses to sleep. The men from the farm had only come during the morning after all, and it was unlikely they'd try anything in the middle of the night. Whatever else was going on in the camp, life made sense at Badger and Tami's.

With most of our giros being spent on rope and a fresh supply of socks, there was a shortage of money being spent on food. This deficit was amply made up for by 'skipping' – raiding the skips of the local supermarket. A completely ethical practice, seeing as the food was getting thrown out anyway. The first time I came across it, was back in the early days in the office. I was sat on the sofa when a girl with a shaved head and a big grin burst in with a shopping trolley, shouting,
"gak attack!" Gak meant junkfood and her trolley was piled high with strawberry yoghurts and cake. It was a marvellous interruption on a dull afternoon and pretty soon

I was setting out with Gordon, Tami and some others, on a skipping mission of our own.

The office was connected by the run of red brick back streets to the edge of the canal. An old wooden warehouse, now offices, stood looking over us as we wheeled the trolley back towards the High Street. The skips in question were in the loading yard of the local co-op and we gathered by the entrance gates, touched by caution, as it was a daylight raid.

No one was in sight and soon we were across the loading yard and I was stood knee deep in cardboard and mouldering lettuces.

The skips had roofs on and little back doors, so it was not unlike being inside a tank or armoured personnel carrier. We passed out cardboard boxes to get them out of the way, along with anything edible. When we left we had enough food to feed everyone for several days, and weeks' worth of yoghurt with two days until their best before. It was a triumph of individual intervention over corporate waste. We wheeled the trolley back through the streets like kings.

Skipping continued, in some form or another, for the rest of my time in Newbury. Most of the missions were carried out under the cover of darkness with wildly varying degrees of caution. It was madness in a way, spending half our nights walking back and forth between town, but it had become a point of pride. And it did keep us well stocked with food.

In other places, supermarkets were wise to this practice and kept their food skips in special compounds, often with crushing units. It was just possible to retrieve the food out of these jaws of doom, though it involved scaling the fence and keeping a look out for guards. I tried this once with Badger at one of the big supermarkets by the main road, but it proved too tricky to get any goods. Later on in the protest, a lad tried the same thing there and got caught trying to climb the fence back out. By all accounts, he got a severe beating.

Earlier on though, sticking to the smaller places, we had an easy time of it. Walking through the town at night meant seeing the place in a different light – the streets were empty of people and traffic and we could stride down the middle of the road, wreathed in halogen and mist, the buildings around us exhaling the depth of their age.

One particular night in December stands out clearer than the others. It was not long after the experience of the cold in Gordon's bender and the frost was still all around us. A freezing fog descended on the trees at night, leaving any water up there frozen solid. Closer to the earth, ice hung to the branches by day, ready for another layer the next night, and another layer and another.

We were low on food and Badger and myself set off to see what we could do. I was muffled up in my overcoat, the hood from my top pulled up, a thick woollen scarf around my face. Over all this I had a grey blanket, folded in two and draped around my shoulders, secured with a tent peg for a pin. But I could still feel the deep cold all around us, even once we were walking.

There was a way into town that kept us off the road for a while – following a footpath down through the woods and out into the fields near the farm. The path took us along by the shadow of an outgrown hedge, the field looming large on our left, white as you like with the frost. The path came out at the end of Donnington village. Our road took us through the old stone buildings, past the low roof of the almshouses and onto the main road and the stone bridge, the Lambourn a torrent in the dark below us.

The road to town was full of minor landmarks; trees by the side of the road, carvings on the lintels of houses; dragons and briars and flowers, anything that would make the distance fly by. Once we were in town there was no shortage of things to be seen. In the ice and eerie quietness that came with it the natural ambience of the old buildings stood out clearer than ever.

The clocktower stood at the northern end of the High Street and more or less marked the beginnings of town. Across the way was the Clocktower pub. A friend had told us it used to be a whorehouse during the Civil War and it wasn't hard to imagine the soldiers spilling out of it and onto the street. The clocktower itself marked the centre of the crossroads that had helped form Newbury in the first place. Roads running south from the whole of mid Berkshire converged here to cross the Kennet, fanning out again south of the bridge. Until the first ring road, the A4 had run through here, the Great Bath Road, still following the same trajectory outside the town.

All of this, all these merging of routes, largely accounted for the two Civil War battles that had been fought here. There was also the legend that the place would never let you leave, that once you'd lived here the crossroads would always draw you back. I think the only real compulsion was to do with whether or not Newbury was your home town, which have a pull all of their own.

We went through an old archway to the back of the pub, to check on the skips of the nearby shops. There were buildings back here that looked as though they must have been stables once. In the halflight, I wouldn't have been surprised at all if ghosts had appeared, stable hands leading the horses about, officers soundlessly calling their men from the shadows. Juxtaposed weirdly with this was the looming stark tower of the modern Vodafone offices, so it seemed as though two worlds were overlapping and in competition with each other, like soldiers themselves or plants in the forest. Delving for cakes behind the Health Food shop, I knew which side I was on.

The skips were rough going that night, our fingers quickly growing wet and numb from the ice on the cardboard. We'd found a bumper crop of cakes though and sat down for a feast to get our strength up before returning. There was obviously a glut of cakes in the run up to Christmas and we found we had inherited more than our fair share. There weren't enough people to eat them all and they sat in the little food bender on site, goading us on to eat more, before finally having to be chucked weeks later. We'd got so many slabs of flapjack-like cake from the Health Food shop's skips - capped in increasingly heinous carroty icing and roughly brick shaped – that someone had made a small wall out of them.

Our skipping days largely came to a stop when we found the containers by the co-op full of not just water, but also dog shit. Other gangs of skippers had come to the fore and this was probably the reason for the sodden and shit caked reception we'd received. Whoever else it was that had started the counter skipping, they'd been leaving piles of cardboard and old food out. We'd always put these back when we'd done so that even if we'd been lairy and made a racket, started dancing on the roof of containers or whooped a bit too loudly with delight, at least we'd left the place tidy.

Outraged by the water and the poo, feeling spited by a petty minded manager, we spent the next half hour arranging a monolith circle from shopping trolleys. This made us feel a lot better about things and doubtless confused the lorry driver with the early morning delivery.

Once or twice, while marching up the High Street, on the way back to the camp, we got stopped by police. We were probably slightly conspicuous thanks to the crates of food on our head.

"Excuse me gentlemen. Er... do you mind telling me what, exactly, you're carrying on your heads there?"

Food, officers, rich pickings and gifts from the Gods. If it wasn't for us it would have been no one at all and how can you steal what's been thrown out already?

"Gifts from the Gods eh? And does the manager of the supermarket know you're taking this food?"

We assured him he did. They were more than a little non-plussed by the whole thing. I gave them a false name when they asked, another step down the line into strange territory. It was probably an unnecessary measure but I felt I'd rather not appear on the police map if at all possible. There'd be plenty of time for that later.

The way back from town was full of the same landmarks, mostly trees. Badger had an eye for fine trees wherever they occurred and was always pointing them out. Near the edge of the woods stood a fine old beech tree in an enclosure of its own. It was a great place to stop, day or night, sat up in the crook of its roots with the ground sloping away from us. If it was night, it was usually the early hours by the time we got there and once we sat down, it felt like we'd never move again. We'd sit there in our layers, quietly steaming; thinking about a time when we could stop moving altogether. None of this was conducive to an early start.

The Hills Are Alive

Further up the road that led to Snelsmore, down backroads that twisted around the foothills of the Lambourn Downs, was another camp. This was known as Winterbourne, thanks to the nearest village and was hidden in a large copse. I only went there once or twice but I got to know the road to it much better, as it took me to the nearest phone box to Snelsmore.

The camp didn't last much longer than the leaves coming down. It had existed up till then on the goodwill of the owner of the woods, but once it was exposed to the neighbour's prying eyes, the game was up. It had been one of the quietest, most organised and tranquil camps I had ever known. I know that one of the men living there went off to be a monk directly afterwards, and there was more than a touch of a monastic sense of order to the bender I stayed in, which contained a gas lamp, a camp bed and nothing else.

The ride out there, and to the phone box, was a trip into the hinterland of the Common. Autumn was in full stride – birch trees stark and conspicuous against the orange sea of bracken, mist gathering in the hollows. It was here I had my first taste of what we were up against. Cycling out to use the phone one evening, I was overtaken by a convoy of dark vehicles. Two black landrovers led the way with two estate cars following on. They took their time about passing me by, and they all had their windows blacked out. Not only that but they turned round down the road to perform a second drive by. And then a third.

On some level, I knew that this was a display of their impotence, rather than their power, and felt that as long as I kept heart, there was very little they could do. Perhaps if

I'd been unsure about what I was doing or felt half hearted about the whole thing, then an encounter like that might have shaken me up a little. But I wasn't unsure and the drive by only compacted my convictions.

Other people on site had had similar experiences. Men in yellow security jackets had been seen near the camp climbing out of unmarked black cars. When they were approached, they got in and drove off. But for a while I wasn't so worried by agents of the government or of road building firms. We had enemies closer to home to think of.

One morning I woke up to hear the landowner's landrovers come crashing along the path to the trees that the bulldozer had left. As per usual, I called for the others in our hash inspired code; "Gringos!" (Enemies in the woods!) and "Underlay, underlay!" (Hurry up! They're almost here!) Today though was not a day like any other. Today we were being visited by Mr Tonensho himself. Mr Tonensho did not have a lot to say for himself, by all accounts. He sat in the landrover, large as a sumo, sporting a white and purple shell suit. But his presence was more than a little disconcerting, knowing the amount of land he owned locally and having heard his name mentioned so many times before.

On the nearby golfcourses, it was not uncommon to see caddies running alongside their employers, who zipped along the gravel tracks in their buggies. Really though, it felt as though they were all of them running to keep up in the business merry-go-round, all slogging their guts out to keep pace with the likes of Mr Tonensho.

They drove off, Mr T. and the farmer, after a relatively short time, leaving an air of excitement and disquiet. Mr T. may not have been the overtly dynamic power dresser we'd imagined, but for the next few days we sat around uneasily, wondering what would come of it. I found myself nursing a private anxiety involving Japanese Triads and midnight assassins. This wasn't helped when I woke up early in the night with the rocking sensation that comes when someone is climbing your tree. I looked over the edge of the platform to see a shadowy figure in black, climbing up the rope ladder to Ed's treehouse. My blood froze.

We were connected by a walkway, which is how the sense of motion was transferred. The figure climbing up looked nimble enough but was taking it deliberately slowly, obviously trying not to bring any attention to themself. I wondered why I hadn't thought to haul the ladder up that night. I thought about cutting the walkway. Eventually, after agonised minutes, I called out and the figure called back. It was Ed, back unexpectedly from Wales, doing his best to move quietly and not wake me up. I was less worried about the Japanese mafia after that.

Thirty foot or so behind the ground camp was the long gravel drive that led to the Stoughton's house. Sometimes, driving out in their estate wagon, their windscreen full of the sylvanshine rolling by, they'd stop to ask us if we wanted a lift into town. It was hard to explain, and I'm not sure if they ever really fully understood, but we were becoming rooted in a sense of place that made taking a car journey not just unnecessary, but completely undesired. It wasn't so much a question of pride, or political self-righteousness. It was more to do with our living in the woods and the effect it was working on our sensibilities.

On one of the first mornings of the new camp, I stood brushing my teeth by the bank of earth looking out over the woods, the fat trunks of the oaks dropping down the slope to the valley floor. I spat my toothpaste out and it fell spattering to the leaf litter. Badger had appeared and as I swilled my mouth out from a bottle, he began – only half jokingly - to accuse me of disrespect, of spoiling the pristine woodland floor with my glaring white chemical toothpaste. Maybe spitting on the bank was in some way disrespectful, and perhaps I was spitting a little too close to the benders. But all the same, I thought he was being a little unreasonable. After all, where could I spit that *wasn't* pristine woodland? Behind the brambles? In the crook of a branch? We didn't have a sink, so the woods were our bathroom. But that's true of everyone – all the world is our toilet, whether we recognise it or not. In the woods, with little outer or inner dimension to our daily lives, the smallest of our actions that damaged the environment stood out glaringly before us, like an accusation from the trees themselves.

The ground around the new communal had originally been full of fledgling brambles, but they soon disappeared with the passage of our feet. As the winter progressed, the leaf mould slowly turned to a general quag. During the worst of it, we had to put planks down which gradually sunk into the mud themselves. It was a strange fact – if we were planning on staying around for long, we'd have been thinking of putting in pavements. Badger even talked about this, cutting coaster slabs off the end of logs to lay down, but it never happened.

It may well be a good thing that more people don't live in the woods – the damage of human activities on such sensitive habitats is not hard to imagine. And as more woodland is destroyed, or is degraded by nearby developments, the ones that remain become more and more precious for the species they support. But there's a lot to be said for experiencing life in such a delicate context and being made aware of the repercussions of our every action. And some harmony is possible still, where we try and tread lightly.

Before the arrival of farming, communities would never have stayed in one place for so long anyway, so the problem of impoverishing an area like this would have never arisen. In England since then, nearly every square inch of land has been subject to human habitation at some point or another, and it's a testament of our ability to cohabit and the endurance of an underlying culture of respect that our countryside has survived with all the richness that it has. Which makes it all the more tragic that so much is now being denigrated and swept away by men who have no understanding of the fundamental connection that was still enjoyed by most people not more than two or three generations ago.

Many woods in Britain could actually do with a stronger human presence – in particular those needing coppicing, which apart from anything else helps preserve a species rich series of habitats. If traditionally managing indigenous woodland like this could be made commercially viable again, then it would actually help preserve the woods that are left – and give rise to the planting of more. For centuries there was a strong culture of people living in the woods in this way, using the trees to make products that were a part of everyday life. Now everyone is surrounded by pieces of plastic and the woods that are left have largely gone quiet, where they aren't being pulled to the ground.

Our material surroundings define our world in a way that most of us can only begin to suspect. With a little more wood in our lives, and a greater respect for the spirit inherent in natural, physical things, we might begin to shift the world the back to something like balance. Our understanding defines the world we live in; the world we create reflects the world we have already created, or allowed to transpire, in our minds. Until we address our connection with the spirit of the material, and in doing so come to grasp that manufacturing a thing like polystyrene or plastic is an actual act of violence towards the world, then attempts at restoring environmental balance will be rootless, however goodwilled.

There's now every reason for wood to play a greater part in our lives once again. Sustainably managed, locally sourced timber is an obvious means of providing heat, at a time where the hunt for alternative fuels is becoming ever more pressing. It would be no hard task to provide even a modern house with a good burner or two, where an old chimney isn't available. We could bring ourselves back from the brink if we all lived a little bit simpler; real fires and natural light aren't just a matter of practicality, they make the world a richer place to live in.

On my first morning in the woods, one of the first things I was told was to "take a spade" meaning "bury your shit." Angela and I started to dig a shit pit nearby but soon began backfilling because the ground was so quaggy. When the second communal was built, a new shit pit was top priority and Badger got stuck into digging it. Part of the reason he earned his name was that, when plenty of others had been up in the trees at Solsbury Hill, he was burrowing underground, to a bunker he'd had to be pulled from when they evicted the site.

Burying your shit, or using a covered pit, is one of the most basic and important things to do when out camping or living in the woods. In the right conditions, i.e. somewhere secluded, taking a dump can be an amazing experience, a kind of daily solitary mediation between yourself and your surroundings, a moment of stillness and reflection.

When finished, our pit was furnished with two planks – one for each foot while squatting. We tried to build a screen for it from dead bracken woven between hazel stakes. But because dead bracken rots down so fast, it never reached more than a couple of feet. We put it on the list of things to do.

There was an ever growing pile of stuff to be recycled, and as it mounted, it became more and more a momento of our environmental shortcomings. At the time, it felt as though we were leading some kind of two-pronged attack against the forces and the habits that were drawing the world into a deepening environmental crisis. Not only were we obstructing the road scheme, but we were doing our best to lead by example in the way we lived our lives. We felt strongly that this was as important as the political protest, and that without seeking to change the fundamentals of our lifestyles, on a very real, physical level, we would be hypocrites. I think it was this combined approach to the problems we face that helped draw so much attention, and which proved the inspiration behind the movement, not some idealised doctrine or wordy ideology.

Living in a house, all the rubbish you generate is taken care of, taken off your hands and whisked away to a landfill site miles away that you may never see. If that landfill site happens to be filling up a little too fast, then it needn't necessarily trouble you, it doesn't affect your life directly. The rubbish you've generated has been removed somewhere else, for someone else to deal with. In the woods though, you have to move it yourself, and every bag sits glowering like a heap of evil in an otherwise immaculate setting.

And inescapably related to the rubbish that gets generated, is the amount of stuff you have; the amount of tat you manage to accumulate. In a house, it's easy to horde tat and everyone knows the amount of stuff they have that hasn't been used in years. Living in a canvas hut with only enough room for a bed, a burner and maybe one or two shelves, there's no option but to keep things to a minimum, and when it comes down to it, it's amazing how little stuff you need to get by.

My tat – besides a few choice bits of bounty from the shops - consisted of everything I could fit in my rucksack; an ex-army eiderdown sleeping bag, a mesh tin, a little paraffin burner, a stainless steel mirror, a compass, some socks, spare t-shirts and pants, a spare pair of cotton trousers, a bunch of old photos and a book of tunes. The mesh tin, the burner, the sleeping bag and the compass, as well as the rucksack itself were all loans from my dad, along with his old para smock. He never got them back and remains in an unprepared state in the event of the outbreak of World War Three.

The most important thing I owned was my knife. I quickly realised how useful, essential, one was – for everything from spreading margarine to cutting rope. The trick, as with any tat you really needed, was hanging on to it. I lost count of the number of times I had to climb down from the tree to look for the stuff I'd let slip. I was on the point of keeping the hammer and saw permanently tied on. I even had to keep myself tied on, as a precaution and it saved my life once; leaning out too far over the edge, losing my balance and freefalling for a terrifying two feet, before my line went taught. As for everything else, I must have got through about five different knives over the winter and as many whistles.

Working up a tree, sitting in the back of someone's bender, round the fire at night – these were all perfect places to lose a glove or a lighter, a knife or a whistle or a hat. And if you had to swing upside down while climbing a tree, then you were guaranteed to empty your pockets, hearing your loose change cascade to the floor, bouncing off the branches with a bright echo.

I began to instil myself with a military discipline about my stuff, to stop myself losing anything else. I had a money-bag, which I kept tied to my belt, along with my wallet and a little holder I'd made for my knife, though I kept knocking it off branches even then. The rest of time, I tried to remember that if you put something down, something that belonged in your pockets, you had to keep your eye on it. Before the pixies grabbed it.

The front room of the office, in its final days, had become a graveyard for old tat. My tent was amongst it, intact but no longer waterproof. And it seemed that everyone who had passed through the campaign in those early months had left some momento – an old bag or a broken soled pair of boots, pots that hadn't been cleaned for too long, random trousers that fitted no one, a radiator. The tat lurked round the room with a presence all of its own; ominous, chaotic and seeking to expand its empire. It gave you waves of despondency just looking at it, which everybody tried not to do.

By contrast, when we were still in the office, Badger came down the stairs and announced he was having a 'tat purge'; giving away every little thing that he no longer needed. It was no bad thing to do – old tat ties you down, binds you fast to the old chapters of your life. I inherited a copper wire ring, wound into a double spiral, which I wore on a stone around my neck. Badger had been given it while at Solsbury Hill and I held it as a token of the family I was still largely to meet.

As well as these realisations, living in the woods had profound repercussions by its very nature, irrespective of our observations or actions. At night, there was only a thin skin between us and the outer world. I became accustomed to the sound of the wind in the trees at all times. It wasn't a thing I necessarily listened to, but the silence that fell whenever I stepped inside a building was eerie and disquietening. The sound was a source of reassurance at night and being out in it stirred the spirit during the day. It was like being connected to a great river, the source of all life.

Sometimes, having maybe just made it back from a mission in town, we would just sit at night and look up at the stars. There was something beautiful about the way they punctuated the spaces between the branches, as though the trees were framing them, putting them within a secondary cosmological framework that normally we were unaware of. The stars blinked madly with the movement of the trees, the distant sound of the motorway made its way to our ears; echoing and distorted by miles of trees until it sounded almost borne of the woodland itself. At times like these, everything was peaceful.

The landscape all around suddenly seemed to rebound with an echo of our arrival and my awakening in this place. It was as if everything suddenly fitted into place, as though unformed questions that had nagged at me for years were now laid out, answered and at rest. Everything was working out exactly as it should, and to be rooted in this place, to have a sense of place within it, made everything seem whole.

To the north, we knew, the Lambourn Downs rolled up to the Ridgeway – the old hillborn track that ran down the spine of the South. The North Downs stood silently to the south, off in the blue distance behind Donnington Castle. Badger said there were more and more stories of people seeing strange things in the woods all round, and that in itself made sense. It was as though the hills were waking up with us and years of separation between us and the Land were falling away like an old skin.

So, it was hard to explain to the Stoughtons why we didn't want a lift, but we were stood in a silent rapture, and didn't want to be removed from it for a moment.

Swords

Some of the best times came when I was down from the trees and sat by the fire at night. The firepit was close to the trunk of the beech tree, with a pallet for a kitchen; somewhere to put all the mugs and pots and plates to stop them getting spattered in leafmould with the rain. If any mugs, or anything else, were left on the ground the night of a shower, the morning would find them encrusted with a thin veneer of forest floor. The essence of the woods began to creep under our skin, everything began to taste of it. Our clothes smelt of it from the smoke and the dry leaf dust of the bender floors. Our fingernails and our hair were full of it. I adopted a motto; "a little bit of dirt does you good." It might not have been true, but it was better to believe it, considering the circumstances.

I got my first rudimentary cooking lessons around the fire, in between messing around with torch beams – rude light sabres formed from the steam, evoking old jedis, but smelling of cabbage. The lessons involved boiling water and whatever vegetables happened to be around, cabbage being an invariable ingredient, as constant as mud. There was a cabbage in the food store that never seemed to die, sustained on an unlikely half-life, where it rose half resurrected every morning, greeting you with a defiant cross section and a vague sulphuric whiff of slow decay.

Added to the cabbage would be salt and some garlic and a handful of lentils; then it was just a question of stirring it and keeping the fire going. When it was raining, we'd cook on the burners, which took all night.

Not that there was any shortage of night – it was midwinter and we knew about it. Even getting up at first light didn't make the days long enough. On nights like

103

this, the woods of the world were very old and big still and town just a distant memory, an electrically lit collective hallucination.

Tami played the guitar and had a voice that would've raised rafters, had there been any. As it was it just bounded around in the canopy and drew you away from yourself. She played songs by Joni Mitchell, Michelle Shocked and Suzanne Vega, as well a few she'd made up herself. Most of her songs felt full of a kind of sweet pining, which seemed appropriate in these woods.

Even without music, I would catch my breath every day at the beauty all around me, and then remember that in a few months, maybe longer, this might all be gone. It was hard not to feel that the woods all around us were in a state of anxiety themselves, or else a deep sadness. A few people who stayed said they thought the woods harboured some element of anger too, though I never felt it myself.

It certainly had an edge though, particularly around the blackthorns over by the platforms. On too many nights I had wandered over there and strayed from the path in the dark, finding myself surrounded by a thicket with my hair getting tangled by the thorns. We all tried to tread softly.

One night I was sat by the fire, listening to Tami and her songs when we heard a wavering cry for help nearby and a muffled sobbing. Soon, the figures of two young lads came into the firelight, covered in bramble scratches and full of disbelief that they'd found other humans in the night. They'd come out as part of a school group but had got separated and lost. It'd been dark for hours. I led them up the Wantage road to the Reserve carpark where their coach was still waiting for them, sat on its haunches and pensive as a mothership.

On one of the days when everyone came over to the treehouses to help out, we established a third platform by lashing on a long, round, ash beam between two upright branches, above where the trunk had forked. This was made possible by my standing on a shorter beam that was lashed further down towards the fork. The beam was hauled up by everyone on the ground, so I only had to lash it into place.

The rest of the platform took shape in the next few weeks with the help of Ed and some others, big pieces of plywood getting nailed to the beams to create a rough, elongated triangle – the whole thing was constructed around the three boughs that forked high up in the oak. These were standard trees, that rose above the shrub layer, growing tall and straight until they were well clear of the hazel and blackthorns and not forking off until very high up. When the wind blew, the tree tops revolved in a slow circle, first one way and then the other. After a walkway was attached, you could feel the tree's movement being constricted where it pulled the lines tight. We wondered about creating a death slide to the tree I slept in, but thought better of it when we realised it would involve coming to an abrupt end against another trunk.

One afternoon found me working alone on the new platform, hammering down one of the boards, wrapped in a tartan blanket from Ed's treehouse. There was a biting wind and it had just hailed, leaving my ungloved fingers frozen and the nails difficult to get hold of. Out of nowhere, an army helicopter appeared and droned over my head, the thunder of its blades blackening out every other noise. I was right near the tops of the branches, the delicate upper hemispheres forming only a very fine frame against the sky, and the helicopter wasn't far above that.

Feeling belligerent, I stuck my fingers up and was suddenly aware, not without a rush of adolescent pride, of what I thought I must look like, out in the hail at the top of a tree wearing tartan. I felt a lot harder than the men in the helicopter anyway.

A lot of talk was later banded around about eco-warriors, from the press and protestors and everyone else as well. The term was used for praise and derision at different times, with protestors more often than not falling over backwards to deny any identification with a role model that was seen as stereotyped and hubristic. It was a fair point that the term was divisive, in that it created a perception that the 'ordinary public' could sit back in awe and admiration while the brave eco-warriors steamed in and took care of everything for them. But people were maybe a little too hot in denying any identification with what was only another term for someone who put up a fight. Though accepting the role for what it was, and with some degree of humility and grace, was no easy thing, so perhaps the self-derision had its place. For my part, I was having it, glad to have joined in the struggle - warrior or not - and appreciative of the attention, though the last bit, at least, would change in the end.

Giving the fingers to a helicopter was another proud milestone down a road that had started years ago, when Sean Connery dropped through a skylight into a ship's hold on an otherwise dull Saturday afternoon, and proceeded to cause mayhem amongst the Lowlander crew. I suddenly realised that people had been fighting with swords for thousands of years. For many, until relatively recently, having a sword by your side was almost as natural as walking itself. Moved to do something about my apparent cultural nakedness, I was soon part of a local fencing club, sparring sabres with a retired general, an overweight chef and three local builders - who were always on the look out for things to swing off.

That in turn, coupled with an impulse for aesthetics – which was only beginning to make a kind of holistic sense now that I was in the woods – led to re-enactments. I knocked that on the head after I turned eighteen and began to realise there were probably better ways of getting yourself injured. It had still been a fantastic laugh and it probably saved me from being narrow shouldered, and scrawny, not fit for much else besides offices. And running full tilt across crowded green fields, screaming your head off so's strike fear into those you were running towards had been good preparation for what lay ahead.

To have arrived in the woods at that place and time felt like the longed for destination of inroads that had spanned back further than I could possibly know. Things had never made so much sense. Life was fantastic.

Far into December, when the cold was cutting deep and a freezing fog would gather by night in the treetops, a man called Olly arrived at the camp. It was beautiful to wake up in the trees after a night of hard frost – branches that were coated on their upper side in thick moss were now underhung with rows of long icicles. Olly was in his middle ages, had a bushy brown moustache and kept himself to himself, conserving his energy, keeping the stove going in the communal and a kettle on the fire outside. He had been at Solsbury Hill and in the army sometime before that. He had an air of sortedness and dignity and always seemed faintly amused, as though he had a lot to say, had he been feeling less charitable.

His stories of Solsbury Hill painted a clearer picture than any I had already heard. Badger had described life on the camp, had alluded to a vast family that I was now a part of, and spoke about things like the talking stick – a kind of conch that was used to keep meetings in order. He was full of anecdotes about particular people at particular times, which somehow always related to the matter in hand.

Sharing muesli and tea with Ed, and he was full of talk about the tree village that was created on Solsbury, and about how we'd have the same thing in Snelsmore soon. He was always putting pictures in my mind of what life would be like when that happened – thirty huts in the sky, people holding parties on their platforms and using each other's living space as a route through from tree to tree. People living in hammocks. People living in double-decker platforms. Triple-decker platforms. Tall tales of returning home drunk along wobbly walkways.

But Olly spoke with a quiet passion and a calm mind about the time he first arrived at the hill, when the tree village only consisted of one man in a hammock and when the cut of the coming road was visible like a white scar on the horizon. He spoke about what it was like to see it get closer every day, working its way across the landscape like a bad dream that woke with you every morning.

Olly, when he came to us, had bought maps of the route. The route of the Newbury Bypass stretched for nine miles to the west of the town. It crossed two river valleys; both triple SI's, a Civil War battlefield and would destroy thousands of acres of woodland. It started in Hampshire, finished in Berkshire and condemned every piece of land between it and town to practically inevitable infill building.

In the south of the route, it crossed the site of the First Battle of Newbury; where Charles I had blocked the return of the Parliamentary army to London but lost the battle after his army ran out of gunpowder. Five thousand men had died in the fight, many of them still buried on the battlefield. There were a further twelve sites of archaeological importance, including a Romano British

108

Villa and the Lambourn mesolithic site; which was classified 'Of National Importance'.

Olly's maps were detailed; full of technical lines and symbols and showed the extent of the cuts through the hills. We couldn't believe how wide these were. Where we stood, on the site of the ground camp, approximately two hundred feet across the top of the hill would be cut into and levelled flat. I had only envisaged a path of destruction the width of a dual carriageway and hadn't accounted for the hills. My stomach churned and my head spun to think about it. Suddenly the woods here seemed very small and fragile, able to be blown away by the merest change of wind, or flick of the pen.

On a day when the clouds hung low, Badger, Olly and myself took a walk along the route. It was paradoxical and cutting to take a walk in beautiful countryside, knowing that every place you visited was faced with complete oblivion.

First we went out of the woods and up to the brow of the hill past the platforms. We were high above the town here, and had a view over much of the valley. The North Downs stood large and still blue to the south, rising up after mile upon mile of damp woodland and meadows. The hills were passive and distantly watchful and homely to look at, for me; reminding me of hills further south. The borders of Snelsmore were visible behind us on either side of the ridge, the woods rolling up towards the Lambourn Downs. The Common formed a part of these downs, which were designated an Area of Outstanding Natural Beauty. The road would cut through this AONB three times. The North Downs rolled West towards Salisbury Plain – the heartland of the South, and standing here on the hill we had a good idea of exactly where we stood in the world.

One of Mr Tonensho's golf courses spread down the slope from the brow of the hill, and we walked through it towards Bagnor village. It was a still, overcast day and no golfers were in sight. At the foot of the hill and the edge of the houses, the gigantic trunk of a beech tree lay on its side, crumbling away to show its middle and big enough to live in, if you wanted. A row of equally big beeches rode up the hill back towards the camp. They stood out of the hedge like giants; elephant skinned with wrinkles fat as your fingers where the branches creased out from the trunk.

On the way down, Badger had pointed out the new v-shaped notches cut high up where a bat roost had been removed. There were no niceties in operation here – cutting the roosts killed the bats within. They'd wanted to remove the roosts before they came into use for hibernation. But, as with the badgers, it was a rush job and they were running late. They'd still been cutting in November and bats started to hibernate from October. It was a real life chainsaw massacre. Lines of spike marks in the trunk marked the spot where the tree surgeons had stuck their boots on the way up, the newly exposed wood of the old roosts standing out with a raw brightness.

Near the village and everything was quiet. The river Lambourn, renowned for its purity, rolled under a bridge, clear and well bedded with green weeds. We stood on the bridge for a while, leaning on an old style iron railing, watching the water go by. The peace hung around us, tangible, blurring and focusing things all at once. A white washed pub was nearby; a long, low Seventeenth Century building, and one or two people were climbing out of cars and hurrying inside, trying to get out of the cold. There was very little traffic. It seemed like the backend of nowhere, and all the better for it; the sort of place you didn't think still existed and which you knew you'd never find on your own, or which you'd find just the once and never get back to, wondering just where it went. The pub

110

was called 'The Blackbird'. The road would come very close by.

Our path took us down a long avenue lined with more giant beech trees – Bagnor Lane. It was majestic even in the winter. But here, too, lines of spike marks led up the trees to where more roosts had been taken out. The road would cut across Bagnor Lane at an angle, toppling many trees in the process. The removal of bat roosts and the nests of dormice, most of which were in a wood known as Reddings Copse, was one of the biggest scandals of the early part of the road clearance.

The reasoning behind chainsawing the roosts and nests and relocating the badgers was ostensibly for the protection of the species concerned - to remove them off route and out of harm's way. But you couldn't help thinking that it was all a bit convenient – removing protected species that could potentially stop the road if an Environmental Impact Assessment went ahead. Nevermind the fact that the job was being done poorly or late, putting the creatures at serious risk, where they weren't being killed in the first place.

When I first arrived, and for several weeks after, the campaign had been in the middle of a cat and mouse game with the tree surgeons contracted to cut the roosts. Cutting the roosts like this was highly illegal, so all that had to be done was find and tail the surgeons and point a camera at them. They'd then scurry back to their landrovers and move onto another site, trying to shake off our attention in the meantime.

For a while, there seemed to be a very real chance that we could stop the butchery going on and thereby help the case for calling an Environmental Impact Assessment. And with an EIA, there might be a good chance of the road being scrapped altogether. Unfortunately, we were facing disruption from more than one quarter.

The campaign, in addition to having an office, was equipped with a blue and yellow 2CV and walkie-talkies. But by the time I got there, the car had somehow fallen into the hands of a man known as Spikey Mike. We were reduced to hunting the tree surgeons on foot and, obviously, not doing very well at all. On one of the first days after arriving at the office, we heard that they were working in a piece of woodland in the south of the route - Reddings Copse. By the time we got down there, they were long gone and we wondered around disconsolate, looking at pheasant coops. That was the first time I'd met Balin, who was waiting when we got there, having just missed the surgeons himself. Black haired, black bearded and big as they come, he emerged out from under the trees as if he'd been expecting us. It was around this time he was sleeping out on the route, in an effort to keep ahead of the game.

Spikey Mike, on the other hand, had a heroin habit and managed to cause a right load of trouble. He almost put me off going to Cadbury Castle by saying it was a tribal thing, in a way that implied outsiders weren't welcome. Fortunately, a nearby Australian woman interjected with "It's all one tribe." Which set the record straight.

Spikey Mike had shaved hair with a little bunch of rat tail dreads at the back, his exposed head seeming unnaturally boney and grey. His eyes were laced with a dark rim and his smile was a little too sharp. It was he who'd sat at the dark heart of the old office living room, laughing a little too loud. While we were at Cadbury, he claimed to have been using the lounge for a bit of black magic. It was fair to say I wasn't a very big fan.

It was his bender me and Len had slept in. When Spikey Mike found this out, recognising my lantern when I took it out of my bag in the office, he turned on a mix of whining and aggression, demanding money for the candles we'd burnt. We might have used one or two, but his outrage was out of all proportion. Later, I came across him in the backstreets by the mills and he sidled up to try and drag some change out of me, pleading with a razor-keen underlying force. He felt like my nemesis, appearing out the shadows and homing in during uncertain moments. I had a feeling that if I ever went to India, or somewhere equally remote, I'd find him at the back of a cave there, staring out with his sharp grin, waiting to fuck up my head. He'd taken the car and done in our hopes. When I looked at his eyes, I felt weird. It was due to characters like him that Snelsmore was founded in secret.

Between the trees at the bottom of Bagnor Lane, we could see our next destination – a copse of trees standing out on a low ridge. It stood silhouetted against the low sky, the blues of the ridge and the trees palely offset by bands of thin silver behind them. At the end nearest us, it looked as though the trees had been thinned so that those that were left stood out clearly with the light behind them. We got there to find that all the trees within that end of the copse had been felled, leaving just a ring of beeches at the perimeter for the sake of aesthetics. There was a palpable sadness, like a war grave.

Further on, past some solitary oaks in a field, and over the A4, we found another woodland where much the same thing had happened. The ground sloped here, running down to the Kennet river basin from the high ground of the A4, the Bath road. At the bottom of the slope, across a watermeadow, the ground was broken up by a crisscross of waterways, keeping us from the woodland where the road would run.

This was Speenham Moor, part of the Speenham Estate. We continued on down into the woods to the left of the water. The trees here were low and thin, due to the waterlogged soil, oaks branching out into snake like contortions, other trees dense with their ivy. It was very quiet, the moor was a world of its own. Somebody found some white swan feathers and we all carried one with us, walking in silence along by the water, overshadowed even in the winter by the swathes of gnarled trees. The earth was very damp and full of moss and gave way easily to our boots. A train echoed past from the south, way off and from another country altogether. Everything echoes in the cold, when the clouds are close. I put the feather in my hair and there was no one to stop me.

We eventually found a bridge that would take us across the rest of the moor and away from the maze of waterlogged pockets of woodland. It was a fisherman's bridge, which is to say it consisted of four planks, two planks wide, with a support in the middle driven into the waterbed. We had passed one of these earlier, but half of it was missing and we had been worried that there might be no way across.

The fisherman's bridges seemed ancient, the rotten ones obviously were, and felt like signs of a half hidden culture; the sole remnants of the moor's retiring population. The old wardens and fishermen, lock keepers and other old men of the moor were nowhere to be seen, as though they were already dead, or watching us; cunning and quiet from the bushes.

The rest of the moor was mostly open to the sky, which seemed very large in this flat expanse of land. A strange melancholy began to sink in as we walked south. The deep tranquillity of the place was laced with the knowledge that soon it wouldn't be tranquil here at all, soon it would be full of machinery and engines and the coming and going of people who didn't know where they were. When we got to the river, it was getting dark, with all the heaviness of a winter evening. We worked our way eastwards until we got to the town and the High Street, feeling hungry and strangely displaced.

Rope

One of the best things about working and living in a tree was going down to the ground again. Having a climbing rope threaded through the branches allowed you to abseil your way to the earth. Even when you took it slowly, it was exhilarating; a few moments of free falling among the stilled hush of the woods.

The main thing you needed to abseil, besides your climbing harness and some rope, was a palm sized piece of steel called a figure-of-eight. It was literally 'eight' shaped, one ring attached to your harness and the other to loop the rope through and around. Figure-of-eights became the most noticeable feature of anyone in a harness round a firepit; curvaceous and futuristic, hanging down from their main carabina like strangely alien genitalia.

Swinging out for the first time, attached by the figure-of-eight, was always a test. Your natural instincts told you that the rope would only slip through, leaving you to plummet desperately to the ground. To prevent this, you had to hold vertical the rope underneath you. To let yourself drop, you moved the rope up towards horizontal. Doing it for the first time was dangerous, in case whoever it was had looped their rope around incorrectly or panicked on the way down and let the rope slip from under them. We always had someone experienced to show how the rope was looped on, as well as someone on the ground to help hold the rope straight – just in case. Badger also advised pulling the ropes up at night to prevent ill-wishers cutting off the bottom of the rope at night, leaving you to a very rude awakening.

However many times you'd done it, abseiling always carried the danger of getting your hair caught. If you had

116

long hair, it was always an idea to tie it back freshly before going down, or to stick it all under a hat. The thinnest wisp could get drawn in by the conveyor belt motion of the rope and, once you were caught, it was very difficult to free yourself – especially with one hand needed to hold the rope down.

It happened to me once – one stray dreadlock getting caught, pulling painfully at my scalp. I was extremely fortunate that a big branch was near enough for me to grab onto and haul myself up. When it happened to Angela, she wasn't so lucky, getting caught ten foot off the ground and way below any branches. We heard her cries from the other side of the valley and it was a good ten minutes after that before it was over. She'd ended up standing on somebody's shoulder while someone else passed her up a knife to cut her hair free – which had more or less already been pulled half out.

Ed's tree and mine was connected by a rope walkway – two lines of parallel rope, one over the other, spanning the distance between one tree and the next. You shinnied across it sideways on, holding on to the top line while your feet shuffled along the bottom. They were always crossed wearing a harness, clipped onto the top rope. We wore our harnesses all the time when up in the trees, and only took them off to sleep.

It was a short walkway – only about ten or fifteen foot long – and good to start on. The lines stayed pretty taut, not being stretched much by the sway of the trees, and they didn't swing too badly one way or the other as you stepped along them.

Another walkway was put up between Ed's treehouse and the third, higher, platform across the stream. This was much longer and you had to lean into it to keep control, your feet swinging out behind you. If you didn't, you ran the risk of the top line flipping back, leaving you to hold on at a nasty angle, which wasn't good, that high up.

Ryan, who was part of the communal bender posse, but who came over to help far more than anyone else, thought he might put a platform in the next big tree on the far side of the stream. Ryan had returned from abroad to find his childhood haunts trashed by building contractors. Now he was setting things right. With dark dreads and beard he was vaguely piratical, with a faint air of the international traveller. He was a good man and a brilliant climber.

The tree he had his eye on was a big oak at the edge of the woods, silhouetted against the sky and spreading its branches out far and wide to catch the light. We both decided, separately, that it should be called Hern – it seemed somehow fatherly and old, dark and antlered and guarding the threshold.

We tried to connect it with a walkway, and spent a whole day throwing weighted lines from either tree to the middle, trying to get them to clear the many branches. If they both got to the ground in between the two trees, one could be pulled up and tied fast at either end. It was a complete disaster. The distance between the trees was massive and we were dealing with a lot of rope. We were soon getting the ropes tangled in a heap and snagged in branches to boot. I'd helped Ed with the last walkway, and thought making another one would be pretty straight forward. We eventually abandoned it as it got dark, having spent the last hour and a half trying to get the lines back in the order they started in. It was a big lesson in how much I still had to learn. Maybe Hern wasn't meant to be lived in just yet.

In general though, with all the hauling stuff up, the walkways and climbing rope, we were beginning to get pretty handy with ropework. After the incident with the third walkway, I began to get obsessive about keeping the lines in order, rolling them over hand and elbow whenever I was hauling up. It was definitely the way forward, and helped speed everything up. Tami had some Kangaroo Moon song she sang whenever she was tying things on, with lyrics about heaving and hauling away, which added to the feeling of being at sea.

By night I sailed some pretty strange waters. I woke with the memory of fantastic dreams. In one, I was with a girl in the bright sun of a spring day. We were stood inside the soft turf of a small hillfort, surrounded by young trees. Small and beautiful flowers were everywhere underfoot, like stars, and we followed a grassy road out, knowing in the way you can only know in dreams, that we were following in the footsteps of King Arthur.

In another, I found myself alone, high in the branches of a solitary oak in the middle of a field of wheat, or long grass. An assortment of police and press were scattered in the field below, stood around their vans, all looking up towards me. Kate Adie was stood by a red van and looking up at me, reporting on my condition. The eyes of the world were on me. As this unsettling fact began to sink in, I heard a shout from directly below the tree. I looked down to see Olly, who had become a golden coloured centaur. I jumped on his back and he galloped away, taking me clear of the glare of the world's eye.

I went back to my parents for Christmas. It felt like I'd been away for much longer than three months. The house seemed much smaller and I slept with my windows open, despite the cold. Up on the Downs and there was no doubt that these were the depths of winter; a thick frost hugging the northern slopes. I went to some small chalk pits after some peace and sat for a while surrounded by the white earth. The chalk pits were like small caves, the earth overhanging them full of roots that bound the ground together. The cold felt very close and I found myself thinking about fire, about how important it was to life in the depths of winter; the primal spark that kept bones and hopes afloat. Having sat round one for so many nights, it was strange to be outdoors without one close by.

The friends I saw were taken aback by my dishevelledness. I was slightly shocked that they'd find something so trivial of any importance. But it was true I was not the same person who'd said goodbye three months back. I'd more or less worn the same outer layers ever since, and they were covered in layers of woodland dirt and the green that rubbed off from the trees.

When I returned to the camp, just before New Year, I was given the news that the road had been called off for a year. Brian Mawhinney, the recently appointed Transport Secretary said the reprieve offered an opportunity for a 'great transport debate.' The shift in popular opinion against roads had become impossible to ignore and a report from the Royal Commission on Environmental Pollution at the end of October widely condemned the government's transport policy. New evidence of the habitats affected on the route of Newbury's bypass was mounting all the time, presenting a very different picture than that given during the major public enquiry, six years previously. The Nature Conservancy Council – the predecessor to English Nature - had presented a survey of wildlife and likely environmental impact that was emerging as incomplete, at best.

Roads in general, and Newbury in particular, were receiving more and more coverage as time went by. We'd received a visit ourselves – a BBC news crew coming to film us at work in the trees. As a result, I'd seen myself on

TV while at my folks – a fuzzy headed figure in an overcoat, crossing a walkway. A storm was raging around us, but since I'd entered the fray, I felt a certain level of peace about matters, a kind of assurance that came with the knowledge I was on the right road, and doing my best to prevent the worst outcome.

I'd missed a party around the trees when the news came through. It meant so much to us; whereas before we were expecting clearance work to start early in the year, we now had much longer to prepare. We weren't sure whether we should carry on building the tree village; it wouldn't have expressed much faith in the 'great debate', though we probably had good reason to be cynical. And considering the uncertainty now surrounding everything, it would have been foolish not to make the most of the reprieve.

For the time being though, there were other places that needed more people, and that decided things for us. Just keeping the camp going, never mind building treehouses, was getting more and more of a strain, Badger and Tami pretty much holding the ground camp together.

The spare wood was hauled up and lashed onto the platforms. I was glad, having long grown tired of my solitary existence in the treetops. New places beckoned, along with new people, and I felt as though a heavy duty had been lifted off my shoulders. Newbury had grown too quiet. The landscape itself seemed full of a heaviness; a deep longing that I couldn't understand and was glad to be clear of.

II

Fairmile

Arrival

Fairmile was a camp on a hill, centred around a huge old oak. It was a giant, one of the biggest trees I had seen in my life. A copse ran behind the camp but the oak stood forward on its own, free to stretch its limbs in every direction. A large, round bender stood on one side and a caravan on the other, a firepit in between. It was a sunny winter's day when I arrived and the oak spread itself out in full glory on the hill above me. Ribbons on a string fence defined the boundaries of the camp. I entered through a heavily decorated gateway to the cry of "fresh meat!"

I had set off from Snelsmore three days earlier, originally in the company of two others; Olly and another elder man called Rick. We were hitching and they'd been one step ahead in reaching the motorway, maybe by two or three hundred yards. I arrived at the roadside, turning a corner onto the sliproad, to find myself alone. The lift they caught obviously couldn't wait, or hadn't had room for all three of us. They'd left me a bag of half past it tangerines as a momento.

During December, Snelsmore had been visited by lads my own age; long haired envoys from Fairmile; down in the South West. They badly needed people, the Newbury road had been postponed and I was only too happy to be off, thirsty for something other than the dense quiet of the Common.

I caught a lift to Bristol, then snow and the onset of darkness coerced me to get a bus into the city and a coach down to Exeter. I had the name of the nearest village and was confident I'd find the camp once I got there. It was New Year's Eve.

At Exeter bus station, the man on duty found it all quite amusing,
"There's no buses today sir; et's New Yer's Eve, es'n et?"
Not knowing what to do now, I headed for the pub, asking some likely looking people where a man like myself might be welcome.

I was carrying, besides a fair selection of my own stuff, a tool bag that had been rotting for months in a tent by the big beech. It belonged to a man I was told was on the camp in Devon, and I decided to take it down to him. Its weight was the reason I fell behind the others, making their disappearance a particularly harsh manifestation of some law in life I'd yet to learn.

There was a dark piece of wasteground next to the pub, and I stashed the toolbag up by a culvert in the wall. There was only so much baggage I could deal with in a crowded pub, and I was worried I might be turned away.

Inside, I quickly introduced myself to some dreadlocked folks before the spirit of isolation noticed the newcomer and took root. They were friendly and genuine with it and soon I was talking to a mixed table load of students and travellers and someone was buying cider by the jug. They knew how to do things properly here. I could feel my long days of hermetic isolation at Snelsmore fall away from me like a shroud. Jugs of cider held about four pints and as things progressed I became happier and happier that I'd made it down to Devon. Then we went to a club.

I was funnelled along strange, wide streets and the next thing I knew I was shouting in a woman's ear at the back of a brightly lit dancefloor. The ceiling was very low and drinks kept on appearing at my side. I had the distinct feeling that something new and wonderful was about to happen. The girl, who had amazing eyes, was shouting back at me and I couldn't understand a word. It didn't matter though; we were all smiles and it was fun sticking my face in her ear half the time. As the New Year came in, I felt happier than I had done in ages, out on my own in the world and surrounded by excellent people. I even had a place to sleep – the students I'd met were having a party and said I was welcome to crash on their floor.

I woke up to the sound of bouncers knocking on the toilet door. I knew they were bouncers because they were telling me to get out. I'd collapsed with my head next to the toilet bowl. I'd a vague recollection of trying to be sick before I'd passed out. The cider had done its worst. I managed to convince the bouncers to let me rush back into the depths of the halflit club to pick up my stuff. Then I was being shoved out into the cold.

There were a few people dotted around the steps, but no-one I recognised. To make matters worse, this was the back entrance, which disorientated me completely. I'd only had the vaguest of clues as to where the club stood in relation to everything else, but now I was totally lost.

The feeling and the knowledge of being totally alone in a strange city slowly sank in. I found myself walking along an old stone bridge in a state of bewilderment. If I'd known how to find the pub I'd been in, I might have found my way. But that seemed suddenly very far away. It started to snow.

A car pulled over and the man inside leaned over to ask if I was alright. He knew how to find the pub and I got in. He turned the heating on and everything suddenly seemed hopeful once again. Outside the pub, I picked up the toolbag and started off towards the party. I'd looked at a tourist map earlier on, the kind you get stuck on a big board, and the students had written down their address, so I had I rough idea where to go. But the bag was very heavy, the day and the drinks had taken their toll and when I reached a small piece of park, my fatigue crowded round me and jumped on my head.

New Year's Day found me inside my eiderdown sleeping bag on a patch of grass, twenty yards from a big road. There was frost on my hair and all over my sleeping bag. I felt cold and sick and a right idiot. I don't think I'd ever felt so wretched in my life. I forced a couple of tangerines down for breakfast (which didn't help my guts) and set off, resolute for the bus station. I must have looked as bad as I felt because an old couple stopped within minutes and gave me a lift.

"There esn't any buses today" I was told "Et's New Yerr's Day es'n et?" This was not the news I'd wanted to hear. At that point, the sensible thing to do would have been to find the students' house. Somehow though I felt too gormless, like the night before had been a fantastic time, but the cold light of reason was back in the world and in my mind. It was a bright day though, and Exeter was a beautiful city. I stashed the tool bag again, this time down an alleyway near the Cathedral Green and set off to do some exploring, armed with a carton of Devonshire milk and cheese and onion pasties.

In the evening I ran into two old boys of the street. They tried to convince me to come to a hostel for a night, but I steered well clear. It might have been pride on my part, but they were hectic characters and I'd sooner spend the night elsewhere than in what might have been bedlam.

I had a fixation at the time that church porches offered a safe haven to people on the move – not just from people but also from anything else that might be abroad in the night. The first church I found faced directly onto the street, so I moved off to find somewhere more illustrious.

This turned out to be the Cathedral itself. I knew I'd feel safe there, because the doorway was behind a big iron gate and a stack of fold up, wooden chairs. It was still early evening when I climbed in there – I could hear families outside, walking back from their New Year's excursions - but I felt I was tired enough to sleep soundly all night.

I was wrong. There was an alcoved seat near my feet and I kept on waking from an uneasy sleep with the distinct feeling that someone was watching me from the shadows there. It was quite a clear feeling I got; an impression of an old woman, a concerned and kindly presence who was keeping watch over me and keeping me from a sound sleep at the same time.

Every so often a loud thump would emanate from the bowels of the cathedral, the sound echoing round the vaulted ceiling until it died out. I had strange dreams of shadowy forms of monks dropping empty cowls. Later on I heard the click, click, click of verger's shoes as he walked up to the door and flicked the lights off. The sound of his retreating footsteps rang out in diminishing echoes. Later still, I was awoken by the creaking of a large wooden door followed by another couple of dull thumps. Suddenly there was an almighty noise, as though someone had dropped a large bible just the other side of the door. An old clock started to strike midnight somewhere, its internal organs stringing out winding mechanisms. I decided to get out of there, clambering over the iron railings in a half panic.

I spent the rest of the night under the stone vaults of a medieval bridge. When it came to sleeping rough, I was a bit choosy like that, a kind of heritage tramp. There shouldn't have been many ghosts under a bridge but, suddenly, this was something I couldn't rely on. It started to snow as I fell asleep. A bush next to my head rustled in the wind all night, its dry leaves rattling against each other in the cold.

I went back to the Cathedral in the morning, out of curiosity's sake. I asked a portly verger if anyone would have been walking around the Cathedral at midnight. He gave me an wide eyed, impassive look, but clearly searching me with it, before telling me there hadn't been anyone in the Cathedral that time of night and, if there had, they would have set the alarms off. He then told me a story how a woman who'd been at a service on Christmas day had looked up at the vaulting to see three medieval workers on a piece of scaffolding. There were two thin men and a fat one. She thought they were some kind of re-enactors until the thin men crept up behind the fat man and pushed him off, the whole spectacle disappearing as the fat man plummeted into the air, arms failing.

After that, I decided to take a walk around Exeter's Roman walls. I felt sure I'd catch a bus today and thought I should see some more of the city before I left. I hadn't got far when I came to a cemetery, accessible by a wide, sloping causeway running down along the outside of the wall. Walking down it, I looked up to see a woman's face on the walkway below me. She was very close and I could only see her eyes and above, the rest of her face being obscured by the dividing stone wall. Her eyes were very kindly and seemed to be smiling at me as if she knew me. She was wearing a black, fur lined hood. I remember wishing that people wouldn't wear old looking clothes like that; it freaked me out. At the bottom of the causeway, I turned around to get another look but she'd gone. She must have cut down across the cemetery through the thick lines of Yew trees because there was nowhere else she could have gone. I asked the people walking immediately behind her, who said they hadn't seen her at all. This was getting very disconcerting.

I got back to the station to find there were still no buses running. As things were now getting beyond a joke, I decided to go and find the student's house. One of the girls I'd spent half the night talking to – pale faced, and ginger

130

haired – answered the door in her dressing gown and took me through to a three bar gas fire. As the fire began to warm my bones, I began to realise how cold it was outside. When it slips below freezing and the streets are quiet, the world outdoors becomes another country, like the twilight or somewhere half submerged. Things aren't the same when it's cold.

A lad with a car was coming around in a little while – a quick call confirmed that he'd be up for driving me up to the camp. He'd even been there once or twice himself, so there'd be no problem finding it. Now I was here, sat by the gas fire, it was hard to explain what had taken me so long. I recounted my ghost stories so as not to feel too stupid about things. My friend had a cold and was looking extra white – as though she'd seen a few ghosts herself. There seemed a fine line between hangovers that wouldn't quite die, cold that got in your bones and joining the land of the dead. Only now, safe in the warm, did I feel like I should have been shuddering.

Schemes and Scars

Fairmile had an air of sortedness to it. The firepit had been cobbled to help stop the winter mud getting a look in and pallets had been laid down around it to form a dry route from the bender to the caravan. A kitchen bender offered a work surface and filing cabinet to keep the food in, away from the rats. There was a stockade of logs on one side of the fire to help keep off the wind and to put the sawn wood behind to stop it rolling down the hill. People got up in the mornings. They washed up their plates. They looked for things to do in the day, to make the camp stronger.

The general togetherness was largely attributed to Kit, one of the caravan residents. Kit was in his forties, ex-army and more than a little reminiscent of Ghengis Khan, even down to the drooping moustache. It was no surprise that Ghengis Khan was one of Kit's heroes. He'd spend large amounts of time expounding his knowledge of ancient warfare. For a while, Kit was a kind of father figure to most of us – sure enough, he might shout and rant on at any given opportunity, but you kind of forgave him because he generally knew what he was talking about and he got things done.

Kit had been a prominent figure at Solsbury Hill, where he'd helped to found the tree village. As one of the stories went, he'd been sat five foot off the ground on a branch, having a rant at people on the ground. In the middle of his diatribe, the branch had snapped. Sat on the ground now, and stunned for only a moment, Kit drew breath and continued exactly where he'd left off. He was a very difficult man to argue with.

The other caravan dwellers were Ceilidh and her son Finn. Finn was as large a character as any you could hope to meet, which was pretty impressive because he was only three years old. His mother was equally fiery, a red head ex-actress who was more than capable of meeting Kit head on. Together Kit and Ceilidh acted as unofficial parental figures – not the kind who would mother you, butter you up, but they were sorted characters who'd been living outdoors a lot longer than we had. The rest of us, with the exception of Olly, and Rick, were all under twenty years old.

I didn't know how to cook. A rapid departure from home had left me unendowed with my mother's rudimentary leaving-home cookery lessons. All I could knock together was something resembling watery stew, thanks to Badger's intermittent tips up at Snelsmore. It didn't help that all my first lessons were on open fires, which were an art of their own just to keep going, never mind to cook on. But everything was new. The very way we all lived had been turned inside out so that life gleamed raw before us.

For months, maybe years, I had a private cooking phobia, a fear that I would be discovered one day as a firepit failure, a fraud in charge of a pan. And there were days when this was extended to everything around me, when sawing wood, rearranging the fire, even making myself toast was carried out under the gaze of half a dozen others, all of them unaware of my private havoc. I was still a teenager after all. I could have done with half an hour to myself first thing in the morning, but living in each other's pockets like we did, solitude was hard to come by.

Numbers ebbed and flowed in the communal bender but for most of the time there were half a dozen of us, more at the weekends. It was a big structure and while it didn't feel overly roomy, it was amazing how many people could be packed in there when times called for it. An interior row of blankets hung as curtains, marking out an inner porch. Here muddy boots could be taken off out of the weather and breezes could be caught before they reached the inner warmth. A home made burner chugged away to one side of the door, made from a large gas bottle and packed around with orange earth. The earth heated up and acted like a storage heater at night; radiating warmth long after the flames had died down.

Around the edges of the bender, strips of foam had been laid down to form mattresses, and that's how we would all sleep, side on to the rounded walls. Any overspill of bodies would be left to the hard open space in the middle. The whole thing rested on pallets, with carpet laid over them, so it was as warm a place as you could wish. After a while someone found a double glazed window, so we could have light during the day. It felt like the invention of the wheel, only brighter.

They were long, dark nights but the world inside the bender was full of warmth. There was usually a spliff or two on the go for a start, and it was well insulated and lagged with blankets between the framework and the tarp. But it was the company we kept together that made all the difference.

I soon counted as good friends two lads more or less my age; Ed and Richard. Ed was from Cambridge, had long ginger dreads and smoked like a trooper. But he was also one of the hardest working people on site and had been here since October. He liked to get up early and make everyone porridge; nice, fancy porridge with raisins and apple and cinnamon. In the evenings, he'd carve bits of wood. He mirrored Swansea Ed, who I'd been building with at Snelsmore, in that he was another Red Head Dreaded Ed and he worked his arse off.

Richard was a little older, had blond hair in a ponytail - which was always on the point of matting up completely - and played mandolin amazingly. He'd come up from

Exeter, where he'd been studying, though that was now an increasingly receding world. We'd play some tunes together now and again, him keeping time with a foot in a half crusty sock. He was cheerful and friendly and good to have around.

Another character who was usually there was a girl called Nina from Brighton. She had closely cropped ginger hair and a ring in her lower lip. She was always chewing her lip, like people with lip rings do. Her laughter erupted at regular intervals, despite her best efforts, like life was always goading her on. She rolled a lot of herbal spliffs. Olly had an ongoing campaign of trying to teach her how to light a fire, but it never worked.

If we weren't making something, we'd be playing cards or reading stories, or discussing the campaign. In such good company, it was like some cheesy sweet dream; you pinched yourself to check you weren't dreaming, found that you weren't and took it all in again. It felt like life was full, and even here, especially here – stuck in a candle lit hut on a windy hill in January – the evenings were precious time and life was worth celebrating.

And Kit talked about his days in the convoys, travelling all over Britain in buses, outfoxing the police, finding ways in past exclusion zones to Stonehenge. Free festivals, free parties; it felt like an unbroken stream of subculture of which we were only the latest manifestation. For decades, people like us had been finding a way to live in this country without buying into a model of progress which was taking the world further down the pan. For decades, people had crowded in trucks or candle lit benders like ours, or sat under the stars around fires and talked about dreams and thought themselves part of a family. And now all these strands; travellers, free party goers, besides the more overtly political, were coming together under the common threat of the Tories' attempts to stamp it all out. Sitting on the hill at Fairmile, we felt we were right at the front of it all.

Hanging from the hazel poles, dangling above our heads as we slept, were everyone's harnesses. They were there to hand, in case we needed to get out and up in a hurry. As the winter progressed, they became a kind of extension of ourselves – our primary means of getting about in the trees and, increasingly, an expression of our identities. They hung there incessantly, as a promise and a threat. We were ready at all times; something which played on our nerves and strengthened our resolve at the same time.

The discussions about the campaign could have gone on all night. We were constantly hatching plans. Kit wanted a series of earthworks dug, to turn the hill into a fort. 'Coffin Drops'; holes just big enough to hold a person upright, would keep heavy machinery at bay. Though the ultimate plan was always to turn our hill into an unassailable fort. As with an Iron Age hillfort, Kit wanted defences that would dissipate and confuse the hordes of security guards as they climbed the hill. Kit was a man who desperately needed an army.

These defences would make the back track, the farmer's road that ran the other side of the copse, the only feasible line of approach. There was a plan to dig this up and cover the hole with railway sleepers, so the farmer could still use it, none the wiser, in the meantime.

The plans could change and meant nothing till they were put into action. The only thing we could be sure of was that, sooner or later, whether we were heavily defended or not, the eviction would come. We could delay them as long as possible, cost the contractors as much as we could, but as far as this road was concerned, the writing was on the wall. As the saying went; "They put a price on our environment, and we will raise that price." And

136

perhaps, somehow or other, our actions would have wider repercussions than we might expect.

In Newbury, when the cat and mouse game was being played out over the bat roosts, there was one occasion when Moonflower got to the tree before the contractors did. Moonflower quietly put it to the man with the chainsaw that he held a great choice in his hands. He could fell the roost, take the money and walk off with blood on his hands. But if he refused – and he fully knew the dodgy premise over which the roosts were being felled – if he put down his saw and in full consciousness walked away from the job, then his actions would ripple out through society and change would be set in motion. The man was a tree surgeon and not without an environmental awareness. He understood the shaky footing his contract rested on. And perhaps Moonflower was simply persuasive because he did, in the end, put away his chainsaw and walk away.

Back in Devon though, half the battle had already been lost. Nearly all the trees on route had been felled before Christmas. Driving up to the camp from Exeter we had seen it – swathes of woodland cut down and lying all around, still waiting to be sawn up and gathered up and despatched to who knows where. The trunks lay down, over and over each other, in the numbing tableau of a flattened landscape.

Arriving so late, I inherited stories of the woods, rather than memories. Most of these consisted of how few protestors there were, and how larger than life their efforts consequently became. Ceilidh perched on a tree at the edge of the felling, scores of yellow jackets in front of her. Ed and Kit facing off diggers single handed.

The appearance of people on the protest seemed like a manifestation of the feeling of the woods themselves, as though everyone had stepped out of themselves, beyond themselves, every action speaking doubly, echoing a sentiment grander than anyone could put their lips to; an urgency and a deep sense of sadness at the loss.

Down the hill from the camp was a river and a small church. The churchyard was round, giving itself a prehistoric brand of antiquity. It felt like an old place. A wooden bridge ran over the river here. I remember it most clearly at night, crossing the bridge in the dark, the river running loud and invisible below me. Sometimes there'd be pieces of light in the water; like stars or bits of the moon, like the whole sky was under our feet as well as above us.

On the other side of the river stood the sawn off remains of an old orchard. The owner of the land was a supporter of the camp, letting us fill our waterbutts from a tap outside his house. It was a long slog up the hill after that.

I was glad I hadn't seen the orchard before it was cut. It was harsh enough to look at it as it was, even without the barbs of a more pristine memory. Standing on either side of a short waterfall were a pair of small stumps, all that was left of an image that might have been Holy. A swathe had been cut through the forestry plantation on the hillside opposite, an unsettling opening on the horizon. And we were next.

Diggers

A major focus of the protest was the digger diving at a place known as the Brickyard. Perhaps it had actually been an old brickworks; it was certainly full of clay. It had now become a muddy building site, adjacent to an ancient pond, which they wanted to 'relocate'. Everyday, bulldozers and diggers were working to shape an artificial pond from the thick clay. Whenever we could, we went down there to get in the way.

On my first trip, I piled out of one of a convoy of cars (an odd irony, but there were no bus routes anywhere near) and found myself scrambling over a barbed wire fence, with a crew of yellow jacketed security running towards me. I jumped free of the fence and under the arms of the lumbering guards, but it took such an effort of contortion to escape their grasp that I soon tripped on my own feet and fell flat on my back. I quickly sprang to my feet, avoiding getting grabbed by inches. Unsure of what would be done to me if apprehended, I made a beeline back to the fence and cleared it in an ungainly arch. It was an audacious debut, but an utterly useless one.

The idea was not only to get over the fence, but to avoid getting rugby tackled by the security and make it to a piece of machinery. With any luck, you'd be able to lock yourself on, d-locking yourself to a pipe or entangling yourself in the cogs and axles underneath the carriage. Once the machinery had come to a halt, others would climb on and the wait for the security would begin. They would prise people's fingers away - in this case taking care not to hurt us or themselves – and drag us to the fenceline, usually depositing us the other side of a big gate. Then the whole game would start again.

We had a good relationship with the security there – most of them we knew by their first names, and there was an understanding that neither side would deliberately physically harm the other. We also kept them in employment, and they knew it. Occasionally, things overstepped themselves in the heat when tempers got frayed. I got my thumb bent back on itself as a security man was peeling my hand off a bar on a digger. Back behind the fence, I taped my thumb to my forefinger and climbed back into the thick of it. For some reason I'd stuck a feather I'd found into the tape and found myself on the receiving end of a particularly harsh tackle by one of the senior security. As soon as he realised it was a feather, he was all apologies, having thought I was running into the compound wielding a knife. I took the feather out.

Other times, tempers were frayed for no particular reason and there was no getting round it. Stood by the fence, on a particularly rough day when a man from London was running rings around the security and winding them all up, I was accosted for wearing my dad's old para smock.
"You're wearing that but you don't know what it means to fight for your country." This really wound me up.
"I am fighting for my country…" I said between clenched teeth, "…times have changed."

The area surrounding the compound consisted of woodland underplayed with a thick orange mud. A lot of the time we'd try to sneak up on the guards through here, hiding behind low mounds and getting plastered orange up to our elbows. Most of the time it didn't work and the security were ready for us when we reached the fence. But occasionally it paid off.

I was alone in the woods one time and managed to get to the edge of the compound unseen by the sole security guard who was stationed nearby. He had his back to me, busy looking at the action going on over the rest of the site. Directly in front of me, only a few metres in from the fence, was the large entrance to some kind of tunnel, rounded concrete disappearing into the blackness. I climbed the fence and stole into the tunnel, still unseen.

I moved along it as quickly as I could, towards the light spilling in from the shaft at the other end. The whole thing couldn't have been more than twenty metres long. When I reached the shaft, a thin metal ladder awaited to draw me up towards daylight. This was going very well, and from the sounds of things, I would be emerging right in the middle of the compound. This was going to be good; a moment of triumph as I burst out to general amazement, leaving a trail of glory across the compound, security falling over sideways in dumbfoundedness, scratching their heads. Maybe everyone from the camp would start cheering.

Just then, overly excited, I trod on a wooden bracing which I thought would take my weight. It tumbled down the shaft and to the floor, raising an unholy clamour as it did. Suddenly stricken, and in no doubt that this mistake would draw unwelcome attention, I scurried back down the longitudinal tunnel, racing to the middle and lying down flat.

I could hear heavy feet working their way down the ladder and soon the voices of two guards were echoing throughout the concrete, trying to sound out if anyone was in the tunnel or not. They called to another guard who was looking in from the other end. The length of the tunnel gave just enough darkness to make my body obscure. It was an agonising moment. I tried not to breathe. None of them wanted to climb in and check the tunnel for themselves and they tried to unearth me with a ruse;

"Let's send the water through just incase. Flush 'em out."
I didn't move. The water sounded pretty bad but I knew it was highly unlikely. Far worse would be the prospect of getting found by the guards down here. They wouldn't be impressed with my little stunt and might not be so friendly away from other people's eyes, where nothing could be proved.

Another few moments of trying to mask my breath and they were gone. When I thought the coast was clear I returned to the shaft and climbed back up the ladder as quietly as I could. I emerged into the compound, rushing out in a near panic before I could be seen and caught in the tunnel again, not waiting to pick my moment. I was bought to the ground almost immediately and dragged to the fence without ceremony.

Another day, I was sat on a digger with Olly when a miracle happened. We got talking with a digger driver. Digger drivers didn't have a good reputation by and large. Just the other week, one known only as Mad Tex was sent home after spinning the top section of his digger – the arm and cab - round and round with half a dozen protestors clinging onto it. So to be engaged in conversation with one - and a pretty good conversation at that - was a bit of a novelty.

The driver and a security guard nearby were saying how you couldn't turn back the clock, how we couldn't go back to horse and carts. Myself and Olly, who'd spent his fair share of time in Africa and India, were arguing that that was exactly what we ought to be doing. At least so far as it was possible. And the driver's grandad had driven a horse and cart. But that was all gone now, he reckoned, a different world. Despite our different arguments, we suddenly had an understanding.

Over on the other digger, fifty foot away, it was a different world again. Everyone had congregated on the one machine and were drumming and chanting and throwing daft abuse at the guards. No one was drumming very well and the songs they were trying to sing sounded awful, more half screams really. It wasn't as if the guards were listening anyway. It would be far better to sit there in silence, I felt.

As work went on and the pond relocation got more and more behind schedule, the niceties began to fade away. The guards got rougher and we ourselves got more bolshy in return. One time I was dragged by two security to the edge of a steep slope and thrown down it onto my back. I was ten feet lower than them when I landed. Seriously winded, I turned my head to see a rusty pole of iron sticking out at an angle, just yards to the left of my chest. "That'll fucking teach him" one of them said.

The security were unmoved by the fate of the ancient pond, pointing out all the time the new artificial pond that was being dug alongside to replace it. A sophisticated tunnel was being built between the two that would successfully transfer the extensive stocks of the pond's fish.

When it came to it, and the water was being pumped between the two, the tunnel proved to be a complete failure, scores of mature fish left to thrash and jump in the rapidly diminishing water, then to flail about in pitiful multitudes amid the drying mud. The security had believed every step of the way what they'd been told; that they'd been protecting a genuine environmentally sensitive scheme. Now they stumbled around in bewilderment like everyone else, desperately transporting fish to the new pond in their plastic hard hats, cursing and suddenly savvy to the realities of habitat relocation schemes. Chances are, the engineers still hailed the new pond as a great success and proudly referred to it on glossy promotional material as a mark of their environmental credentials.

As a way of getting to know me better, or maybe even to sound me out, Ceilidh took me out wooding one day; a long walk over the land surrounding the camp. The camp sat on the furthest limit of an estate that had originally been landscaped by Capability Brown. As a consequence it wore the look of semi real pasture, broken only by clumps of aesthetic mature beech. There weren't that many sheep, but plenty of stiles.

Ceilidh asked me what it was that had drawn me to the protests in the first place. It was a story I'd told often enough before – how long walks on the South Downs as a teenager had eventually brought about an awakening within me, a stirring of sensibilities. I took to walking up the hill I lived on every evening to see the sunset, and experience the unsettling of the twilight air. I started lying around in the woods, watching the green lances of young ash trees dance in the sunlight about me. I found secluded places among the gorse and hawthorn where I could lie back and watch the clouds form. I went for long walks at night, when the pulse of the hills beneath my feet was all the more detectable for the lack of light. The ridges were old sleepers and as I awoke to their power, I became increasingly disturbed that they could be cut through, that roads were cutting them in two all over the country. The hill I lived on was due the chop in a matter of a few years.

Somewhere amongst all this rising awareness, images of protestors began to seep in. Later, they would jump out. There were people in the trees in Ambridge, raising a racket in the kitchen while I made myself snacks. I imagined pink mohicans, piercings and people in jeans and leather that didn't fit very well. Somehow, somewhere along the way, this grew into a more lucid picture. Pieces of half heard news cobbled themselves together, confused but strangely far from off the mark.

The people are banded together like a tribe or family, squatting in and amongst a belt of stubby hawthorns on a steep bank of downland. There's a sense of fellowship, and they're all smiles to one another and even to me, standing amongst them in my mind's eye. A biting spring wind is blowing and everyone seems to be sheltering from some trouble further down the slope. It's evening and the sky above the bank is soft with purple and pink, echoing their dyes.

Things moved rapidly after that. It became clear that if I really valued the treasures I had uncovered on the Downs – and the worthiness of a great many other things were still far from proven to me – then I was obliged to help defend them. I felt privileged to have got to know the hills as well as I had, and therefore honour bound to act on their behalf, to live up to the only truth I could be sure of.

It had been a summer of discoveries. Nearly all my friends were off to university in the autumn. Most of them said they were going for lack of anything else to do, that a grant off the government and a chance to mess around were as much as anyone could hope for. I couldn't see myself getting along with it. I couldn't trust myself to work at university, doing something I had no passion for, and I couldn't jump on the wagon of partying as much as possible; another distraction from the very real problems we were all faced with but which nobody wanted to acknowledge, never mind do something about.

And going abroad, as some of my friends were thinking, was something I could only see myself doing years in the future. I already knew there was a lot of Britain I still had to see. Jumping on a plane and immersing myself in another culture had little appeal when I had so much to learn about my own inheritance.

I'd opted to do a third year at college, having had a change of heart over what I wanted to study. At the end of the summer term I sat at my hometown station, having just got off one train and missed another. I watched it pull out, musing how it felt as though all my friends were already aboard. When I left for Newbury in the autumn half term, jumping at last on a train that stood to take me somewhere promising, it took some effort to trust the ground would rise up to meet me when I came to step off.

Tami had been a fairly regular visitor to the treehouses back at Snelsmore. We had long chats about what had drawn us both to this place. She talked about a hillfort that lay on top of the hill behind her parent's house, in the Welsh Borders. I saw it clearly in my mind, sunlit and green and melting away into the mountains, augmented by my memories of hillforts on the South Downs. We had both awoken to the land around us and felt the calling ringing in our ears, as though we'd been asleep a very long time.

It was the same with Ed, who had had some kind of experience with the oak at Fairmile and had known, once he'd returned to his hometown, that he had to go back. Once you'd felt it, there was no mistaking it. Ceilidh understood all this very well and we returned to the camp with our arms full of fuel.

Spooks and Sparks

If Ceilidh had been sounding me out, it was not without good reason. The farmer's track along the back edge of the copse would have been a good way for unfriendly visitors to sneak up on us. We'd laid a tripwire by the main gap through the hedge. It was rigged up to pull the pin out of a rape alarm if anyone walked through it. On the night before a planned action on a local MP, somebody set it off. Kit went to check it out and we got the word back that nobody was in sight. It had probably been a fox or a badger. The next morning, Rick, who was always in the early stages of growing a moustache, pulled me aside for a quiet chat. The two of us had already agreed to go up on the MP's roof together and drape a banner from the guttering.

"There *was* someone on the back track last night" he told me.

"He came to talk to Kit only we didn't tell anyone so we didn't freak anyone out. He said there was an informer on site. I'm telling you because you need to know because you're doing this action today. Be sure to check the rungs on the ladder, you never know what they might have done to try and stop us. But don't tell anyone else – we don't want to freak everyone out, and we don't want them to know that we know."

It wasn't until much, much later that it occurred to me that it might have been him.

Rick was a photographer and had managed to sneak in to the eviction of Claremont Road in London. Claremont Road was full of squatted houses and represented the zenith of the protest against the M11 extension. Houses had been heavily barricaded, nets had been slung across the road from roof to roof and scaffolding towers had been built looming out of the roof tops – all ploys to make the eviction last as long as possible. When the police turned up, the protestors on the rooftops said they could see a line of riot wagons stretching unfeasibly into the distance. It was an unprecedented level of police presence. For four days, the road was under a state of complete siege. So for Rick to have miraculously snuck in was a feat of unlikely proportions. But we put it down, at the time, to his luck and his cheek.

We were dropped off in the village – with a ladder and a banner – as a kind of advance guard. The MP was a strong advocate of the new road, to the obvious pleasure and fairly likely financial encouragement of building consortiums. On the way to the house Rick made it known that he thought the action had become incredibly dodgy, which he attributed to the meeting that morning where someone around the firepit had announced to everyone present what the plan was. Rick said he was still freaked out from the eviction in London, where Riot Police on the ground had laid into whoever they got their hands on.

By the time we got to the house, he'd convinced me there was practically a riot van around every hedged corner, just waiting for us to seal our fate. We sat on a wall and smoked fags, waiting for the others to turn up. There were a lot of unhappy faces when they did. In the end, the banner got put up by Ned and Swampy; two characters from a smaller, sister camp called Allercombe. Allercombe was a very, very muddy place to live, which is how Swampy got his name. Though his hair had something to do with it too. An ongoing discussion had quickly arisen over what to do with the banner, which Swampy and Ned cut through by grabbing the banner and climbing a drainpipe onto a garage roof, then using the ladder to get to the roof of the house.

Everyone else sat down to a picnic on the MP's lawn, while a few photographers and journalists hovered around, having got a press release that morning. A little later I left the lawn to get some mud from the track at the front of the house, looking for something for facepaint, and found all the journalists chatting casually to the police, sounding almost farcically grown up and dismissive of our little stunt, which they obviously saw as quite childish. They were probably fairly disappointed that they couldn't arrest us or slander us for harassment or criminal damage or something more conventionally antagonistic. Having a picnic just seemed a bit... nice. And yet they couldn't afford to ignore us, and we'd made our point, not least to the MP in question.

Much earlier, on a quiet evening in the communal bender at Snelsmore, with nobody else around, Rick made it clear to me that we were being spied on. He put it into my head that there could be microphones behind every tree and I had to accept that any and all of my conversations could be getting monitored. He was upbeat about it, saying I shouldn't let it stop me passing on information – the word had gone round over the summer he said, about how to do things. New techniques and strategies had been shared; something a fear of surveillance would have prevented. But it was wearing to believe I was the subject of such unwelcome attention and I felt as though a great burden had been put on my shoulders.

It was very likely we were being watched, though the extent of surveillance was probably greatly exaggerated. Moonflower was firmly convinced that the office on Berkeley Road was bugged, which it probably was. He used to address the invisible listener in half his conversations; "I know you're listening but you have no

149

power. Put me in prison and I'll just do a degree. I'll become your worst nightmare." It was an unsettling stirring of awareness.

The phone at the bottom of the hill from Fairmile clicked when you put the receiver down, which I knew from Seventies TV programmes was a sure sign of being bugged. I took to lying about the camp when I was on the phone to my mum, who was always asking awkward questions and getting wildly exaggerated replies. There were dozens of us, if I was to be believed, instead of a hardcore of about ten. And we had many, many treehouses.

But in truth, there was a lot going on in the trees behind the camp. I helped Ed lash the first beam of a platform into the branches of a large beech. The tree formed the main entrance to the copse and was also the hub to the whole walkway system. There were a lot of walkways. Thick rhododendrons covered the lower storey of much of the wood so that abseiling through them was like submerging into another world, or descending from Asguard to Midguard as I liked to think about it.

We had some amazing days of early spring weather and I found myself up in the trees for most of them, where I was building a platform of my own. I saw it as a 'battle platform' – something that would only be used for an eviction, or just for messing about, and had plans for a more habitable treehouse further down the tree. The battle platform would be sturdy enough to make my removal from within it very difficult and I even planned to have it reinforced internally with a welded cage. I realised that might overburden the tree though and, as Kit pointed out, no one wanted me to make a martyr out of myself and get stuck in a fire up there. We weren't that far from Tolpuddle, so it was best not to tempt fate.

As time went on and I finished the flooring, an image of what the platform could become began to crystallise. Half sloping roof, half turreted lookout post, I would name it Chateau de Fromage, painting the sloping triangle like a lump of cheese. It was a conception of genius, I felt, and I worked towards making it a reality, putting in the wooden frame piece by piece. The tree it was in stood out on its own from the main copse and formed one of a line over an area of scrub. There was a large badger sett here, someone reckoned one of the largest in the country. You'd hear them at night, bundling along in the undergrowth near the tree line, coming to raid our bins.

Working in the treetops in the bright sun – not quite in winter and not quite in spring – was a fantastic feeling. A man visiting the camp who had just returned from Africa climbed up to the top of the beech where someone had strung up a net to sit on. He sat there for a long time, singing. It made you want to sing, being at the top of a tree. Sometimes music would drift up from the campsite, someone around the fire with a guitar or a mandolin. It felt like a soundtrack then, that we were living as part of an unfolding film, a bright dream that grew more vivid every day.

I'd look down from my platform sometimes to see buzzards float past, gliding on the early thermals. To the south, a line of black hills strung themselves along, separating us from the sight of the sea. Occasionally hail and rain would come in and I'd weather it out, not having the time to descend and avoid it and knowing there was blue sky on its back.

One time I heard the distinctive sound of a helicopter approaching, the rotors displacing the air with an ongoing cycle of dull thuds. I stopped work and looked around to see if I could see it, searching the sky. It was getting closer but wasn't anywhere in sight. It got louder and louder until I was sure it was almost overhead and then I saw it – army green and moody looking, fifteen foot below me. I could clearly see the pilot and a man leaning out of the door. It rose up over the treetops, just clearing them. We were good practice for fly-bys and presented a pretty close approximation of the Third World targets the hardware would probably be used on, when it got sold on the sly to a variety of dodgy regimes.

A band called Heathens All - who sang a goat skinned brand of nature orientated songs – were putting on a benefit gig for us in Exeter. We piled into all the cars available and made for the venue at top speed. The Cavern was just that, satisfyingly subterranean and hidden away among a network of lanes. It was fairly big too; old vaulting hanging over pillars in the halflight, a bar of dark wood strung out along one long wall. Everyone was getting painted, larging up the tribalism. I painted a blue band across my eyes and dropping down my cheek bones. It was a good crowd in the Cavern and I sat by the doorway for most of the night, painting girl's faces with Celtic triskettes.

After the music, Kit got up on stage to talk about the road scheme. It was a characteristic rant, full of the kind of passion more usually associated with the outbreak of violence in a pub. A woman called Angel also got on stage to help drum up support. She was a white haired elder woman of Allercombe and was soon to earn fame for walking naked into Coventry Cathedral. They were holding a service in honour of the "holy invention of the car," complete with a vintage beast parked near the altar. After posing as an upright member of the congregation,

Angel stripped off and walked down the aisle in her altogether proclaiming at the top of her voice that she was invoking the spirit of Lady Godiva. Lady Godiva's trip around town in the buff was done to get her husband to revoke his harsh taxes, therefore placing her high and above Coventry's good and great. Angel's stunt was a grand act and a fitting antidote to an unholy outbreak of ecclesiastical idolatry. It was probably fair to say that, had cars been around in her time, Lady Godiva would still have preferred horses. Motoring naked down the A46 wouldn't have had the same class.

For the most part, Kit's rant was about the Exeter-Honiton bypass being a toll road – a DBFO. This meant a road that was publicly financed, the contractors being paid by a system of shadow tolling that would come from the taxpayer for years after the completion of the road. It was highly likely that people would still be paying for the new road long after it had fallen to congestion and gridlock.

DBFO stood for 'Design, Build, Finance, Operate' though we had dubbed it 'Destroy, Burn, Flatten, Obliterate' or 'Dodgy Blokes Felling Oaks.' It almost went without saying that the bypass would be built to supersede a road that had been constructed in the Seventies.

A random straggle of grim housing had been built up along the roadside since then, which included the pub at the bottom of the hill from the camp. It was owned by a couple who had become landlord and lady late on in life. They both wore a look of permanent regret. The pub was festooned with a drab dazzle of lighting outside, an effort to drag in more punters. It stood on a busy road but, for all the people inside, it might as well have stood on a desolate moor. In midwinter. During a plague. The walls inside were part stone, in the style of a European theme park or a mid Seventies, Flintstone cladding job. We drunk our pints with our boots off, feeling slightly deranged by the fruit machine.

It was a far cry from the dark peace of the camp. The winter nights had a serenity all of their own. We built a new kitchen and it became somewhere new to sit out at night, the view from the door framing the vast span of the oak's limbs perfectly. The oak never got any smaller and it never failed to raise a sense of wonder to look up and take it all in.

For the sake of security at night, and also as a step along the road towards Kit's envisaged hillfort, we began to fortify the string fence. The hill dropped down from the camp to a meadow and this was full of a tangle of trees that had been felled at the same time as the orchard. We used these trees to make a proper fence, a kind of dead hedge, dragging sawn off segments up the steep bank and wedging them together. It became a personal mission of mine and I worked on my own for much of the time, getting grimy and working up a sweat under my layers. We were short on numbers and other people were busy getting on with the walkways in the trees, wooding and looking after Finn. Gradually though, more and more people joined in with the sawing and dragging until a sturdy fence began to appear.

The day after the gig found me sawing away with a hangover. It was cold and misty and the face paint hadn't been washed from my eyes. Ceilidh said I looked like a ghost. The warmth of the fire seemed a long way away and as I looked up I noticed two men, watching me from the other side of the river. They were yellow jackets, surveyors armed with tripods and theodolites. They seemed as unnerved by my presence - half blended with the tree mesh in my grey smock - as I was by theirs. By rights, if I was going to do my job properly, I should have taken them on, run through the river and got in their way, or else gone up to the camp to get help. But it was a grey, dead day, my hangover was clinging to me like old sweat and it seemed easier just to leave them to it and get on with some sawing myself.

We had other watchers from over the river. Behind the orchard, a road ran down towards the estate house and a few times each week a white van would materialise, lingering on the verge by the remains of a hedge. We never went to investigate – it was a long walk – but we felt in no doubt that there was a lot of equipment in the back of that van and that this was surveillance. There may have been something uncanny about it, but mostly it bought out a defiant streak and added to an already heightened idea of our own importance. I'd already made an appearance in the Exeter Echo; an enlarged shot of my figure traversing a walkway - which in turn enlarged beyond all proportion my sense of significance.

More surveyors turned up and this time we let them have it, running down to meet them. I was with Ceilidh and Richard and we hopped over the fence into the field they were working in. There were two men in their twenties, huddled over a theodolite, with the air of a long university education behind them. They had no idea how to handle us and were flustered even before we got to them. Ceilidh did her show of 'I'm a pretty woman who wants to be your friend but will nevertheless make your life a complete nightmare.' I stood in front of their line of sight and then somebody started unwinding the clamps to the extendable tripod legs. That really wound them up. They eventually left in a mess and a panic. Part of me felt a bit guilty at making their life so miserable, but then again; what did they expect? They were helping build roads, after all. They could have got a proper job.

The orchard was still littered with the trunks of felled trees. They'd been sawn up but were liberally scattered around, covered in ivy, with old piles of sawdust long gone soggy in the rain. One morning, our breakfast was interrupted by a four wheeled, yellow earthmover making a move on the trunks. The firepit we were sat around had a view over the whole valley and there was an unreal moment where we carried on drinking our tea, unwilling to move so early and unexpectedly. Then we downed our porridge bowls and legged it down the hill towards the digger; the yellow of it like a red rag. Richard and myself cleared the river with relatively dry feet and the digger turned round at once, making a beeline for the road. We herded it off at full tilt, ecstatic at the easy victory but a bit nauseous from the porridge and the run.

As spring drew nearer, it bought with it a growing awareness that we'd need more accommodation on site. We set to work on a new bender, set across the firepit from the first. It was going to be a giant. We marked out a circular space with stakes and string and then set to work levelling it, working with spades and forks in the pouring rain. The men in the white van were watching, which pleased us all greatly, knowing that our efforts weren't going unnoticed.

The Exeter-Honiton bypass was of course not a bypass at all, but part of a super highway that was being built all the way along the South Coast. And this in turn was part of a road building scheme that encompassed not just Britain but the whole of Europe, an EC directed, trans European highway network, to get more lorries everywhere faster.

To show the opposition to the South Coast highway, a series of beacons were being lit on the hills all the way along, and we were duty bound to have one ourselves.

Beacons are lit in times of dire threat to the country and this was no exception.

In the weeks leading up to the fire, we began to gather wood and slowly the heap and the tension began to rise. It was going to be a good party. Ed got excited about the prospect of using large amounts of petrol. The day before the fire, a man turned up and carved a labyrinth in the meadow by the river. This would be full of fire on the night.

As it worked out, I was in Exeter on a mission and only made it back once the labyrinth and the beacon had been long lit. I'd led half the students from the house with me, along with one or two other ragged characters, tramping over the fields from Feniton station. It was such a random seeming route that they all thought I was lost but didn't want to admit it. There was general bewilderment when we arrived over a stile into the back of the camp.

Though the labyrinth was now no more than a blackened shadow in the night, the beacon was still going strong and fierce to stand near. After a while, a load of us retreated to the inner firepit, where we could sit down on the logs and still be warm. It was a fantastic night with no shortage of booze. I discovered playing the whistle was the last of my faculties to be rendered useless – even after speech and walking. I eventually crawled along the pallets back to the communal, where I collapsed in a heap among a mass of bodies. The beacon was still burning come the dawn.

Hitching

I was still signing on in Newbury and every fortnight I'd set off to hitch back up there. The M5 and the M4, pivoting around Bristol, took me almost directly there and I'd start the day by catching a train from Fairmile to Exeter, where the M5 pretty much began. Trying to hitch from the road near the camp was always a bit optimistic.

The train station in Feniton, where I'd led the students from to the beacon burning, was a couple of miles away, over the fields and through the estate. Fields in winter, the ploughed ones at least, are sombre characters, a sodden reflection of a dull sky, but there was something meditative about walking across them, something that left your mind upturned and cleared out.

I got to know the motorways pretty well, and whichever way I went, it always felt like I was coming home. I looked at the motorways as a kind of hyperspace; warps in normal reality and the everyday passage of time, not far off from teleportation itself. But, hitching, I wasn't adding to any extra traffic on the roads and sat through these interludes in conventional physics with a certain smugness and easy conscience.

More than a few times, as I got talking about "what I did" this easiness spilled over into a brand of righteousness. It seemed imperative to force home my feelings at every available opportunity and while my views were often met with complete sympathy, on other journeys it felt as though I was fighting a slow tide of apathy, a caution of the spirit that threatened to wear down my resolve, windscreen wipers mopping the despondency in further.

So at a point in the dialogue with another manifestation of an uncertain mind, my defences clicked in, the red rag had been waved and I ploughed into the fray, fighting my corner once again. As far as I saw it, there wasn't room any longer for hesitation or circumspection; the land was being torn in two and everybody had to act on that knowledge. If we weren't ourselves in danger of being lost (and in the long run, in the wider environmental sphere, we most probably are) we stood to lose something very precious and irredeemable: the uncut hills of our country.

Two essential bits of kit for any hitching mission were a good piece of cardboard and a fat marker pen. A clear sign showing where you were headed and what road you wanted to take next made all the difference. Leaving your piece of cardboard on the dashboard of the car you'd just got out of was a pretty bad thing to do, though you could sometimes pick up another piece – in grotty but useable nick - down the embankment from the road if it wasn't too wet.

My first hitching trip – the journey towards Cadbury with Len – was marked by the absence of a marker and we had to make our signs with a biro; small lettered and painstakingly coloured in. I once made a sign that said EXETER that was large enough to hold with my arms spread wide. I never used it and it ended up rotting at the back of the communal at Snelsmore. Gordon always talked about making a series of signs that could be put out on stakes at intervals leading up to your hitching spot: PLEASE. PICK ME UP. I'M A REALLY. NICE BLOKE. AND I ROLL. GOOD BIFTAS.

Choosing your spot was important too. You ideally wanted a lay-by, but most of the time you were using sliproads that only gave half a car's width to pull over in. There'd be plenty of space for other cars to get by, but a lot of people said they were put off by it, so it wasn't ideal.

You had to stand where people had a good chance to clock you and stop. Half the sliproads came off roundabouts though, making this tricky. Sometimes it seemed like motorway junctions had been designed to make hitching difficult. Like Brasilia, motorways were a land invented for the car, not living things with legs. Occasionally you'd get dropped off at a junction of doom – a place that was designed so efficiently that the traffic never slowed down, where you could stand for hours in the dark, getting moved on by police and waiting for angels.

On a random blat to visit my old girlfriend in Lincolnshire, I got dropped off at a junction on the M25. Police in an estate car soon appeared to move me on, waiting to watch me go. "There's something you need to be on a motorway..." they'd told me,

"...and you haven't got it. Any idea what we're talking about?"

I dunno officers, let me see... An umbrella? A kaleidoscope? A packet of filter tip fags?

I had to walk for miles in the fields above the cutting, past mildly stunned horses and electricity pylons, under a rain threatening sky until I got to decent sliproad onto the M1.

One time I got a lift back from Exeter with a man who drove me all the way along the M4, convinced we hadn't got to the Newbury turning until it was far too late. Another time I was having such a good chat to the driver that we stopped in a services carpark where our routes divided. We carried on talking for so long that it was dark by the time I got out and he could have driven me all the way to Newbury and back. We were talking about ghosts.

On a long wait, you played tricks on yourself to pass the time; count the white cars, get to a hundred and count all the red. Watch the clouds go by; see the hail come in, stand out in it till the blue reappeared and then watch the next batteries begin to roll towards you. Look into people's eyes, searching, willing them to stop. So many faces washing by, so many cars with just one driver, a thousand moments of connection with faces you'd never see again. But always standing there; upright, waiting, letting the time and traffic roll around you like water around a rock. Then there was no hardship or thoughts of lifts left, only a question of standing. Sometimes you could sing songs to yourself, but it tended to make you look mad.

Once I got a lift with two French truckers who did a U-turn on the M5 and who drank whiskey and milk all the way. Once I got a lift in the back of a balloon seller's van. I shared the back with a guy with a smack habit from Bristol who was trying to escape the drugs of the city centre. Helium Mickey Mice hovered inches from our heads. When the smackhead got freaked out and tried to bat them away, they swung back tenfold, leering even closer like a bad trip. And it didn't help much either when my fellow passenger sparked up a fag, dispatching handfuls of Disney faces into balloon Valhalla, and shouting at them in shock every time.

A man picked me up once who barely said a word but passed back a copy of the Telegraph for me to read. He was a very well turned out businessman with tidy grey hair and a plush estate car that smelt as though it had just come out of the valeteer's. He told me I should be more organised. I'd been hitching the wrong way.

Once, Badger and Tami came down to Fairmile too and we hitched back together, not on the motorways but up the A roads; the `303 and the A34 from Andover. We set off in a howling gale, stood one behind the other, behind a swing sign to a garage, which itself soon got blown over. The garage itself still stood. We tried to jump on a train at Feniton but were turned away by the elderly station master, who had "no time fer waifs and strays, no time at all!" He bumbled off, thin and cheese headed, bewildered and fuddled by our strange silence. Badger had suggested we tried to flood him with our heart chakras.

We eventually got a lift as far as Glastonbury with a crazy Greek chip shop owner. When we hitched out a few days later, we were picked up by a man in a buff coloured Volvo, who wore dark glasses, smoked a cigar and talked about the overland trail to India in the Sixties, when "Hippies were real hippies." We sat there together, taken aback by this slur on our integrity by a man who, when all was said and done, was now driving a Volvo. Didn't he know who we were?

Later that day we climbed out the back of a white pickup (Tami had sat in the cab), stiff from the wind and the hail, just outside Andover. There was a large area of scrubby trees by the sliproad – stuff that had presumably been planted after the road had been widened. Most of the leaves – delicate birch leaves and hawthorn and larger limes and aspen – were still on the trees with the mildness of the wet weather. They were rotten and every shade of brown, red and mottled yellow, a damp montage of creeping deterioration.

As we stood there, three dogs came trotting out of the shrub forest. They were wild dogs; mongreloid, with matted fur hanging in thick dreads around their bellies and collars. They had a thick winter coat too, thicker than any other dog I'd seen, and a look to them that told on its own that these were no domesticated animals. They looked free, their own masters and they looked wild eyed with it and mad. The three of us stood there looking at them, Badger and Tami in woollen ponchos and me in a torn barbour and rapidly degenerating trousers. The dogs took us in with rolling eyes and trotted back into the trees.

Beyond Junction 13

Junction 13 was the gateway to Newbury from the M4. From there it was a three mile walk through the woods, the vast hinterland of the Common, to the camp. Walking back one time, a sole point of movement amongst the stillness, I began to think on what someone had said about the Common having 'an edge.' I was unsure about this, it didn't feel like an unfriendly place exactly, and yet there was something about it; a presence perhaps or a feeling of being watched. Crunching along the frost on the empty tarmac road, entering into the woods, I became aware of the trees all around and began to think that maybe there was a way I could become less of an intruder here, maybe I could somehow align myself with the oldness of this place.

The branches passed by over my head, heavy with a sentience and an answer began to form; I'd make myself a hood. I bought the material a couple of days later - burgundy and beige felt - stitching panels together and curling bits round to form a long taper that ran down my back. I thought it looked good, at the time. It made me feel as though I was somehow more close to the woods, under their protection but shielded from them too, where their wildness felt a little too raw.

Arriving back at the camp in the dead of night and it was hard at first to see where everything was. Soon, treading softly in the blackness off the path and the outlines of the benders would begin to show themselves – just patches of an extra nebulousness initially so it was hard to tell if they weren't simply your eyes playing tricks. Then they'd become clearer, the rounded outlines marking themselves out like barrows or old sleepers.

Inside, the darkness was complete, it hung in your mouth with the smell of the leafmould floor rising up to meet you, a memory of the stars outside your only light. Once I had a dream of entering a bender to find a pool of black water on the floor, lilies floating on it and Tami sat the other side. The stars outside blinked in and out with the movement of the trees so that the sound of the wind in the branches was also the sound of the stars.

Back in the black inside, it was essential to have some source of light on you, some matches, a lighter, a stub of a household candle in your pocket. Then, with a scratch of flint, the light would be born in your eyes; the round walls of the tarp, the gleam of the hazel, the reflecting surface of the burner, a tumble of bedding. All this would spread out as the glow of the candle sunk in and, after hours in the dark, you were suddenly home.

Quite often, I would stay in Badger and Tami's if I was only around for a few days, the site being pretty deserted besides the three of us. Everyone else had moved off with the postponement of the road, leaving Badger and Tami as the sole keepers of the place. Quite often they'd use my appearances as chances to escape for a while; to check out Newgrange in Ireland, to camp on Silbury Hill or to visit a budding tree village that had been started by friends in Lancashire. I'd be alone on the camp for a week at a time then, but it was a good quietness, a long draught of peace after the intense communalism of Fairmile.

Staying at Badger and Tami's had the advantage of not having to chop and burn wood unnecessarily. They only had a small burner, which they called 'Puff', and all the wood had to be sawn to size – about half a foot long –

before going in. Badger often complained that he spent most of his days chopping wood, but then we could have all got up a little bit earlier. If Fairmile was the land of almost militariesque early starts, then at Snelsmore we experimented with hibernation. And without electric lights, it seemed fair enough.

Badger and Tami had built a guest room – a "North Wing" – which consisted of a tunnel like chamber leading off the main 'room', with enough floor space to sleep on, and to accommodate several boxes and shelves. In the evenings, we'd get properly stoned. At times the tarp was just a thin shell around us and our ears were tuned to the woods at large. They were alive with the sound of the wind meeting the branches, even on the night of a gentle breeze. Some nights there was no wind but still a noise; the hum of distant things - roads and planes – getting transformed on the air by the insulation of miles of trunks; muted and bark warped, a sound like the moonlight on bracken, a near nothing sound that still brimmed with unspoken transmissions. Otherwise there was just a needling stillness, the deep quiet that comes with intense cold. The stars hung still and bright and a part of all this, the silence the heart of their song.

At other times, I'd spark up the burner in the communal. Badger and myself had rebuilt this, stripping down the old one and uncovering an abandoned rat's nest in the process. We got rid of the pipe stove square burner, leaving it to rust in the rain, and reinstalled the gas bottle burner that had been in the very first communal 'over the border' by the treehouses. A drainage ditch had been dug along one side of the old bender and we made a little wooden bridge over this where the flue from the burner could pass out, packed all around with earth.

We'd rolled a huge log to one side of the burner, along a flat wall, which formed a good bench. It was beautiful to look at just that; the bark of the oak log, the bare, swept, earth floor – caught in the sunlight coming in through the doorway – the symmetry of the hazel wall rising up straight to give room to sit down by it, without bending your back. Pallets had been rearranged to form three separate beds, in a C shape round an old cog for a table. The whole thing tapered down to a narrow storage tunnel at the far end, which I closed off with a blanket. The new communal felt much more welcoming than the cavernous space of the last one. It felt like a place I could call home.

I was having trouble using an axe and persuaded Badger to give me some lessons. He didn't take much persuading, teaching coming naturally to him. He was full of wonder at everything and our conversations were full of his inexhaustible supply of revelations. You could say it had something to do with his liking a smoke, but he was always full of excitement about something or other; an element of the campaign or the mechanics of a leaf. He looked at things in a way that stripped them down to their deepest ingredients and then reassembled them; inside out and all the fresher for it. His insights were like practical jokes of the trees and to be exposed to his imagination was to be alive amid the mind of the woodland. He taught me how to use an axe.

Badger had been trained in Kendo – the Japanese art of swordsmanship. Here, with my experience of fencing, we had something in common.

"Don't look at the axe when you swing," he told me, "look at the wood, see where the cut will go and then cut it there. Focus and destroy Jim. Focus and destroy."

It worked, not all at once, but by the end of the evening, logs were falling in two fairly happily, if not quite leaping apart. The trick was keeping them balanced while the axe came down. This was usually done by removing your fingers from the log during the fall of the axe; catching it with the blade before it had a chance to escape. Other times you could just hold the log with the blade up to it, hammering it on the ground until the axe had taken hold and splitting it from there.

I never had an accident with an axe. But with a bowsaw – a far more innocuous tool – I wasn't so lucky. Once at Fairmile I let a bowsaw bounce on the wood I was sawing. I ended up with a double cut on my left forefinger. Like a gangster's double bladed slash, it took a long time to heal.

The trees by the river at Fairmile were covered in fat strands of ivy, two fingers thick. I'd heard ivy was good to carve – soft to work with and then drying hard as you like – and took several pieces to cut chessmen with. The pieces were for Gywddbywll – a Celtic variant of chess where the one king had to escape from the middle, past enemy pieces; a fight between order and chaos. I was looking forward to having my own set.

Back at Snelsmore, with Badger and Tami away, I was cutting a carved piece off from the main strand of ivy with a small hacksaw. It was twilight, I was holding the ivy at a weird angle, my finger hooked round the wood and suddenly bit into my flesh with the blade. I held it up to the light, to see it was bleeding all over the place. I'd cut it between the two top joints of the finger and when I began to curl my finger around, half the flesh above the main mid knuckle stayed where it was, standing upright while the finger above the cut curved off as it should.

I went to Badger and Tami's bender, scrambling behind the doortarp for the first aid kit. Then, on cue, it started to snow, a sudden storm that blew up out of nowhere and had quickly carpeted the bender roof and the woodland floor in more than a fair powdering. By the time I'd got a dressing on my finger, there was a bright patch of blood on the ground, red on the white. The snow stopped as quickly as it had begun.

The treehouses in Snelsmore were left empty, though occasionally one of us might spend a night in Ed's, just for variety. With all the spare timbers and plywood hauled up and lashed down to the roofs, the woodland floor was left free from detritus. The most insidious of the litter we'd cleared were the scraps of blue polyprop that had been produced whenever anyone had been cutting rope. They hung around, melting into the leafmould like plastic slivers, separating into ever decreasing fibres that were hard to pick up. The electric blue stood out garishly from the rest of the woodland, like a synthetic insult.

There was a little scrap of paper stuck to the inside of Ed's treehouse, just above the window. It was an advert torn out from a paper; a man with a megaphone shouting "Where is everybody?" The woods looked back in answer; silent and empty of life. There was no doubt about it – this was a very quiet time. There were now only three road protest camps still existing that I was aware of: Fairmile, Snelsmore and the tree village in Lancashire. There was a distinct feeling that there were only a few of us keeping the fires going, whereas the previous summer the papers had been full of massive protests, most noticeably the tree village at Solsbury Hill. This had been the first of it's kind in the country and as such had received a lot of attention.

So where were all the people now? Winter had a lot to do with it.

I talked to Badger about it and remember clearly his response; that it wouldn't matter if there was just one person at Newbury. One person acting in the right way could set off a whole chain of events and reactions. One person sat on a digger could stop work for the day, could make the driver reappraise his views, could force the contractors to hire security, could make the world believe the woods were teeming with protestors, just ready to reap havoc on the road builders. It was a good philosophy to bear in mind. But I still wondered where everyone was.

There were exceptions; even in Newbury we weren't totally alone. For one thing, there was a heavily supported anti-bypass group, who had been active for years. When I first got to Newbury, they were doing things like putting leaflets through everyone's doors. The campaign 2CV and the office were supported through their funds. I was largely unaware of them as a functional entity at that point, never going to any meetings myself. Occasionally though, in town with Badger and Tami, we'd bump into women who knew who we were. They tended to wear big black overcoats and made a big fuss, full of kind words about our living on route. It was embarrassing and touching and I never really knew what to say in return.

The group were called 'The Third Battle of Newbury'. The last two battles had been fought during the Civil War. Some people reckoned there had actually been three Battles of Newbury, which confused everything as it meant the group should have been called 'The Fourth Battle of Newbury'. But technically, it wasn't true, the 'third battle' having been only a skirmish, not some proper set to of national significance, drawing in thousands of people.

The in-town anti-roads presence was augmented massively in the New Year when a group called Road Alert moved their offices up from Southampton. It was a foresightful move that increased the air of expectancy about the coming battle. Together they were Tim, Becca and Phil. They'd been involved in road campaigns since the very start of Twyford Down and put together a newsletter that was pretty much the gospel of what campaigns were happening where. They now lived in a flat above a hairdresser's, in the dingy bit of the town centre, south of the railway line. It was on the main road, though their back garden overlooked a patch of wasteland and a large, lowland sky.

The sense of emptiness and quiet was added to by the depths of the winter and by their lack of any office furniture to speak of, besides some filing cabinets and a photocopier. Above their main window, they'd pinned up black and white, grainy A4 photocopies of American Indian tribal elders. Tim was tall, had short black hair and a mildly wired enthusiasm for everything. Becca was warm and purposeful and Phil was pretty quiet and softly spoken, though with the same underlying force and energy of the others. They were all as hardcore as you like.

The walk back to the motorway from Snelsmore was a very different experience than the arriving journey. It was never in the dark. Sometimes Badger would roll a big spliff to see me off and we'd sit on a log to observe the old ritual. It kind of annoyed me at times, because I'd have a long journey ahead of me and wanted to get going while I still had the fire of the morning in my bones. But I always forgave him as I melted into the woodland around me. It made me feel as though I should always make more time just to stop and observe the woods around me for once, rather than hammer around in my little bubble of ideas and busyheadedness. The woods magnified themselves at times like these, colours shone out and birds became louder, a whole pattern of the life all around us unfolded itself and I was very still and very small amongst it.

Walking the first leg, up the Wantage road, Badger and myself would yip to each other as we got further apart. Yipping was our call sign, a cry high in the throat that we'd sound off whenever we wanted to call to each other. It was a greeting and a farewell and let people on any camp know we were friends before they heard us coming. It also meant 'nice one' and we were all distinguishable by our style of doing it; a kind of rural, vocal tag.

Walking to the motorway, through the thick woods and it was amazing how far away we could hear each other. One day we just carried on yipping as I walked further down the road. Each time I cried out, Badger's call came back a little fainter, but all the more vibrant for still being heard. Yellow leaves were hanging thickly everywhere up here, even now, the mildness and damp of the winter making the woods one steady slow world of drawn out and fruitful decay. Badger's voice seemed to ring out from the heart of the woods, lit bright and clear with the thin winter sun. Each time we called out we cried louder; a cry for life, an exaltation in everything neither of us wanted to end.

Up the road from the site was a very different kind of camp; an Iron Age hillfort. It was sort of en route to the M4 and Badger walked up with me to it one time, so we could check it out together. It was in the middle of the woods, a thick plantation that offered no view, though it was good to see it all the same. The floor was carpeted with silver and copper leaves. The fort was small, with a shallow bank and ditch and had once been at the heart of an

171

ancient community. It would have looked down from the top of the hill once, down over the valley where the Chieveley services now stood and over the place where the work on the new bypass might soon be beginning; an inroad to the pensive woods from the existing A34. There was nothing to see with the trees in the way – something I wasn't used to when visiting hillforts – but the sound of the motorway was a little too close to home. The boundaries here were blurred and uncomfortable. Our homages paid, we made our way back, then off down our separate tracks.

Solsbury Hill

We'd heard there was going to be a big reunion gathering on Solsbury Hill and decided to walk there. Badger was elated; "You're going to meet the family Jim!" We set off at dawn with a friend who'd been staying at the Road Alert office – Richard Dragonhead. He'd been helping them sort out their filing system. He had spikey blond hair and observed things with unshrinking accuracy, which was alright, as he found half the things were worth laughing about.

I was the first to wake up and gave the others a shout. I'd been sleeping in the communal and Richard had been in Badger and Tami's guest wing. It was still dark. From the sounds of things, the others had had second thoughts about the journey overnight. But eventually they crawled out into the early light. Tami decided to stay behind and look after the camp, but she got up to see us off.

Badger reckoned it was an easy fifty miles from here to there. A friend of his had done it in two days, sleeping in West Kennet Long Barrow overnight.

By the time we made it to the canal, walking down into town and across a big park, the sun had come out – a sharp bright sun of early spring, the trees and bushes all lively with the wind and full of rich smells. Badger had borrowed a black, felt bargeman's cap from Tami, and he looked like he belonged on the waterways. He had a large, rounded bell hanging from his rucksack, which added to the feeling of being on a pilgrimage.

Our first obstacles came just a few miles down the way, near Hungerford. Two walkers we met told us they'd had to turn back as the footpath was flooded. The flooding seeped out from the edge of the canal, a sluggish brown underwater cloud, skimmed with brightness here and there where the open sky still shifted between gathering clouds. We stripped off our footwear when we got to the water's edge. A cloud of dust and dead skin rose into the air as I peeled my socks off. I tried to keep my socks fresh, but between one thing and another it wasn't always easy. It felt like the first time my feet had seen the light of day all winter. Richard reckoned I was just another crusty – an unwashed breed of traveller – and it was hard to deny.

It started to rain and we stopped off not long after – eating sandwiches under a bridge like trolls over bones. We were soaked. I eventually broke the stony silence with a deadpan,

"This is the life." The other two just looked at me.

We were still walking as it began to get dark, rounding a long curve in the canal near Savernake forest. Canals make for compulsive walking; everything is on the flat, and that carries you on with it, pulled by some strange power of monotony.

It had been a long day already when we bumped into a fisherman packing up; a dark shadow on the towpath. Badger was keen to get to the longbarrow that night but the fisherman reckoned it was at least another fifteen miles further on. Badger's enthusiasm was unchecked, though I had my doubts. I began to feel as though I could drop into the water at any moment; partly through fatigue making me stagger but also because I couldn't see the towpath clearly in the dark. The water lay there in a still black mass, merging with the darkness all around us, threatening to overwhelm all my other senses and pull me down into it.

I was relieved when we stopped, a little further on, by the mouth of a tunnel. It was a long tunnel, with no towpath through it. Badger reckoned this was where the bargemen had to 'walk' their boats through, in the days before engines – lying on their backs on the boat roofs and treading against the ceiling, keeping up the boat's momentum.

We crashed out on a flat opening, sheltered from the elements only by the tall brick wall next to the mouth of the tunnel. The ground was hard and gravelly and the sky was impenetrable with clouds. But to me it was sweet just to stop.

We woke to a watery dawn. A village hung not too far down the way and we stopped here for water and supplies. A large pool full of ducks seemed to be the central piece. It was peaceful here, and beautiful with calmness of the pool and people going about their business with an air of understated reverence. But on the other side of the canal, it all seemed a little too quiet. There was a square of bungalows here and I was hit by a sense of oppressive stillness, of people leading quiet indoor lives, a patch of sun on their patch of lawn, telly on the go in the shadows. I felt a rush of gratitude to be living out in the open, under the sun and the wild clouds of the spring.

We passed a place called Honey Street and sat to eat lunch by a lock, sunlight on the water dazzling us into a sense of serenity. We didn't have the money to get beer in the pub, but it didn't matter. Everything was suddenly fantastic. The walking and the sun and the night in the open air had worked on our senses, beguiling our nerves into an easy, absent minded bliss.

We knew we were near Salisbury Plain by the dark thuds of distant guns. The gunfire continued in a dull thunder as we walked on. We'd thought it was actual thunder at first and had argued about it for over a mile before it got clearer.

We climbed up on a little brick bridge to get a better view of a White Horse carved into a green hill. I had a feeling of having covered a lot of ground now, the hills around us felt different and had begun to close in on us.

The trees and the bushes had thinned out. The canal didn't get any higher; this was the heartland, the upland centre of the South. It was also the threshold to the West. We'd come a long way.

A hill soon came right down to the water's edge, projecting out from a chalk escarpment to the north. It was a fantastic hill, curling away like a dragon's tail. Behind it, Badger pointed out Tan Hill; site of a Donga gathering the last summer. One of them had resurrected the ancient Tan Hill Fair by selling a mate a horse up there. It had been a kind of place of transference for the tribe, after the evictions at Solsbury, and with Newbury set to take off.

I wanted to leave the canal then and walk up into the hills. Behind them, Badger told me, lay the sacred landscape of Avebury and West Kennet. I wanted to explore it all then, but knew it would have to wait for another time.

We arrived in Devizes after dark and descended on the skips. As Badger had promised, it was a good haul. Out the back of one of the supermarkets, a lad who was working there appeared to throw some stuff out – he saw us rifling through the cardboard and ducked back inside, returning with the best things he could find that needed chucking. We wanted to have food for people at the gathering, so filled our rucksacks up to the brim. They were suddenly twice as heavy.

Afterwards, stood by an old window with my arms full of French bread, Richard turned round and said,
"You look medieval Jim." It wasn't just to do with my hood and spliced trousers. I felt medieval too. Standing against the building I felt I could very easily melt into the ambience of the old stonework. There was something

about the old towns that got under my skin in a way I quite liked.

Devizes was on top of a hill. Back by the side of the canal, the hillside dropped away sharply, leaving no clues to the path of the water from here on in. A cold wind was blowing out of the darkness and it would have felt as though we were on the edge of the world were it not for the thousands of lights that lit the valley before us. We weren't sure whether we could see Bath in the distance. Even the lights seemed somehow ethereal, as though this was a very different country opening out. We'd made it to the West.

We descended the hill, looking for somewhere to crash out. The locks went by one after the other, dark shadows in the night. At the bottom, Richard and myself waited at turnings off the path, while Badger went to scout out a place to sleep. First he tried a shed in a builder's yard, but that was blatantly ridiculous and I was glad when he climbed back over the fence, saying the door was locked.

I was so tired I felt like I could melt into the path. Eventually, Badger returned saying he'd found somewhere really good. It was a big, open sided barn with a corrugated roof and was full of flat straw bales. We climbed up onto it and into Seventh Heaven.

We slept in late and breakfasted on cakes. The straw gave off a slow heat that was blissful in the cold of the morning. In the next town along, I met a man who could only rightfully be called a tinker. He was too refined to be a tramp. We had just passed a boatyard and a strange grey building on high concrete stilts and there he was: sat on a bank of grass by a wall, a thin middle aged man in tweeds and corduroy, a smallish green hat on top of his whiskered head. I sat down next to him for a while and he told me in an Irish accent like running water that he was heading down to Cornwall for the summer, following the canals as they were such easy going. He seemed at once bewildered

177

and all knowing, as though his knowledge had broken him and broken him till there was nothing left now but this watery soul who moved in a state of silence and solitude and grace.

We got into Bath that night, the canal snaking round as fat hills closed in on both sides. Then it was dark and Solsbury Hill was looming above us at last. Badger told me we'd have to walk across the route of the road to get there. We turned off the canal and along a footpath bordered with red and white tape. I got the impression of churned and muddy earth stretching away on either side, vast in the darkness and not unlike the Somme. Not long before, this had been watermeadows.

We re-emerged into a village on the side of the hill – Bath Easton. Badger pointed out water running across the road, a small stream emerging from a bank and then following the gutter before it crossed the tarmac; plentiful and silent.

Solsbury had been a source for many springs. It was also said to act as a natural aquifer – the weight of the hill acting as a pressure head that pushed the main hot springs of Bath underground, before they emerged some miles distant, in the old city. The spring, because it is hot, is perhaps the most notable in Britain and was worshipped long before a town and temple were built, when the Romans came. And they had only chosen to build there to help keep the indigenous population under their grip, understanding very well the political power of religion. The Roman Gods subsumed the older Gods, but still carried something of their spirit with them.

Bath was a sacred city, and Solsbury a hallowed hill. But the bypass had cut deep into the side of the hill and several springs had been blocked up. Now they were erupting all over the place, not to be denied.

Soon we were climbing up the steep side of the hill, using a gravel path. Badger told me how the path had been used a lot by the protestors, who'd often go barefoot. The road builders had put the gravel down. It was rough and spikey and the size of small coals – the kind you'd normally see lining railways.

The campsite, when we got there, consisted of a fire in an open space among the trees and bushes, a few benders set up around the edge. It was on the side of the hill still, and the clearing was full of tussocky, lumpy anthills, almost as though they were natural seats. Badger seemed to know everyone there. I talked round the fire for a while before going back to a bender and falling into a deep sleep.

More people had arrived by the time I got up the next day. I went for a walk up on the hillfort, which was full of protestors milling around. It was a big fort, flat topped like Cadbury Castle, but harder to map in your mind – you kept on thinking you'd walked round the whole thing when another length appeared, and then another. Large rocks stuck out proudly from the turf of the ramparts, boulders buttressing out above the old ditches.

I spent most of the day wandering the hill, getting lost in the thick woods there. When we got back to the camp, there was a furore in progress over some unknown protestors who had turned up and done an action of their own. They'd all been dressed in army camouflage and black balaclavas had managed to make the local news with predictable results. Nobody seemed to know who they were and everyone was generally disgruntled by being represented like this. Although it was a free enough world to protest however you wanted, and while these people had something to do wih the wider movement, there'd been a family on the hill before, and these protestors had nothing to do with it. Besides which the feeling was, at that time, that balaclavas were detrimental – a barrier between you and the rest of the world and playing into the hands of journalistic stereotypes. And if you wanted to do something cheeky, you could always do it at night, when no one was watching.

In the evening, hordes of people turned up. I helped put up a bender as the light faded. There were at least thirty of us sat around the fire, two men duelling with each other with huge djembe drums. Kit was there with Ed from Fairmile. I turned around to talk to him at one point and found two voices answering me. Ed from Swansea was there, sat next to the Fairmile Ed, both of them grinning at me with long red dreads cascading down their backs. I'd been suspicious for months that they never appeared in the same place together, so it was a bit much to take when they did. Especially after so much to smoke.

I sat up all night, listening to women sing incredible, soulful songs. When dawn came, there were just a few of us left awake, passing round tea in a porcelain bowl. I'd caught a few hour's half sleep, curled up behind the people round the fire, trying to ignore the cold. There was a companionable silence when I awoke and a strange feeling of blurry excitement. Partly, this was an effect of a night of little sleep and many spliffs, but it was also the quiet warmth of the people around me and the shift in the day as the tide turned towards dawn.

A heavy mist had fallen and I decided to walk up the hill. As I neared the ramparts, an outline of a tall woman became distinct from the fog. She had a wild mass of hair and seemed to be wearing some kind of coverings over her long legs. I felt sure she was one of the women who had lived here, who had now come back to visit. As I continued to get closer, I got the impression she was looking out at something past me; a neighbouring hill coming clear through a patch in the fog, or the sudden appearance of a bird or the sun. I turned around to look at what it might be and as I did I got the sensation of something darting off at the edge of my vision, a shadow slipping off behind my shoulder. There was nothing behind me and when I turned back round I found there was no woman, only the rough outline of a concrete trig point.

I walked up onto the top of the hill and began to walk across the middle, through the mist. After a while I came to the further side, the edge dropping away in front of me. But a few steps further showed that this wasn't the edge, only a small dip in the level ground, accentuated by the fog. It was a convincing illusion and one which kept on repeating itself, no matter how far I'd walked. I began to worry that I was caught in some otherworldly trap, destined to walk across the face of a never ending hillfort until the end of time. I looked around me, the mist clinging in droplets to my hair and clothes and saw I was surrounded by the rounded outlines of posthole huts. I was stood in one, and others radiated out all around, overlapping each other and covering the ground as far as the mist would let me see. Eventually, with great relief, I found the further ramparts and began to walk back round to the trigpoint.

Later that morning, after the mist had cleared, there was a press conference on top of the hill. This started with a couple of men in wellies with mandolins, singing predictable songs about pixies and elves. After several rousing anti-road speeches, we formed a massive circle of hands, several hundred strong. Then we all raised our arms and let out a massive cry, scattering to run down the hill, the cameramen struggling to keep up. We were heading for the building site.

We raced down the gravel path. Kit was there, climbing the fence of the compound and then the arm of a nearby digger. The security guards all seemed to know

181

him well and there was the half friendly greeting of old rivals. I continued on down with the main rush of people, storming past a thin line of security where a footpath crossed the site. Then I was running through the mud towards a massive blue machine, suddenly out in the open, my heart pounding. I scrambled onto the machine by the caterpillar tracks; huge pieces of metal, caked with grey mud. On the main chassis, a middle aged security guard and rolls of razor wire stopped us climbing any higher. I was joined by two local teenage girls who had been digger diving here all the last summer. One of them made a doll out of the sticky site clay that covered the machine. She offered it up to the security guard when she was finished, who was worried they might cut their hands on the wire.

I climbed round to the back of the machine, trying to evade the guard. People were clambering onto cranes and diggers all over the site. The guard followed me round,
"Now you're not going to try and climb any higher, are you son?" I told him I wasn't while I tried to figure out a way round the huge ventilation plates. But I knew I didn't have much chance with him above me. As we chatted, genially enough, more security arrived with a ladder. A crazy faced black guard with eyes like he was on speed was the first to appear.
"Are you going to come down or what?" There was a moment when I knew it was hopeless to argue, that whatever I said or did would inevitably lead to my removal from the digger. Maybe they'd let me climb down the ladder. But it seemed such a cop out to go quietly and I found myself staring back at the guard,
"I'm not here to make your life any easier." There was nothing to cling onto. I don't know how far it was to the ground, ten foot perhaps, but I was soon lying flat on my back on it, totally winded. Before I could begin to get my breath back I was being dragged – a guard to each foot –

over the rough ground towards a big metal gate. They didn't take their time about it and soon I had been shoved out, among a throng of other protestors.

A line of lorries was building up on the access road to the gates. Everyone was linking arms and sitting across where the gates opened. Before I knew it, I was linking arms too. A scrawny police sergeant appeared and stood in front of us. He told us if we didn't move, we'd all be arrested. He stabbed his finger at us, widened his eyes to make the point. People were shouting back, telling him about things. The police had only just arrived and were keen to get things under control, though it was clear they weren't prepared for this. There were only a few of them and a load of us. One or two officers stood to one side, whirling silver pincer cuffs, looking scared.

The atmosphere changed, everyone was suddenly on edge. I got the impression the Sergeant had just had an earful from someone very important and very unhappy. It was overcast and cold and the lorry drivers were getting agitated. I watched as someone in green and black, something pulled up over their mouth and nose, climbed up and opened the door to a lorry cab. His speed and the purposefulness of it was striking, almost disturbing, like a spell breaking or an opening shot. There were shouts and thuds from the cab. Maybe the lorry had begun to move, perhaps people had crawled underneath already, locking their necks to the axles. Maybe no one had told the driver. It was possible too that the guy who'd climbed up was a bit of a nutter. I heard later that the driver starting laying into him with a lump hammer.

I climbed the fence back into the compound, where it suddenly seemed much safer, in time to see someone slide into the spinning drum of a cement mixer. Everyone who wasn't laughing or swearing was shouting at the driver to turn the mixer off. I ran past the digger and towards another crane. There were no security on it so I climbed up past the body and into the shaft itself. The diagonal bars here were well spaced, but it was relatively easy to clamber up, the body of the crane getting smaller below and the view widening out all the time. Four of us got to a small platform and had a rest – Fairmile Ed was there, along with a blond, dreaded girl from Brighton and a man in a black woolly hat. Two or three people were above and below us. It was freezing up there and we all hugged to keep warm, an early spring wind cutting through our layers.

Below us, the crane body was already crawling with protestors, the machine having become a rallying point. Badger was sat on some scaffolding nearby, his face painted half green, half white. He was holding a flag proclaiming EARTH FIRST! We had a good view over the whole site, which was brown and massive and desolate. Pinpoints of steel girders projected outwards in places while, elsewhere, the monotony was broken by deep rectangular pits, lined with thick walls of brown metal.

Security were gathered around the base of the crane, trying to pull people off. But everyone had their arms locked together and were difficult to budge. I felt a huge surge of relief to be above the thick of it, away from the hassle and stress. We had the upper hand, which people kept on demonstrating by knocking guards' hats off. Security guards hate having their hats knocked off. It was the best thing you could possibly do. One of the security decided he'd had enough and, declaring he was leaving his job, stormed out of the compound, throwing off his jacket and hat behind him. Everyone cheered.

The balance shifted as more and more security arrived. In twos and threes, everyone was gradually prised away from the crane. With nobody now below us, one of the security threatened they'd use a hosepipe on us to get us down. We thought he was probably bluffing, but we'd had enough anyway. It was dark and even colder with it, so we all climbed down, stiff limbed and numb fingered.

After that, we trooped round to the house of someone in the village, who'd cooked up a big stew for people. There was still a bit left. When I got back to the camp, I crashed out in a heap in the bender, dog-tired, just behind Badger and another drummer. I hadn't slept properly for thirty-six hours and was oblivious to all the noise around me. I hitched down to Fairmile the next day, getting a lift to the main road in an ambulance full of hippies. People in it were full of talk and excitement about the coming spring. Stood on the side of a road again, I wondered what spring would have in store for me.

Leaving the South

I kept in touch with the students in Exeter, the ones who I'd met on New Year's Eve. Every week or every other week I'd hitch in to see them, to get a shower and to hang out in a pub. They were very hospitable with a kind of half reverence, half wariness at my apparent outlandishness. My baggy black jeans now had a split at the front running from top to bottom one leg, the sides frayed into clumps like dreads or feathers. Under this I wore one of two trousers – red and white stripes or green and black checks, these last ones a satisfying woolly type that I'd bought at a stall on the street.

The market was on one of Exeter's main streets, I'd been directed there by one of the security at the Brickyard, who'd noticed I'd needed new boots. The Doc Martens I'd left home in weren't really made for outdoors, and had been steadily rotting all winter. This wasn't apparent to me until all of a sudden they began to fall apart at the seams. I spent a few days at Fairmile barefoot. Being barefoot in the cold wasn't so bad if you put your mind to it, and kept the rest of you warm.

The security guard, one of the rounder, friendlier team leaders, said they sold old policeman's boots on the stall – they were good and solid and cheap. My new boots, when I got them, were brown and second hand, the heels worn down on one side. They were as good a pair of boots as you could wish for and I felt righteous wearing them, plodding the streets like a lawgiver. It felt like they knew their own way around town.

While I was in the city, I'd do a bit of busking. I'd signed off in Newbury, feeling that I wanted to spend all my time at Fairmile now. I wasn't keen to sign back on, so was relying on busking to keep me afloat. It wasn't as hard as it sounded – I had no rent to pay after all and communal food at Fairmile only amounted to a tenner a week.

Spring was coming now, a few sunny days in the Devonshire March, and I'd place myself randomly in lanes and against the red stone of old buildings. I played the tin whistle but was determined not to let it stand against me – they weren't the most popular instrument in many quarters. If I stood up straight, and looked proud to be there, I was sure it'd make all the difference, though I never did too well if I wasn't in a good spot. And that was the art – to find a good spot and hang onto it.

One day, I met a lad with a drum and we ended up playing together. He knew how to play and laid down sound beats to all my tunes, which made the music dance out twice as good. He was typical Devon; laid back and engaging and with a life somewhere between sketchy and sweet.

A week or two later, I met him again. He said some friends of his were down from Lancashire and that maybe we could all play together. We rounded a corner in the lane to find a tall man with long dark hair playing guitar and a small girl with a fiddle and a purple hat. She looked like a beautiful elf, with a gorgeous broad smile and eyes that seemed to be laughing and friendly at once. The hat had little plaits coming off the back with a bell on each end, which danced around as she played. I was sure they were a couple, having hitched down from Lancashire together and doing their trick of standing on one leg while they played, to see if it earned them more money.

The music we made went well, a kind of spontaneous thing that you could never put together by willpower alone. That night, they invited me back to their friend's house, which we reached by walking out on the long roads to the north, until we'd reached a place we could hitch from.

Long lanes full of hedgerows led us at last to the house; their friend's parents had gone away for the week, and they were having a party.

That night, sat in an alcove of a stone walled room, with a mad American man on the piano, I'd figured out that the elf girl, Sarah, wasn't seeing John the guitarist. She sat facing me now, yards away, playing the tune we all knew. I felt like I was being bewitched, that she was placing an enchantment on me with her eyes, willing me on to something. But this was good magic and I was happy to be drawn into her spell.

The following night, back in town, while everyone else had gone to a dub gig, we sat in the cemetery together, under a Yew tree. It was a mild night. She lay back on the grass looking up at me with the all the signs of invitation. A moment had arrived and there was no mistaking it. We lay for a long time looking at the sky through the Yew branches, which disrupted our vision with their myriad needles, throwing a bleary eyed optical effect all over us.

I took her back to Fairmile. She liked what she saw. With the arrival of the warm weather, new faces had appeared. The camp was blossoming into something wider and beautiful. Someone was always playing something round the fire now. Further off, behind Ceilidh's caravan, someone would be getting fiddle lessons. The trees were alive with activity, half of which was climbing instruction; people finding their feet among the exultant heights of Asguard. Kit was working on a triple decker platform in the beech. And a ditch had been started, circumnavigating the dead-tree hedge, the first firm step down the road to a hillfort.

A day of action had been called on the Brickyard and we trooped down there again, this time with a double decker bus among the convoy of cars. There'd been a good turn out from town. The plan was to shut the site down and hold a mass picnic. I'd brought along a load of French bread and jam, last minute acquisitions from a supermarket in Exeter. That was about as far as my picnic skills went.

The diggers stopped working when they saw us all coming and we sat down on the orange earth to eat. Sarah and Richard and myself played tunes in the sun. We'd been playing a lot back on site too and were thinking of forming a band- though Sarah was supposed to go back to university in Lancashire, nothing seemed impossible.

After a while, the security told us the digger drivers had all been sent home for the day. We had a chat and decided the best thing to do, to make the most of all these people, was to drive back to site and have an afternoon of work on the defences. Kit was particularly enthusiastic, seeing it as his longed-for deliverance of a team of slaves.

We piled back in the bus and drove off. Looking back, I saw the arm of a digger start up through the trees. We'd been very easily fooled, though I didn't mention it to anyone else, not wanting to spoil our sense of momentum. Thinking about it later, I should have sung out and had us all pile back onto site again. A day's work means a lot of money. But by then it was far too late. I'd led everyone down the lane and onto the site earlier on, walking in front with Ed and playing my whistle. Now I'd let everyone slip off while there was work still going on. What a fool.

On the way to the site, some security had made comments that I was leading a load of rats, though they might have been kids, even if I'd no home in a mountain to take them to. Though sometimes I think you could see it, the place in the back of the hills, with some of the tunes that we knew.

After another day's digger diving, Sarah and I found ourselves visiting Allercombe; a camp in a meadow, all the hedgerows surrounding it seeming like thick woods. On one side was a stream, cutting deep banks out of the soft earth. The riverside gave rise to one of the camp's worst problems – rats.

That night all the usual inhabitants of the camp, besides the rats, took our presence as an opportunity to escape and go to the pub. As with squats in town, squatted land needed to remain populated to prevent it getting requisitioned. The Allercombe camp didn't get many visitors and we were happy to let them get off site for a while – we still had all the company we could ask for in each other. But they hadn't told us about the rats.

We were tired from a long day and as it was a fair looking night, decided to sleep out in our sleeping bags. But as soon as we quietened down, the noises began. The kitchen bender wasn't far away from us and a fierce screeching soon erupted from it. The rats were fighting. All the food had recently been put in metal boxes and they were probably feeling the pinch. Pretty soon the screeching was accompanied by scrambling and thumping; the rats apparently knocking each other all over the bender. The noise they were making now was out of all proportion. They sounded as big as dogs. The two of us took our sleeping bags and relocated to a far end of the field where, away from the fire, the stars shone out all the brighter, the meadow dark blue with their light. Technically we were leaving the camp unattended, but by that point we were past all caring. We could still hear the dog-rats making a racket in the kitchen.

All the time, stories filtered down from the tree village in Lancashire. Badger and Tami went up to visit the place and came back with their eyes lit up. It was in a valley, with a river running through the middle and more than

190

anything else it sounded wet. But there were a lot of treehouses, with everyone spending half the days cooking stew on their tiny stoves. I liked the sound of it – so many treehouses in the sky in one place. It was also in a part of the world my father's family came from, and it seemed fitting to go up and give them a hand.

So when the call came, when the word came down that they were expecting an eviction, I didn't see there were two ways around it – I was going up there. Also, Sarah needed to go back to university in Lancashire – if only to jack it all in properly – and it seemed more than mere coincidences that had drawn us together.

But I was scared. I'd seen a video of the Solsbury hill eviction; chainsaw operators leaning out of the cabs of cherrypickers – a kind of crane on a truck – cutting away at branches just yards from people's faces, women getting pulled from walkways, a friend I knew screaming and crying as the police dragged her away. And every time a tree went down, it fell to the sound of women screaming. Olly had talked about this, about how it was all too much, as if it wasn't enough bad enough anyway without the air split by wailing. But it was a kind of keening, a cry that left no one in doubt that this was the death of a friend.

The footage made brutal watching and seeing it in the knowledge that I was going to go through the same thing made me feel cold. A tension set in, bloody mindedness fighting for control over a very unsettling fear.

We left first thing in the morning. I realised in a sudden wave what a home Fairmile had become for me. It was full of brothers and sisters and as we left the gate I knew that I'd never really see it like this again, that whatever was going to happen would change everything. I hugged Kit last. This man had become like a father to me. I was leaving my family. The camp receded behind us in the sun, happy in its springtime and seemingly oblivious to our departure.

III

Stanworth

The Road to Lancashire

Now the hitching began. The first leg was easy and we arrived in Newbury towards evening. Wild Ben was there to greet us, begging in an alleyway, reclining on a sunbed. Women from the florists had given him a big bunch of yellow flowers. His sunbed had yellow flowers on it too.

By the time we got near Snelsmore, it was dark. Everything had changed. A thick mast was now covering the woodland, making it utterly black beneath the trees. It was like another country. We got lost on the way and Sarah grew impatient, asking me whether I knew where the camp was in the first place. A few months ago, such a thing would have been unthinkable – I'd walked these tracks under moonlit and starlit nights a hundred times. Now the woods here were one vast dark soup, that swallowed everything up.

Eventually, the small light of the fire appeared, with the soft sound of burning wood and the smell of the smoke. Tami and Badger heard my yip and came out along the path to greet us. Back at the fire, a man called Matt the Cook was sat with a friend. He had a brown beard and long dreads and read from 'the Hobbit' most of the night. Badger, mildly derisive as ever, had introduced me as, "Jim, a flying protestor."

Badger, whose hair had long grown out from the tonsure in reverse, built the fire up steadily throughout the night. He didn't seem to know how to stop. More and more logs cascaded from his arms until we had to crawl behind the sitting logs to shelter from the heat. Matt carried on reading 'An Unexpected Party.' Someone's lighter had rolled into the fire unnoticed and exploded minutes later. Just before we finally came to eat, Tami made the final adjustments to the stew and the top of the pepper pot came off. It was good to be back.

Just to be sitting in the glow of a fire among the mammoth trees, back in the heart of the woods, was a good feeling. The winds in the leaves were full of warm rumours and assurances. That night we slept in a net.

The net was slung fifteen foot up in the arms of the beech tree, easily reached by free climbing. Badger was beginning to call it a climbing tree; an entrance or causeway to the ever expanding ghost village.

As the mists rose around us and Sarah drifted off into an exhausted sleep, I lay wide awake, listening to the forest come alive. The mist moved through everything like sighs or silver strands of brain matter. I could feel the sap rising all around me in the veins of the oaks. It was a strong tide pulling at me now under the moon. Insects wound themselves up, clock tapping beetles clicked into life like a snapping of twigs. Everything was stirring in the silence. The spirit of the place had arisen and now moved no more unseen than any other thing. I could feel it all around me; my rhythm drawn in, inhaled into it. I breathed it in and could not sleep with the pulse. The place sang to itself and I rocked in the hum of it, a small boy, listening to the leaves. This was a shore.

The next night we slept in a place over by the platforms. It was a place within a place, a grove of moss open to the moonlight, a green chapel watched over by the silent woods on every side. It was a special place. I felt welcome here.

After a few days we set off again. Badger wrote a letter for me to carry, for the people he knew in the village up North. Now the hitching really began.

The first lift that stopped was going towards Oxford. We decided to take it, even though it would take us off the motorway network. After an hour or two on the side of the

Oxford ring road, we opted to head into the city itself. Apart from anything else, it would be a good place to busk and we were running low on money. We took our first pitch that evening, by an alleyway leading to a Greek chip shop. It had been a long walk in from the outskirts. We made a fair bit of money, though I kept playing too slow and Sarah kept racing ahead. A man came and told us there was a good Irish session the next night and we decided to call it a day.

I'd visited Oxford the summer before and now led the way down a towpath out of town; a route I was sure would lead us to woodland and a tranquil place to sleep. But I'd obviously taken the wrong canal – a few of them converged in the city – and we eventually crashed out on the towpath itself, black water lapping at us from either side. Posh types coming back from the theatre were full of dismay and disgust at the apparition of these sleeping bagged bodies, tutting and throwing protective arms around startled women in shawls and high heels.

"Hardly an appropriate place to go to sleep!" one man huffed, shrill and indignant, but we were too exhausted to care and let them tread gingerly over us.

The next morning we woke early and hung around a stone garden, an avenue in the mist between two roads. We busked again later on and sat in the grounds to Christchurch College, staring across at the walls of old windows and stone. The whole place, the whole town, felt like a beehive somehow, some incessant buzzing of industrious, pretty much feverish minds. This made us glad to be sat in the sun, with nothing to do but eat pasties.

That evening we made our way down to the session. We were the first to arrive and sat among the old men and fruit machines, listening to Christy Moore on the stereo. I'd never been to a proper session before and was wondering what to expect. After a while, people with instruments started to turn up and we all piled into the next room. It was a long, old room, with the musicians crowding round a table at one end and the rest full of chairs for the people who'd come to watch. By the time we started, the place was rammed and it felt like we were sat in front of a big audience, crowding round like there was a dogfight or like they all had money on who would play best.

It was a bright evening, candlelight spilling all over the tables and all the tunes were new. A bundle of Irish lads in suits were sitting next to Sarah and myself and they asked us questions wide eyed, somewhere between disbelief and derision. Somewhere into it, Guinnesses appearing in front of me like a bad animation, I jumped on the back of a tide of emotion. It drew me under with an old man singing and I began to think that there ought to be songs for us; for Snelsmore and Fairmile, for the oaks and my friends and all the sacrifices that were being made. A song for the tricks that were still to be pulled from the government's dark cloud of a hat and a song for the spirit we were meeting our uncertain horizons with. There ought to be a song for me too, come to think of it, but the Guinness would do in the meantime.

After it had all played itself out, at stupid o' clock in the morning, the landlord took me and Sarah aside. He was a gruff man, with a professional moustache, and he got straight to the point.

"So, do you have anywhere to go tonight, the pair of you?"

"We were thinking of sleeping in a park down the road. But we need to figure out a way of getting across the river. There's a pavilion and stuff. It looks quite good…"

"You'll sleep here tonight, but be sure to be out early in the morning, or you'll get me into trouble."

As a wave of relief washed over us, he led us out into some kind of conservatory, pulling cushions off seats for us, to keep us warm and away from the stone floor.

We were woken early by an old woman bustling around with a mop and bucket. A lining of dry drink was caking my throat and the panes above us gave way to a grey sky. But it had been a good sleep and it was all that we needed.

We got on a coach that would take us to the M40 and soon we were back where we'd started; stuck on the side of a road. It was a long crawl around Birmingham and we hopped from services to services, seemingly never the nearer to wherever it was we wanted to go. We'd lost all sense of distance or destination now and clung on above the roar of traffic, with blank and bloody minds.

We camped that night by some trees at a services, dining on overpriced and insubstantial cheese and onion pasties and wrapping ourselves in a blue plastic sheet to keep off the dew. At times like these, exhaustion was our saving grace.

The next day carried on much the same, though a moment of light relief came at the next services. On the sliproad leading out onto the motorway, a whole queue of hitchers stretched back in stages of jadedness. We put our thumbs out round the corner, still on the grass of the services and got a lift within minutes. Later our karma caught up with us when a police BMW parked opposite for an hour, stopping any hope of a lift. A man in a dodgy motor finally carried us clear from all this; plucking us out of the mire of exhaust fumes and endless windscreens sheltering frightened or impassive eyes.

He took us all the way to Sarah's house in Lancaster – a good hour's drive out of his way. He was rewarded with food and tea and spliffs. Sitting on a sofa with a full belly was heaven and it seemed hard to believe it could get any better. When I finally slept, I felt sure I'd never been so knackered in my life.

Arriving in the Valley

Stanworth Valley was big. The forest floor swept your eyes downwards through the green undergrowth, towards the distant silver of a thin river. You wouldn't know, to walk through it then, that it was home to such a large tree village. The platforms, the walkways, were so high up you had to crane your neck to see them, though here and there there were signs of life on the ground; piles of old tat at the base of a tree, a bucket on a blue rope. Even people.

We'd hitched down from Lancaster to the nearest village; Feniscowles – a sprawling bungalow town from what I saw, hemmed in by stone walls on the edge of the roads. Together with Stanworth, it lay between Preston to the west and Blackburn to the east. The road being extended was the M65. A campaign had been going here for some time – the Valley was just the latest, and possibly finest phase.

The entrance to the Valley came by way of a group of brick buildings; some garages, an old disused factory and a mill. There were a couple of vehicles parked up – a long caravan and a bus behind it. The garages had been squatted and one of them now formed some kind of office. A bunch of cackling women sat or stood round a battered desk. They were all smiles and welcome, even if they did accuse me of stealing the blanket that lay, rolled up, over my shoulder. It had been going spare at Fairmile, though they'd had one just like it somewhere else, which had gone missing. It wasn't even a nice blanket; a sort of Seventies style mix of brown and black triangles that I tried to pretend amounted to a russet camouflage. Badger's letter, when they opened it, ended with the message: "We are more possible than they can powerfully imagine."

The road to the woods took us up by the corrugated sides of the mill, a large vent pumping out steam above our heads. The track was full of large, grey stones. We were definitely in the North. From a tree overhead a burgundy, embroidered banner hung with the words:

WHOSE LAND
IS IT
ANYWAY?

Up past the mill, at the top of a slope, the path took us over a canal and across an exposed hillside. It was April and the wind was still cutting. A line of stunted thorn trees crossed the hillside, bent into themselves like old women, grey barked and bare of leaves. To our left the hillside dropped down into thick woodland. This was the Valley. A couple of treehouses were visible against the skyline a little further on and beneath them, out on the open hillside, large bulldozers were working back and forth across the earth, their engines thundering doom.

We entered the woods and began to make our way down through them. There was no sign of people and we walked in silence at first, dwarfed by the trees that grew taller and taller around us as we descended. Suddenly a voice opened up,

"Welcome, visitors to the Valley!" Someone was sticking a very small head out of a platform high above us.

"Hold on! I'll come down!" A man with a Northern accent and a wrinkled face had soon abseiled down and was stood before us, grinning, introducing himself. Percy wore black wellies, a fisherman's sweater, dirty black jeans and an old woolly hat. He seemed animated by a huge sense of humour, or sense of something else, which I was sort of sensing too, having arrived. I explained I knew Olly and Percy took us down to meet him.

204

Talking all the while about how harsh it had been here over the winter and about the good old days in Solsbury Hill when everyone's harness was made out of carpet and polyprop, Percy led us down by a flight of rough stone stairs. They'd been building them over the winter on account of how muddy it had been. Huge, arm thick slabs of granite were pinned in place with fat hazel rods, arching down to the Valley floor like an unlikely but beautiful illustration. I couldn't quite believe it. It was like entering a dreamworld, a world more deeply real than everything I'd seen before.

Olly, when we found him, was stood talking with a barefoot man on the Valley floor. They were on a flood basin by the river and everywhere under their feet was carpeted in thick tongues of wild garlic. Olly knew a lot of people here from Solsbury Hill and had come up several weeks before. A lot of people called him 'General Olly' or sometimes just 'The General.' The barefoot man wore a woollen suit with breeches, had a wild crop of curly black hair and eyes as bright as the place we stood in. His name was Pete.

The two of them had been looking at the ropework above them; a new net had just been slung up and they were surveying for other possibilities. The trees and the net stood in silhouette above us; high, thin branches gnarling into each other even further up, with an ambience of great age. The leaves were coming out, but only just; a thousand darts of green catching the sun in an inverted ocean. Pete seemed like he'd somehow inhaled the green buds into his soul. The breeze seemed to pour through him. He was smiling. It was hard not to smile here.

The river Ribblesworth divided the Valley between east and west and was spanned by a bridge with wooden slats underfoot. It wasn't a particularly wide river, but it was deep. In the middle of winter, at the height of the rains, it had run twice the height that it did now. It was telling that the bridge was slung so high above it, a five foot drop beneath it to the water. Large tracts of meadow-like platforms either side of it were only now becoming solid enough to walk on after the receding waters. A steep bank bordered these, lined with the roots of trees.

The whole Valley had been a muddy quagmire over the winter, prompting the tree dwellers to stay airbourne for most of their days, cooking in their treehouses and visiting each other over the walkways. There were still large areas of impenetrable quag, I was told. Occasionally security guards sneaking around at night fell in and had to be rescued.

A path worked its way up from the eastern meadow – the opposite side to the one we arrived on – and disappeared between thick bushes of holly and rhododendron. Up here somewhere was the major focus of the site – the firepit. It wasn't exactly glorious, but I got to like it all the same. It was sheltered on one side by a half bender and bits of pallet were shoved around the fire itself, for the sake of something to sit on besides the mud. You could pack a fair few people around it. Pride of place was an old car seat looking west, a communal 'baccy stash hanging by its side in the form of half a coconut shell. It was an optimistic fixture and as far as I knew there was never anything in it. Everyone seemed to spend half their time blagging fags off everybody else. Sometimes, when it was wet and drizzly, "two's up on your fag mister" was about as far as conversation went.

Stuck here in these woods in the North, reluctant to leave the Valley and unaware of any lifts going anywhere, I was very low on money. Olly gave me a hard time for it, "If you're not signing on, you're a burden to people around you." It was a peculiar inversion of contemporary morality, but here made complete sense. In any case, it seemed mad to sign on when the eviction was only just round the corner. And I didn't want to go back to signing on, not if I could help it. Soon I'd be free to go busking again. I thought I could, just about, survive off skip runs and donations until then.

I hung around the fire pit quite a bit, in case any skipped or donated food was bought in. There was no communal cooking as such but once I initiated war on a bag of potatoes. Once the words 'chips' went around, people descended out of nowhere to help dissect spuds. It seemed particularly strange as I'd never cooked a chip in my life, though fortunately somebody had some idea what to do. The ensuing frenzy of starch and vegetable oil just left us hungrier than ever.

The firepit could be a grim place to be when you were hungry – the wood always seemed damp and mossy so it was hard work just to warm up a tin of beans. Sometimes we'd just eat them cold. On days like these I felt weak from hunger and just the walk from one side of the Valley to the other could wear me out.

I justified my ungiroed existence by the work I did in the trees. Although there was no rope for new walkways, Olly and I had plenty to do in repairing the old ones and checking on knots. Sometimes these were definitely on the dodgy side – tied off with a hitch or two too few.

One guy in particular was notorious – he was another 'flying protestor' from London and seemed on a mission to put up as many walkways as quickly as possible. He was manic and looked unsafe in his own movements, they were so rushed. We kept an eye on him and afterwards retied his hitch skimping knots. Even this was tricky though; whereas we would tend to leave a good overhang of spare rope on every walkway, he'd cut the rope close up to the knot every time, leaving little to play with when retying it. People called him Gleefoot.

Later on, in the semi panic leading up to the eviction, he dismantled the bridge, reasoning that the steel cable it was made from was too valuable in the trees. But the lengths he salvaged probably weren't any use in the trees anyway; they certainly weren't long enough for the kind of long walkways steel cable was actually useful for. And a lot of people weren't happy when he took the bridge.

The bridge across the river was formed from four lengths of steel cable; the bottom two supporting wooden slats, forming a solid base to walk on. The other two were left as hand rails. Many of the slats were missing, or half hanging off, probably being swept away when the river had risen in the winter storms.

Besides the missing slats, the whole thing wobbled around alot as you crossed over it. I preferred to hop across on the large grey rocks that now protruded from the river bed. It was a bit of a balancing act, but it was do-able. A third bridge was right at the northern end of the Valley, which was cut here by an earth bank; supporting the canal overhead. The river came through from a tunnel. The bank was strewn with pieces of building wood, thrown down from the canal. People loaded up a pontoon further down, near where vehicles could park, and floated the wood down from there. They offloaded it without ceremony, where it waited for anyone building a platform.

This bridge was a fallen trunk, right by the tunnel and it was not uncommon to find men fighting here over the river, with staves of yellow telecommunications tubing. There was a lot of digging not far away on the Preston – Blackburn road and the tubing was, by all accounts, just lying around.

The tunnel would have appeared to swallow the river up, but it was flowing the wrong way. All the same, the tunnel had a reputation – nobody wanted to go in there, and if they did, they came out in a cold sweat. The story went there were strange symbols carved into the rock in there and, all in all, it was better off left. I walked through only once myself, without noticing anything strange. But that was after the eviction, and nothing was the same after the eviction.

As the river divided everything into east or west, it stood to reason that everyone in the Valley was either a Westender or an Eastender. I would be living on the Western Front.

Olly took us back up the hill, to show us a treehouse that stood empty. The man who'd built it had gone away and not come back and no one else had claimed it, not wanting to put themselves too close to the diggers and the frontier. It was close to the edge, maybe by only twenty yards or so, one or two treelines in. It seemed like a good move to inhabit it – not only would we have somewhere sorted to sleep but it would do everyone a favour to have more of a presence on the front.

We moved in that night. A smaller, adjacent, tree was good for climbing – cutting out the need for lengthy prussiking – and it was a short trip on the walkway from there. It was a bender in a tree – a white tarp tied over the rounded, hazel frame. A net was slung underneath full of tinned and packet food – provisions for an eviction. You entered by a trapdoor in the floor to find a cosy space; carpeted and well lagged with blankets against the cold.

Sarah went back to Lancaster and to wrangles with the university while I got used to the reality of life on the front. On one of my first mornings I awoke to women shouting and stuck my head out of the trapdoor. A team of security had been posted at the edge of the woods and my nearest neighbours were out in the treetops, exchanging abuse with them. I climbed down onto a branch below the net, so I could sit in relative comfort while I kept an eye on the security. I wanted to be sure they weren't about to launch an incursion into the woods and hanging out of the trapdoor with my head upside down for much longer wouldn't have done me much good.

This kind of rude awakening became pretty familiar as the days wore on. One morning I stuck my head out of the trapdoor to see a team of yellow jackets climb out of a landrover. They began to walk purposefully towards the edge of the woods and were holding shiny metal objects that looked suspiciously like chainsaws. I didn't wear glasses, though I was pretty short-sighted. The only times I missed them in the woods was when I looked up at the moon, or came across a deer in the brambles. But this was one of those times. I gave the three yips, which was the code for 'yellowcoats in the Valley'. Shortly afterwards all the guards stopped short of the trees and began to ram their silver rods into the ground. They were some kind of surveyors – I'd made a big mistake.

After a while, a man appeared on crutches, hobbling up the steep stone stairs with a pair of sheep dogs at his heels. I explained what had happened, he wasn't exactly impressed. He was on crutches because he'd fallen from the trees at Solsbury during the eviction. It was a miracle he was alive, let alone able to walk. He lived in a raised bender at the other end of the Valley, with a series of planks attached so his dogs could get in and out unaided. The resilience shown by his presence was encouraging, but

210

his condition was also a reminder of the coming eviction and the gravity of the situation we all faced.

Tinwhistles and Generators

From the moment I'd arrived, I'd got it into my head that a treehouse was needed right on the edge of the woods; something along the lines of Chateau de Fromage perhaps – a battle platform we could intimidate the security from.

I took it on my shoulders to build it and was soon scurrying about on the banks of the canal, looking for pieces of wood. I chose an oak above an access road, that snaked its way right up to the treeline – a very visible and depressing threat. The road was gravel lined and cut into the earth around it. It was probably designed specifically to bring machinery down to the Valley floor and was another ugly reminder of coming realities.

They posted teams of security under my tree while I worked. They seemed alright, as security guards went, though I never really tried to get talking to them. It was better than swapping insults, or getting drawn into their never ending talks about football.

By the end of two weeks or so, I'd finished the treehouse. I'd borrowed an old hand drill off someone, angling holes in the edge where bender poles could be stuck, and I'd gone on a trip to the local builders' merchants with a local bloke with white hair. I bought a big bag of nails. The hand drill fell apart as I used it – the ball bearings in the handle dropping out from the worn down sides. I replaced it guiltily back under the tree of the man I'd borrowed it off. I told myself I'd tell him when I saw him again, which I never did, until the eviction, and it didn't seem to matter much then.

The treehouse was easily the worst piece of building I'd ever done. The floor was just big enough to fit one person lying down and it sloped so that you always felt in danger of rolling off. I'd used a few bender poles, with a piece of telecommunications tubing as a kind of lintel. The tarp was see-through plastic. It was a miserable piece of work. I only slept in it once.

Olly pointed me in the direction of another treehouse in the West End that was up for grabs. Someone had built it and then gone away. It was still further west than most of the inhabited platforms but was set back far enough from the security guards to give me a bit of headspace. You reached it by a zigzagging pathway of walkways that grew steadily higher. The platform itself loomed higher than these, navy tarped and triangular roofed, foreboding and faintly like a gothic pinnacle. It was spartan inside; uncarpeted, unlagged and with holes at two corners where the wind cut through. But it suited me fine.

Being so near the top of the Valley, and built in the top of the branches, it was one of the highest treehouses in the whole place. Through my breeze leaky window, over and past the East End, I could see the line of the moors, white with snow for a few days and shouldering the unmistakable outline of Pendle Hill.

Pendle Hill was a massive, brooding shadow and a very personal beacon. I'd had some imagined attachment to it for years, reading about the witches there and listening to the Stone Roses, when Manchester and Lancashire seemed pretty much the same; the music lighting up long winter nights, with thoughts of the North spreading out like relations. Half my father's family came from around Pendle Hill – Recusants from the Lancashire/Yorkshire borders who'd kept an older Faith, hidden among the moors from the magistrates and their penalties. This old brand of Catholicism had been handed down to me, and I'd held true to it until my seventeenth Easter, when I'd met a

213

girl in a beertent in a green dress. We'd walked Pendle together that summer, in a heat that had made the bog streams run hollow, exposing huge banks of brown earth, topped by thick caps of green moss. I'd had a great Aunt who'd lived down the bottom of the hill somewhere, apparently in an old house alive with grandfather clocks.

Pendle is famous for it's witches still – the Devices family of the Seventeenth Century and Alison Nutter, who'd been hanged at Lancaster prison. Among the cranky old crones who might have used curses for begging there were many kinder women and men, who'd use whatever skills they had for a more benevolent end. The new physicians rose to the fore in the wake of the strangling of this old knowledge; a sharper profession to rule over a narrower age.

So to see Pendle Hill on the horizon was a reminder of many things and no small compensation for being on the other side of the country than my family and friends. I wasn't so far from home, after all.

And I was making good friends in the Valley. Apart from Percy, whose treehouse I was now not far away from, there was the bright eyed, barefoot Pete and his girlfriend, Janie. Janie had long, ginger hair, a pointed nose and was as caught up in the magic of the place as anyone else. In the East End, people used to sing,
"Too much magic bus, too much magic bus…"

Janie played the whistle and made up nicknames for everyone, which were half the time ignored by everyone else. But she knew what she was doing in the trees, and she had a beautiful, strong spirit. It was excellent living so close to Janie and Pete.

Their platform was truly fantastic in the proper sense of the word. It had a ladder leading up to a kind of cabin; covered in a dark green tarp with a hurricane lamp inside and a green glassed, mullioned window. This lead up from a huge, open platform painted with a spiralling sun and perfect for sitting out on as the weather improved. On every side, a vibrant green sea sank and climbed away.

Things were quiet now, I felt I'd done my share of treehouse construction and there was no rope to be building new walkways with. So I'd spend a lot of time sat on Janie and Pete's open platform, surrounded by the green bloom of young leaves, reading a copy of 'The Adventures of Robin Hood'. We were along way away from the ground.

Percy's platform was also a good place to hang out. Getting up was a bit tricky, if you were climbing straight up from the ground, because the edge of the platform protruded out from the branches you were climbing up. Once you were up, out on the porch, you had to be careful where to sit because half the plank ends were unsupported beneath. Pecry knew how it all fitted together, so you always looked at him for approval before sitting down. A lot of people would pile into the bender, folding themselves up so that everyone could get in. Time would fold in on itself too as you sat there, smoking a spliff or eating jammy dodgers. Percy's treehouse was a vortex that swallowed you up, like a good book or like London. Only miles better. I always lost my gloves in there.

On the very night I moved in, the security guards set up a huge floodlight that shone down into the Valley until dawn. It was a harsh white light, bleaching the tree leaves, invading the darkness. The lights were powered with a loud generator, so that even if you couldn't see the enemy, you could hear them. Now and again, I'd poke my head into the first treehouse I'd stayed in, the one with a white tarp. It was occupied by two geezers now; chaps with shaved heads and hoodies and a heavy hash habit. They were good to hang out with, drinking brew and playing cards. They weren't new to protests and as someone burst into tinwhistling, somewhere off in the night, they said that that was the classic sound of protests; tinwhistles and generators in the dark.

Percy had his views on these new incursions too. He'd had a dream where he'd been swallowed by a caterpillar and had emerged with an understanding of all insect life. He'd done his fair share of drugs, had Percy, and was respected as a kind of tribal elder. He reckoned the floodlights messed pretty seriously with all the insects in the Valley. He'd seen them at night, beetles in the garlic, caterpillars on a thread. They were confused, they didn't know which way up the daylight was. It disturbed me to think about it.

I used to play my whistle when I got up, stood on a branch, my chest against the tree. My mentality was in some kind of halfway house towards being a piper; there was something about looking out over the Valley and seeing the day in as I played. And all my best tunes were Scottish. There were a lot of whistlers in the Valley; throughout the day there always seemed to be at least one tune echoing throughout the treetops; you usually had to wait for a quiet moment – for 'airtime' – before you could play.

Sometimes, on my way to the firepit in the East End, I'd stop by the river. The trees were like a cathedral here; graceful trunks reaching up taller than anywhere in the Valley before their limbs vaulted out into an interlaced canopy. The effect when the leaves came was stunning, the woods transforming themselves into something younger and brighter. There was some serious whistling going on down in the cathedral – the sound of six or more whistles would continually float down from the treetops – mostly from different trees but all playing the same tune. It could have been the sound of the woods themselves; a thin airy chorus, augmented from every direction and impossible to hold to one place.

It seemed there were people who never left the trees. There were a lot of people in the Valley I never really met because of this. I only explored a tiny proportion of the village in the sky. It was so big, there were so many walkways, it felt like it would take you half a day just to get from one side to the other. Walkways fanned out from every tree you came across, multiplying themselves, offering more routes than you could rightfully choose from.

If the whistlers over the river never seemed to leave their station, there was one whistler who could never be found. People doing a nightwatch would invariably find themselves asking the same question come the morning,
"Was someone playing the whistle in the middle of the night or what?" The Phantom Whistler of the Valley was a strange phenomenon, it would catch you unawares, a mere hint of music that would have you wondering at first whether it was your imagination or not. He, if he was a he, existed on the fringe of your consciousness, a playful echo from the Valley itself, climbing in sideways through the gaps in your hearing.

I was visited by a different kind of music. On a night when Sarah was due back in the Valley, I was wandering the pathways, having difficulty tracking her down. Then I heard the music. It sounded like a choir of women. They were singing something distant, vague and yet close. It was beautiful. The words they were singing formed themselves into these as I listened,
"Christmas time, mistletoe and wine," over and over again. Untroubled by this manifestation of Cliff Richard in my subconscious, I approached a fire a few people were sat around, convinced the music was coming from there. There were just a few men there and none of them were

217

singing. Olly was among them and he told me he'd seen Sarah up at the main firepit. Just then the singing came back, this time from a completely different direction. I wandered off into the woodland, abandoning the tracks in trying to locate the source. I found no choir and didn't track down Sarah herself until hours later.

It was strange the way Sarah and I used to keep missing each other. We'd never arrange where to meet, believing the Valley wasn't such a big place. I'd wander the tracks asking everyone I met whether they'd seen a girl with a fiddle,
"Yeah, I saw her just back there" or
"Yeah, she's looking for you I think." It began to seem uncanny the way we kept missing each other. Sarah got it into her head that I might be avoiding her on purpose. I began to wonder if, somehow, something might be keeping us apart. There was no doubt that there was a strange old power in Stanworth, and who could say how or when it worked its influence.

When I first arrived in the Valley I was determined not to fall in love with the place. The eviction wouldn't be long coming and I was here on a professional basis – a 'flying protestor' as Badger had said. It was bad enough already that Snelsmore had my heart, and that it was a place I now looked upon as home. I couldn't afford to set myself up for another loss. The Valley would be going and all we could do was slow the inevitable down. We'd be able to say we didn't let it go without a fight and perhaps, eventually, they'd stop building so many roads altogether. But as far as I was concerned, the fate of the Valley was already sealed. Others were more hopeful – there were a huge amount of treehouses after all and it was a very steep valley. That meant it might be impossible for them to bring cherrypickers in and without cherrypickers, how would they get us out of the trees? If they did bring them in, they'd have to build a road as they went and it would be slow, painful progress. Many people seemed to genuinely believe there was still every chance the Valley could be saved.

I tried to harden myself, to blind myself to the beauty around me, to make my heart as impenetrable as the rocks in the river. But two weeks, three weeks after my arrival and there was still no sign of an eviction. And by then the damage had been done.

There was no escaping it – the Valley was the most beautiful, the most fantastic place I'd ever lived. It was also my first spring outdoors and when the leaves appeared I felt more alive than I thought was possible. The oaks were bursting into an old, bright song around us and this, I now knew, was where all my inroads had led.

Disquiet

A couple of weeks into my stay, everyone had a big party. I was clearing out jam jars in the river, which we'd use as lamps when we'd put candles in them, when the musicians turned up. I took them up to the firepit. They got pride of place by the fire, a big woman who played the whistle sat on the car seat, the others sat around her. They played some cracking tunes. Afterwards we all trooped down to the garages where somebody had set up some decks. There was a big burner in the garages, the size of an oil drum, which made it a good place to go if it was pouring with rain, though you had to get across the windy hill first.

Tonight though, it was packed full of people, a smoking posse sat round the oil drum on bits of old sofas. Among them was a chap wearing a dark blue, North African djellaba. He'd got it in Morrocco, where he'd just got back from a few days ago. I talked to him for quite a while about his travels. He'd hung out in the villages off the trails in the Atlas Mountains, picking up a bit of Arabic in the process, speaking pidgin French. I still felt like the British Isles had a lot to show me, but when I did get abroad, if I ever did, North Africa was a place I wanted to see, so it was good to swap stories with the boy in the djellaba.

Later on, he got stuck getting up a tree. He was prussiking up a rope in the dark when he got the fear. I could hear the girls from the other side of the Western front, my original neighbours, trying to coax him up. I could see him in my mind's eye – a robe swamped figure, spinning in the blackness of a wood in full leaf, spinning out. It was a reminder that not everyone had a head for the heights we inhabited. Prussiking in particular was always an ordeal – a prolonging of the agony, a tortuous inching up from the ground. He had my sympathies, though it sounded like there were plenty of people on the case, helping him out. In situations like that, there was often nothing to be done but talk people round – their panic would fade in the end and then there was just a slow injection of faith, coupled with a realisation that the equipment was sound, that they weren't going to plummet to the ground at a moment's notice and that they were in good hands. It was always excellent when whoever it was made it to the top.

At one point, something alarming happened. People began to disappear from their treehouses. A woman living near the river in the West End left. A black dreaded man called Spencer, who wore a thick, stripey jumper, threatened he was going to leave as well. There were others. The woman who lived near the river had been involved with Stanworth since the beginning and it couldn't have been an easy thing to go. She'd been campaigning for a long time and had been at Solsbury Hill. But that was why she was going – she'd been through one tree eviction already and knew what to expect. It was the same with Spencer and the others. Even people who swore they'd see it through to the end were showing signs of getting freaked out. Reality was dawning beneath our dreams, the tide of events building up to a current that made us feel increasingly diminutive.

I tried to carry on as normal, scooting around the walkways and visiting people, being chirpy at every turn. But the people around me were older and more experienced. I knew that if they were worried, then I ought to be too. So to maintain the appearance of indifference in the face of everything now became vitally important. In the absence of rope, there wasn't much else to do.

One day a load of teenage girls turned up from a nearby college and there were suddenly enough people to do an action. A pair of friends of mine - Brave Sir Robin and Cookie - jumped in the back of an earth moving lorry. The lorry driver hadn't noticed though, or was just being malicious, because he drove off, leaving the two in the back no chance of escape. They fished up in a lorry yard in Blackburn – after a rocky and freezing drive – and quietly ran away.

Another time, a day of action had been promised in the underground press. It was news to us though, and the first we knew about it was when an extra two hundred security turned up to guard the compound on the Eastern Front. We thought we'd leave them to it – there wasn't much point doing any digger diving with so many security and nobody on our side had turned up for the action anyway. Besides, we'd already secured a victory, even in our total slackness; the cost of hiring so many guards must have been massive. It was particularly satisfying knowing that they knew it had all been in vain.

We weren't the only residents of the Valley who had a thing against diggers. A herd of white cows used to roam around, trashing anything on the ground. It was another good reason to live solely in the trees. At Solsbury Hill it had been pigs. Someone, inspired by tales of Bladdud the swineherd, had bought two pigs to live on the hill. He'd managed to get the wrong breed of pig, so that soon they'd grown to three times the size of what you might expect a pig to grow to, rolls of flesh wrinkling over each other down to their snouts. They roamed around at will, sometimes destroying whole benders in their hunt for food. But here it was cows.

The Valley was long and wide and most of the time you'd never see them, but now and again they were hard to miss. I was looking out from the Western Front one time when I saw the herd arrive at the edge of the area being worked over by diggers. The cows looked purposeful and were being led by a large white bull. A barbed wire fence prevented them getting any further. But it must have been only propped up because when the bull trod on the top wire, it fell to the ground easily and the cows all sauntered through. They milled around in front of the earthmovers, forcing them to a standstill. They stood there for a good ten minutes or so before wandering off again along the flank of the trees. They'd made their point.

Huge bulldozers appeared on the Western Front after this. They were easily three times the size of tanks and seemed as big as a house. Little ladders led up to the cabs, which were dwarfed by the rest of the machine. The racket they made was infernal, the ground itself seemed to rattle as they trundled over and back, rubbing in fate, caterpillars shaking out empty spite under a sky heavy with threats. It made you sad sometimes to watch it, the sound drumming into you, numbing your senses. It was better to be angry.

Around the same time, as the weather improved, there was an influx of locals walking around the woods. Before we'd arrived there'd been big signs everywhere declaring 'PRIVATE, NO ACCESS.' I think the locals knew the place hadn't got long to go and they wanted to see it while they still could.

More and more protestors were in evidence too. Tents were appearing along the level sections of the paths. There was a feeling of inundation, people were suddenly everywhere that I'd never recognise and never see again.

I was walking back from the garages late one afternoon. It had been a windswept, April day. But now the clouds were knuckling down to a more settled pattern, the sun had dropped beneath their western boundary, casting a thin, golden light over the entire valley. An old man in a tweed suit was stood at the edge of the Western Front, taking it all in. We acknowledged each other as I past. He said,

"It'll all be gone soon…" and we fell into talking about the Valley and about how everything in the world was being turned on its head. He was old as a bird, soft eyed and with a voice as rounded and gentle as old country cheese.

We hadn't been chatting long when a punk who I'd met earlier came along. He lived in one of a group of tents not far from the front, that had sprung up only in the last few days. He had a bolt through his nose and a mohican. That was fine but there was something else about him I was a little unsure of. In front of my eyes, he turned round and snarled at the old man, an expression of twisted enmity he obviously saved for any perceived enemy. And an old country gent out for a walk in his tweeds was an obvious target. Practically an aristocrat. The punk made some vague verbal attack and, predictably enough, the old man took umbrage.

Soon it was a full blown argument, the punk all aggression and hatred, the old man all wavering indignation and petrified defence. A bunch of other people turned up and joined in, seeing the argument immediately from a 'them and us' viewpoint. Soon the old man had a whole mob on his hands, giving him grief.

I snuck away, ashamed but half afraid of the punk myself and feeling unable to talk round a mob of the loud mouthed. More than anything else I was stunned that it had happened at all, that people could react so swiftly and venomously for no good reason. It was still sinking in some days later. All the same, walking away from it was probably the most shameful thing I'd ever done. The old man had been reluctant to talk at first and I'd pretty much coaxed him into it. Now another chance at reconciliation and understanding had been lost, and another enemy made. And more than that, I'd turned my back on an old man who'd done nothing wrong. The scene was predictable but disturbing and I could hear them shouting it out behind me as I scurried off down the stone stairs.

New platforms were springing up all over the place. John the guitarist, who I'd met with Sarah in Exeter, had turned up and was building a house with his new girlfriend. Others had devised a scheme of building platforms on the ground and then hoisting them up mob handed, whoever was around grabbing a bit of rope in a tug of war against gravity. It was incredible to see one go up; six, ten square feet of solid wood ascending in swooping fits and starts, taking its place in the trees. The dwellings in the village were multiplying at a rapid rate, thickening out in the treetops.

We knew the eviction was coming close when a white haired man turned up from Greenpeace to give us all a training session on handling the media. There were a lot of rumours flying around, apparently, among the rest of the population that we were all in the payroll of Greenpeace, getting paid hundreds of pounds a day. But the hour's talk from this man was as close as those rumours ever got to truth. His main point was that if you got interviewed it was best to keep your comments short and sweet because anything superfluous was likely to get edited and maybe used against you. Sat in the middle of the woods, following nothing more sophisticated than our heart's calling, we had just been introduced to the soundbite.

Around this time, we had another visitor. He was a professional climber and had come to give us all a few tips. His main advice was that we should all get chest harnesses, in addition to the ones we wore around our waists. Apparently, if we were knocked unconscious during the eviction and left dangling from our waist harnesses, there would only be a few minutes before serious damage could begin to happen, as a consequence of dangling upside down from our pelvises. Chest harnesses – essentially only a loop of tape threaded around one shoulder - would keep us upright.

As well as this, he advised having two cowstail clips. Cowtails were the umbilical tapes that kept us secured to the walkways – they ended in a snapgate carabina that could be clipped and unclipped from a rope without hassle. With two, we could be clipped on at all times, clipping onto two adjacent walkways simultaneously whenever we got to a tree. Some people went to get supplies from a climbing shop and we all got properly kitted up. I even got little rubber fasteners that got my cowstail tapes securely fixed to the carabinas, which had always been in danger of falling off beforehand.

Someone had set up a practice walkway on the basin by the river. It was close to the ground so you could climb on and off it and even fall off without any trouble. It was good practice for people who'd yet to get to grips with the walkways in the trees. It met an early end when people decided to test the rope's breaking point. As many people piled onto it as would fit and started bouncing up and down. It gave way in the end, the blue plastic sagging and eventually snapping. But it took such an effort that we now knew a walkway giving way under us needn't be a top concern, no matter how many people were on it.

On the last week in April, stacks of rope arrived. The waiting around was over. I set to work putting up walkways on the Western Front with an almost manic enthusiasm. When I couldn't find anyone to help, I'd work on my own, slinging the two ropes into the gap between the trees and hoping they'd fall to the ground. I'd tie a line to the second tree next and throw this down to the middle ground as well. If all went according to plan, I could then tie the lines together and haul them all up. Threading the lines through the branches was the difficult bit and a clean throw made all the difference between a long job and an easy one.

The walkways went up and by the end of the week it made me dizzy, in places, to see so many lines radiate out from the one spot. It was a web.

A sea of bluebells had opened up almost overnight, a last minute surprise from the woods to blow us all away and welcome in the spring. I'd seen plenty of bluebell woods before but this was truly stunning, especially looking at it all from so high. The flowers stretched away on every side, tiny pinpoints of blue rolling together at a distance into a blurry fleece. This was amazing. But with it, as always, came the plummeting feeling in your chest that it would soon all be gone. I didn't want to think about it and put up more walkways instead.

Now it was the eve of May the First – the old Celtic fire festival of Beltaine. It marked the beginning of spring, when the flowers and the heat came back into the world. It was a time for lovers, not for fights. People had set up a sweatlodge down by the river, a bender lined with blankets to keep in the steam. Hot rocks would be bought in from a firepit nearby and have water thrown over them. The resulting dark, soupy environment was good for vision questing, and strengthening and purifying the spirit. I put up more walkways while this was going on. I heard them all climbing out hours later – whooping as they plunged into the river to cool off.

We'd heard the eviction was due the next day, but had already received several false alarms. A sense of unreality had taken hold. But now this really did look for real. People kept on appearing throughout the evening, wanting to get up in the trees. While I was on the ground, tying some lines together, two women appeared out of nowhere with an ancient, 1950's style screwgate carabina. The octagonal screw had seized up, probably through long disuse. I managed to get it undone using a lighter. It felt like I was opening a jar of jam for them.

A couple of sound, laddish men appeared to occupy my home of the last few weeks - the pinnacled spartan bender with the view of Pendle Hill. I'd told them to be careful of my eviction stash – two dozen or so green plastic 'Jackie's Beer' bottles, laboriously collected from all around the Valley floor and refilled with water from a spring in the East End. Jackie's beer was brewed locally and sold in a nearby shop. It wasn't too bad, considering it was so cheap. It was a sorry loss when the shop declared there was no more left – we'd drunk the warehouse dry.

Sarah had reappeared and was now occupying the white tarped treehouse with a woman called Shel. At some stage a nervous looking ITN cameraman turned up and we agreed to make room for him, as long as he behaved himself and did what he was told. The last thing we'd need was a panicky or rogue cameraman on the loose. The four of us sat in the bender, looking out over the new security compound. The tarp had been raised up to give a good view and make filming possible and we sat there with it framing our vision, as though we had our own treetop cinema.

The compound was in the process of being invaded by naked hippies. We were worn ragged, things were becoming more and more like a dream and it seemed incidental that the cameraman was filming it all. Not that any of what we were watching would ever make the news.

Down in the compound, everyone was yipping and dancing to the drums. People were breathing fire and whirling firesticks; rushes of real colour amid the blanched white of the floodlight. Everyone looked blue in the halflight; nothing seemed quite real. A huddle of petrified security had backed away to their portacabin, unsure what to do in the face of so much nakedness.

The cameraman kept on getting trivial messages on his pager from the rest of his crew – the "guys". They were all wrapped up in a hotel somewhere and obviously finding it hilarious that he was stuck up a tree. He was seemingly a new boy on the job and was beginning to annoy me already, getting flustered and excited every new time his pager went off. I left to finish a final walkway before crashing out sometime in the early hours, drumming and dancing still going on in the compound nearby. With all the space in the treehouses finally full, I was able to claim my bed in the ropey piece of work I was responsible for. The floor slanted badly so that only the bender poles kept me from rolling out. But I was so shattered I couldn't care less.

Eviction!

"Jim! Time to switch on mate!" Percy was calling to me across the trees, trying to get me to turn on the CB I'd been given. It was early, about six o' clock. The sun was only just climbing free from behind Pendle and the moors. I felt like I'd had about three hour's sleep. There was no sign of any security or police, no sign of very much at all in fact, and I climbed down to go to the loo in the seclusion of a holly bush.

Holly bushes had been great friends of mine for this very purpose throughout the last month – I'd dig a hole with a bit of stick and that was that, my bare arse safe from unwelcome eyes. Or, more likely, unwary eyes safe from the sight of my bare arse.

I bumped into Olly as I returned from the bush. He'd just finished cooking himself breakfast on a little campfire. Someone else was wandering around with a spade. There was an eerie feeling of near normality, though I felt edgy on the ground, in case something did kick off. But part of me began to relax and even begin to believe that perhaps today wasn't the day after all. I'd be able to catch up on sleep.

Olly was happy to take the CB off my hands; I was unsure how much use I'd be with it in such a sleep deprived condition. I climbed back into the trees feeling a rush of relief as I left the ground.

They came in around eight o' clock. Six police landrovers appeared first, pulling up in a diamond formation on the access road, immediately beneath my tree. Security started piling out of vehicles on top of the hill, assembling themselves into a yellow block of colour on the horizon. I reckoned there were at least five hundred of them; a neon legion growing bigger by the minute.

As soon as they appeared we started shouting from the trees; yipping – high, long, war cries – banging drums and blowing whistles. We threw up a wall of noise to let them know we weren't afraid, that we were up for anything the assembling horde had to throw at us.

More and more vehicles arrived, more and more security and police piled out onto the hillside until the whole scene had grown so big it had overtaken itself. It seemed ridiculous. Police 'Evidence Gatherers' appeared beneath the trees, pointing cameras up towards us. They had a new uniform – halfway between police and Star Wars extras. We shouted quotes from the Holy Grail at them; "We decline to speet in your jeneral direction you Engleesh peegs" and "Your mothurr smells of elderberries." The Evidence Gatherers said nothing in return and continued to film us with all the emotion of robots.

Police moved in and dragged away anyone who hadn't got up in a tree. This accounted for quite a few people – those who couldn't climb and locals who had come to lend their support. It was the first wiping of the slate. A bunch of people had clambered up the climbing tree near the white tarp platform. Now they were getting pulled down by bailiffs. These men were dressed in chequered lumberjack shirts and hard hats with the rose of Lancashire on them. They were built like brick shit houses and rough handed with it.

At the same time, teams of red shirted, white helmeted climbers were making their way into the trees. They ascended simultaneously in three separate places at the other side of the frontline, near where the press had been herded. They were fast; disconcerting blurs of rapid movement up the trunks.

Scuffles started to break out around the trees and the Valley echoed to screams and shouts and the crashing of people being lowered crudely through the branches. The sun climbed higher and the heat arose, adrenaline hung thick in the air and far below, the bluebells fell in swathes under the security guards' feet. The security had moved down to secure the area cleared by the police and now lined the route of clearance. It felt like the first day of summer – there hadn't been any heat like this before and their coming in like this, on May the First itself, had turned everything hideously inside out.

The first treehouse was taken. It was Ryan's, who'd come up to the Valley roughly the same time as me. He tried appealing to the bailiff's sympathies, asking them not to trash his stuff as it was all he had. He shouldn't have bothered. The bailiffs emptied the water stash over his bedding in response, before throwing it all to the ground. Then they slashed the tarp with knives.

The climbers massed for an attack on Percy's platform further into the Valley, to try and isolate those of us on the front, and maybe to divide our attentions and diffuse our defence. But Percy's tree was full of people and by the time the climbers were bought to a halt, they were coated in layers of water, soup, beans, treacle and flour. With white, powdery faces and the trunk above them smothered in protestors, they beat a retreat to the ground. Everyone started cheering as they descended.

Now and again the climbers would give us a break while they went back to their landrover to discuss tactics. Every time they did they were accompanied by whoops of derision. Somebody shouted,
"You're climbers! You do it because you love nature! You're betraying yourselves!" They were mostly rock climbers, used to clambering about North Wales. This was their first major public outing. Most people were shocked

by the tactic of sending people up in the trees to bring us down. They'd been expecting just cherrypickers, with which the eviction at Solsbury Hill had been carried out. But climbers were more mobile and could attack anywhere without warning. They'd recently been used in an eviction in Pollok Free State in Scotland but everyone had dismissed the chances of them here; it hadn't seemed feasible.

I was spending my time moving about on the walkways, trying to cover as many trees as possible. If anyone on the ground looked like they were about to climb a tree, I'd scurry overhead to shadow them.

So far, most of the action was concentrated on the other side of the front. People started to shout that they needed more help over there and I moved as quickly as I could along the walkways to where the action was. Two men were grappling with a pair of climbers in a tree just past the white tarp platform. They were fixed in a bewildering flurry of movement, clipping themselves on, unclipping themselves as they moved again, the protestors shouting out whether they were secure or not.

"Clipped on!" "Unclipped!" "Clipped on!"

It was like a wrestling match revolving around carabinas and climbing tape and a long drop. Even stood on a walkway, next to them as they sat in the crooks of branches, it was hard to keep up with what was going on.

Other people were stood on walkways, preventing them from being cut. A climber nearby with a strange, mad look in his eye started holding a knife to the top rung of a walkway, in an attempt to get us to give ground. Nobody moved.

"Put that knife AWAY!" people screamed. My heart was in my throat. If I hadn't been constantly moving, I would have been shaking instead. There'd been a pre-eviction safety meeting between a representative group of protestors and the Sheriff. The main point agreed upon was that, under no circumstances would knives or other sharp objects be used.

It was around this point that I climbed down the white tarp tree, stopping about fifteen foot above the ground. I'd brought some barbed wire with me – there was a roll of it up near the platform. I'd started arranging it around the trunk when I noticed a man calling up to me from the ground. He was a vicar, wearing a hard hat.

"I have been asked by the people of the Valley…" his voice was thin and strained but nevertheless carried above the noise of the chaos,

"…to ensure that fair play is carried out by both sides." I assured him that most of us were doing the same, before scrambling back up to the madness.

"They're coming for your tree, Jim." I looked over to see a squad of red t-shirts climbing up the tree I'd just slept in. I'd put a roll of fencing wire around the lower branches, which slowed them up enough to give me time to get over there. They were still cutting through it when I arrived – a big bailiff was painstakingly working away with a pair of snips. There wasn't much I could do to stop them, at this stage, besides put my fingers in the way, and I didn't want to do that. The bailiff looked like he wouldn't have too many reservations about snipping off a finger or two.

Then they were through and climbing up towards me. There's a feeling like no other when someone from the government climbs your tree and enters your territory. It's a feeling of invasion, a physical revulsion at the people moving up towards you.

I'd been told the thing to do at this stage was put your foot against their head, not kicking them but bracing your leg against them, stopping them from climbing any higher.

I put my foot against the white hard hat of a bailiff. It seemed to work for a moment or two.

"Take your foot OFF his head!" A policeman was shouting at me from the ground – not so very far away now – with such indignation that I found myself taken aback and complying. I climbed higher and the bailiff followed, reaching up to cut my bag away from my shoulder. I felt it slip and watched it fall to the ground through the branches. It had a first aid kit in it, put together by my dad during my last visit home.

Shel was there and they managed to grab her ankle. Others had come over to help fend the bailiffs off. Two of us grabbed hold of Shel's arms. We kept this tug of war up for a while before we had to let her go and watched as she slipped away from us, sinking like a lead weight into a sea of muscly arms.

Then I was stood on a walkway on my own, a climber at one end, criticising my knots.

"It won't be long" he told me "before we'll give you three warnings and then we'll cut the ropes." I should have known better, but after what I'd seen already that day, anything seemed possible. Wanda, who'd been in the Valley all winter, had already had a rope cut from under her. Although we were always clipped onto the top rope and her cowstail would have saved her anyway, she instinctively clung on, skinning her hands in the process.

They were coming for the white tarp tree. My mind on Sarah, and how they were likely to handle her, I made a move to get there on a long walkway. The bottom line had already been cut and I was thinking of going hand over hand. Fortunately, somebody talked me out of it and I could only watch as the red t-shirts made their way further and further up the trunk.

Climbers had been and gone in a number of places now and I was franticly trying to restring walkways that had been cut. Locals and others were stood on the other side of the fence nearby, shouting their support. I had some nylon wire and a roll of tape for a weight, throwing it to people in the next tree. When I accidentally let go of the end, and it flew to the ground, I tried again, using my moneybag for a weight – this opened up mid-flight, sending a shower of what coppers I had to the earth, together with a lens of my glasses that I'd saved after the frames had got trashed.

I'm not sure how many I managed to reconnect before I realised they were coming for the gothic tree and we were in danger of being cut off. We had to glide pretty sharpish along the walkways now. Janie was in front and I was the last to leave that section of the woods. The oaks stood wild and pensive and full of the raw power of sap in the spring. I felt like I was leaving old friends behind. Janie turned round to look at me,

"Kiss the trees as you go Jim." The bark was harsh against my lips.

We got to the gothic oak and I began to clamber up to the platform to make what I thought would be my last stand. The climbers weren't far behind. Below, my friends were retreating away from me along the skyward paths, sinking deeper into the heart of the Valley. The Sheriff was below us, shouting up through a loudspeaker not to evade arrest, his words falling out inconsequentially. On the walkway under me, Larch was the last to leave. He was a kind of unofficial spokesman for the Valley and had attended the pre-eviction safety meeting. A bailiff got on the same walkway as him and to shouts and jeers from his mates on the ground began to bounce up and down. There was an unmistakable feeling of being in the hands of animals.

"There's no way you can carry on like this," Larch shouted to the Sheriff "without someone being killed before you've taken the whole valley."

I can still see everyone slipping back from me along the walkways. I somehow knew we'd never meet in the same light after this. So much was lost before I'd see them again.

I got into the treehouse with the climbers right behind me. The two men who'd slept in there had gone. I hadn't expected that. The climbers piled in after me before I had time to think. Somehow the will to fight had been drained from me – it was just me and the climbers now and, despite everything, they seemed suddenly human. I offered them a cup of tea, hoping to delay them that way. They declined, but I was able to show them the view of the Valley. At least forty or so treehouses were left swaying. After a long, drawn out day, they had claimed maybe six. The climbers fell silent. This was the first real look they'd got at the entire valley and the enormity of the task ahead of them had clearly just sunk home.

"Oh my god" one of them said. They didn't want any tea.

Stanworth Falls

I let myself be abseiled the eighty foot or so to the ground. My last words in the tree had echoed Larch's; there was no way they could clear this valley with their current tactics before somebody ended up dead. On the ground, police were on hand to march me in front of the Sheriff, Andrew Wilson. He was a miserable looking, grey faced man up close. It looked as though this was the first time he'd seen daylight in years. A police sergeant stood next to him gave me an official warning that I'd be arrested if I went up to the trees again. An Evidence Gatherer stood on his other side, filming it all. Then I was turned free onto the hillside, a bale of retrieved polyprop over each shoulder, walking dizzily towards a crowd of press and onlookers.

The press crowded round as soon as I was over the line and I was faced with something I thought I'd never see; a sea of microphones and cameras pointing towards me, reporters shouting out questions one after the other. I was fired up for this and managed to answer the questions reasonably coherently, telling them how dangerous the eviction had been so far. All thoughts of soundbites went out of the window. Someone was banging a war rhythm on a big empty oil drum just behind me. When I'd said everything that needed saying, they realised they hadn't picked up anything thanks to the drumming and the whole barrage of questions started again. This time I wasn't so eloquent.

Sarah came up to me through the crowd – she hadn't been arrested either. It was good to see she was safe. We were sat a little apart from the crowd when a grey haired reporter came up to interview me. I stressed again how dangerous the eviction was. As I did so I thought of all my friends still up in the trees. It felt as though the fate of the entire country was encapsulated within the Valley then and, as the enormity of it washed over me, I began to weep. The reporter put his hand on my shoulder.

We went to the sheds after that. As we walked down towards the mill, the shattering sound of chainsaws started up behind us. I almost doubled up when I heard it, as though I'd been punched in the stomach. I was glad I wasn't there to see the carnage.

Back at the sheds we heard about a Scottish girl I'd met in the last blurry days before the eviction. She'd been one of the first evicted and had had her arm broken while being lowered upside down by a bailiff. We were all sat round on old chairs, looking wrecked. A man in an overcoat was giving blowbacks with a spliff; inhaling the smoke and then blowing it back through a tunnel of hands into the face of the recipient. He was a big crazy man giving the blowbacks, bending people's heads back in the process. One lad ended up swallowing the butt of the spliff, gagging on the ember. I refused all offers of a blowback but was so tired that I ended up almost falling off my chair anyway.

Someone led me to a waiting mattress and I crashed out immediately. I was done in. I spent the next day just lying on the mattress, watching herds of reporters coming and going. Ed from Fairmile appeared, as energetic as ever. He was running away because the Sheriff had singled him out for some dodgy deed he didn't do. He told me Beltaine at Fairmile had been incredible and was still going on when he left. Part of me wished I was there, instead of being wrecked on an old mattress at the back of a falling down outbuilding.

The other red headed Ed also appeared. During his arrest, when the police wouldn't give him back his belongings, he told them he didn't like the games they were playing.

"We'll teach you about playing games" they'd said and told him they were going to beat the shit out of him before locking him up for a few extra hours. He was convinced they were going to come into his cell at any minute and start laying into him. They let him go unharmed, but badly shaken up.

The day after that, Sarah and I went back down to the Valley. It was the third day of the eviction. Half the trees of the Western Front had gone. Security guards stood around the new void. The impression again was unmistakably of a Roman column advancing. People were gathered down on the Valley floor, behind a thin picket line of chestnut fencing, sitting on logs playing music and creating a general noise of defiance as the battle continued over our heads. I tried to block the battle out, a wave of raw emotion threatening to overwhelm me every time I looked up.

I sat reading newspaper reports with Sarah. Most of it seemed to be on our side besides something in one of the tabloids that showed "a protestor girl wielding an axe as a security guard approaches." The 'security guard' in the accompanying photo was Ryan, wearing a neon yellow jacket. Even in the photo you could see his dreadlocks. And the axe had just been seized from a bailiff who had taken it into the trees to cut walkways.

On the front page of another paper was a big photo of a tree being felled, the hinge just giving way, the trunk at the start of its fall and the chainsawman lowering his saw. There was a bright gash of new wood where the beak of the cut was opening out. By the mark on the trunk – an old white cross – I recognised it as the white tarp tree, the first I had slept in here. I thought I'd been spared this. It made me feel hollow to look at it.

A pile of returned tat was heaped next to a log. Most of it was from evicted treehouses and was in a sorry state. I found my first aid kit among it. Someone had gone through it – the cream had been squeezed out, the bandages had been trodden on and the box itself was broken. I couldn't understand the extent of their pettiness. There was no sign of the ivy chessmen and Indian inks I'd left in the white tarp treehouse, or of anything else I recognised.

I soon felt ready to return to the trees. I shaved off my sideburns to try and disguise myself and painted my face with a stripe of brown mud down the line of each eye. They could recognise me from my clothes of course, but that didn't occur to me at the time. I'd heard there was a tree right on the edge of the East End that you could still climb into. I set off at twilight, taking a long way round by the canal. It was dark by the time I made it to the tree. It was a large oak, quite low set, the arms sprawling out towards the edge of the woods. One of these came right down to the ground and offered a route up. Everything was cast brown by the falling darkness. Someone had a fire nearby and that only accentuated the shadows.

There were a fair few people around and I thought I was getting up unnoticed until somebody called out,
"Oiy, mate!" I looked up to see two security guards just beyond the treeline. I noticed one was holding a camera up, just before the flash dazzled me. Because of the slope of the ground they were on a level with me and got a good view of my face. Feeling tricked and gullible and with my cards suddenly marked, I climbed up away from the ground.

I stuck my head in the first treehouse I came to. It was occupied by a Greek girl called Sule; frying up sosmix on a little stove. Percy was there too, strongly advocating the consumption of spliffs and alcohol during evictions. He was leading by example.

241

"They're earthing energies..." he said,
"...and earthing energies are what you need when you're up a tree." I picked up a couple of bags of sosmix sandwiches and set off across the walkways in the dark.

Before I'd got far, I managed to drop one of the bags. I didn't feel it slip, perhaps the handles had worn through against the rope. It fell silently and swiftly, dropping down into the dark. I thought of all the hungry people out on the front that it would've help feed. I felt like an arse. In the second treehouse was the punk who'd verbally mauled the old man. Somehow though, this didn't seem like the time to settle old differences and I climbed up from the walkway to talk to him for a while. He seemed glad to have a bit of company and was another one in the Sheriff's black book after he threw a slab of chocolate cake at him. For months, people had scrimped and saved the best food for the eviction, which in some respects was looked forward to as a cushy long siege, where there would be very little to do besides lie back and eat.

The people in the third treehouse were testaments to a very different reality. It was a huge construction, one of the main bases of the East End and was full of people huddled round the edges, wild eyed and battered looking, not far off from nervous wrecks. A bulldozer had been working under them that day and had started to move the roots of their tree, which protruded from a bank of earth. The whole tree was swaying violently and they'd leant out from the platform to see what was going on and then to scream in pure terror. The Sheriff had finally called the bulldozer off; just how close to disaster they'd been was hard to tell.

I was in new territory. I'd never been into the trees in the East End, I hadn't even seen half the treehouses in the West End properly. It was a vast village in the sky. Being in an unexplored part of it made me realise just how big it was. I had to ask directions to stop myself getting lost: "Go straight on for two trees then climb down about ten foot, watch the next walkway as it's a bit slack, then take the second left. That should get you to the next platform and you can ask from there."

Away from the edge, over security controlled ground and everything was lit by huge floodlights. They shone up into the trees, turning the leaves a jungle-like yellow. I had the distinct impression of being immersed in a very strange film.

Someone had told me Badger was about – somewhere on the front line – and it was now my mission to try and find him. I crossed over the river by a long, long, walkway. Facing me, as I scuttled side on to the direction I was travelling in, was what looked like an oak in cross section, about fifty foot away. At the centre of its branches was a little treebender radiating a good light to the leaves all around. It was a bizarre moment of peace in an otherwise bewildering journey.

I eventually made it to the remains of Percy's treehouse. This was now the frontline and had been taken by the climbers, stripped of its tarp and then retaken by the protestors at night. When I got there it had a small crowd within, huddled inside the bare bender frame, lit by a couple of candles. They all looked haggard but strangely triumphant, handing round a bottle of wine. I gave them the last bag of sandwiches. Pete and Janie were there and it was somehow indescribably sweet to see them. It seemed some kind of twilight zone; everything that was good about this place hanging on defiantly in the face of what had started. Without it's tarp the bender seemed overtly cosmological and, inside it, we were all raw spirits in the night. The stretch of the Valley that had been felled looked even grimmer from up here; floodlit, covered in tracks and churned up mud. It was like a lunar landscape. The trees where I had lived were now nowhere to be seen, leaving a gaping, starry chasm.

Pete confirmed that Badger was close. I called for him at the top of my lungs, it seemed a lifetime since I had seen him. He called back, sounding hoarse and a long way off. I had to strain to catch his words. We shouted to each other for quite a while; a strange, disembodied conversation in the dark. He said he was alright, apart from lack of water – they'd cut the walkways around him, leaving him stranded at the top of a tree. He also said one of the climbers had told him they were coming for Fairmile. I took this to heart, though I ought to have known they'd come out with anything if they thought it might do our heads in.

I crashed out that night back at the eastern end of the Valley, with my feet sticking out of a small treehouse. I kept my boots and harness on, wanting to be ready for a rude awakening.

Andrew Wilson himself woke me up, his thin, reedy voice proclaiming,
"Good Morning Vietnam" through a loudhailer. He drawled out 'nam' like an Essex office clerk. I didn't want to move. I knew I ought to, but I felt like a sack of potatoes. Surely it wouldn't make too much difference if I didn't get up just yet... Then I heard the shouts of protestors on the ground,
"People in the trees wake up! They're cutting the walkways! Wake up!"

I looked out to see long, white poles wavering about from the security's territory. They had knives or some kind of scissors on the end and walkways were being sliced in two with a gentle twang. I saw two or three being cut before I had time to react. It was a dismaying sight. It turned out to be part of a police operation to isolate a girl who'd had a chainsaw worker cut through a branch inches from her face. She'd subsequently lost it and started kicking a climber while she hung from a branch. And now they were out to get her.

I didn't want to carry on defending the trees that morning. I'd had enough already and was thinking about Fairmile after what Badger had said. I also hadn't had any breakfast, hadn't eaten properly for days in fact. And I could have done with going to the loo. But that seemed irrelevant now. I was in the thick of it and it was hard to draw myself away. I ended up helping to re-do some of the walkways that had been cut. Then I joined a long line of people, one on each walkway, all of us waiting to get to the front line but defending existing walkways at the same time.

A riot kicked off below me. The police were pushing the picket fence back and the people on the other side were trying to stop them. A middle aged woman fell over and got trapped between the fence and the trunk of the tree I was in. She was being crushed. Anger erupted out of me and I started swearing at the police,
"You're crushing that woman! You fucking bastards!" At the same time, shameful as it was, I felt a rush of relief that I was up in the trees and safe from the frays on the ground.

Not long after that, they tried bringing a cherrypicker down onto the Valley floor. But the ground was soft here - this was the quag – and the cherrypicker was soon floundering in it, engines revving with no result, the whole thing listing onto its side. Everyone starting cheering. It was the best thing that had happened all day.

It was still morning when I decided to come down from the trees. Somehow, and without a clue as to how I'd do it, I wanted to get water to Badger. The nearest I had to a plan was to get in the general area and then start calling for him. If I found him, I could then climb over the fence and scoot up his tree. It wouldn't be easy with the ground crawling with security guards, but I had to give it a go.

I was sneaking through the lushness of the Valley floor, a safe distance from the fence, when a crashing erupted not far away. A man who'd just been taken down from the trees was making a run for it, two guards right behind him. They were running full tilt, all of them desperate to stay out of trouble. I emerged from the ferns I'd taken cover behind and started running in the opposite direction, hoping to bewilder and distract the guards. I think they gave up the chase. When I stopped to hide behind a bush I could hear the escapee, not far off, puking into the grass.

It dawned on me that I had very little idea, even roughly, where Badger was. The fenced off area, the new lush growth and the area of felled trees was all disorientating. I realized I couldn't even have found Percy's treehouse if I'd wanted to, and I had no clear idea where Badger was in relation to that. I also began to feel I was in some kind of bandit territory, with escapees running about all over the place. Perhaps the police were keeping an eye out for me now, now that I'd returned to the trees. I needed to get out of there and I needed to eat. I wandered back towards the sheds and crashed out under a tree by the mill.

I went back to the Valley that night and found a camp set up outside the security fence. There were loads of locals there, women with their kids; their lives now entwined with the eviction. I heard, much later, that my Great Uncle Richard, who'd I'd met only once at a wedding, had tried to make it down the Valley himself, along with his wife. They'd heard I was there and had been carrying a big box of food. They ran into a load of security though and got a rough treatment, never making it to the Valley itself.

Badger was there, a big drum strapped around his shoulders. He told more of the story of his time up the tree. One of his shoes had been pulled off, causing the Sheriff to address him as,

"You there! With the red sock!" He also dropped his hat – a red, velvet, pixie's hat, not unlike my hood. He abseiled down to get it and just as the security were closing in on him he tied himself to the rope and was hauled up by five or six people. When the climbers were trying to get him, he was up in the highest branches, almost out of their reach. The climbers had fixed loops of climbing tape around his legs, trying to pull him down. Exactly what would have happened if they'd succeeded, and he'd let go, probably doesn't bear thinking about. As it was, Badger had his pocket knife and was able to cut through the tape. The safety agreement had already been broken after all, and the tape he was cutting was being employed dangerously. They got him down in the end, but it took a long time.

After a while the security guards, petty minded as ever, set up a big floodlight and shone it into the firepit. Somebody got a big mirror.

The next evening I was walking along the canal with Sarah, not wanting to go back into the thick of things, not quite able to tear ourselves away before it was all over. We came across a man in his forties, thinnish and gently spoken, carrying a bugle. He told us how, every evening that week, he'd walked along to where the canal overlooked the Valley and played the Last Post. It was a fitting tribute from a Northern town. The eviction had started on a Monday and now we were at the end of the week, this was the last of the Last Posts.

The treetop eviction had been the biggest the country had ever seen. More than sixty people had been arrested, with a hundred and twenty getting removed from the trees all in all. It had lasted five days – not nearly as long as we had hoped for, but still impressive considering the weight of the forces thrown against us. There had been huge security and policing costs – which all reflected on the wisdom of building the road. Most importantly, despite the recklessness with which the eviction had been pursued, nobody had died. We'd been very lucky.

Once it was truly all over and my days of drifting disconsolate around the canal and the sheds were finally at an end, a huge crowd of us piled down to a pub in Blackburn. The feeling of being in a film hadn't diminished, even here. Only this was the overly sweet ending; we were all smiles and happy drinking beer with the friends we now loved. But there was a hollowness behind everyone's eyes and if our hearts had once been full of the woods in full leaf, there was now something missing, something ripped up. It was good that we still had each other: we were all feeling highly fucked up.

IV

Intermission

Back at the sheds, a big yellow truck was revving its engines in the dark. Sarah and I climbed in to have a look – the back was crammed full of people we knew and a few others besides. Everyone looked bewildered and wrecked, but surrounded by each other, by the family, and happy enough for that. People tried to get us to stay, to come with them to some party in North Wales. It was tempting, but we'd already decided to head back to Sarah's house in Lancaster for a while. We hopped down and the back was pulled shut, people left outside crowding round and yipping as the truck trundled off down the track. It was a parting of the ways. If we'd gone with them, perhaps things would have been different.

Stanworth took a heavy toll on everyone there. The stress of the eviction made Sarah miss her next period, making us think, for a while, she was pregnant. For me, the full effect didn't become clear until I arrived at the Thanet Way protest in Kent, almost a couple of months after the eviction.

After spending time at Sarah's in Lancaster, we hitched down to my folks on the South Coast. We were planning to return to Snelsmore together, only I'd been hatching a plan that before we did, we'd go down to Sussex first and walk up the South Downs Way to Winchester, and then north up to Newbury itself. It would be a kind of formalised farewell to the South for me, and a connecting of place to place by our feet. The idea was already flourishing into a vivid dream – there'd be plenty of people from Brighton who'd be up for coming with us, I felt sure. I was making a long, tapering banner – blue and white with a stag's head - and pictured it fluttering above us on the downland as we pitched our camp in the evenings. A call had gone out, a song had risen and now we were all walking home in our youth across the summer hills.

Things got strange in Sussex. It was dawning on me, slowly at times, but quite suddenly at others, that I was living in an increasingly different country. Waking up in a squat in Brighton, the successor to the now boarded up Courthouse, and I could have still been in a dream. The room we were in was completely bare and whitewashed. Somebody was talking somewhere. I couldn't tell if it was a radio or not; it sounded impossibly loud but strangely muffled, as if it was coming out of the walls. I got out of my sleeping bag, pulled on my trousers and wandered through several large, bare rooms until I crossed a corridor and opened a door into sudden air and sunlight. The room was painted a rich, dark blue two thirds of the way up the otherwise white walls. A woman with dark hair and leather trousers was sitting on the sofa like a benevolent crow. Directly opposite, the white wood of a pair of glass paned doors opened out onto a short, iron railed balcony and the source of the noise. An open topped, double decker tour bus had stopped in the traffic right outside, the top deck dead level with us, a crowd of faces looking in at us, the tour guide blaring out something incomprehensible before they all lurched off.

I said hello to the woman and wandered out onto the balcony. There was traffic below me, and park and trees in the sun, and the white onion domes of the Pavilion. Sarah appeared in the doorway behind me. We were like Kings and Queens here, I felt, majestic among these blue tapestries. I could see the potential for this room, almost as clearly as if it were there already. It would have curtains, some mirrors and knotwork all around the borders of the blue. I could see the knotwork most clearly – triskettes and slender birds; graceful and fine in their symmetry. But I was excited by more than how the room would look – this was a regal place; great things would happen here, would spread out from here. I could feel it in the mortar as surely as I could feel it in my bones. Sarah smiled at the woman on the sofa.

Later, in Lewes, sat on a mound we both knew, Sarah and I talked about Stanworth. It was a sunny day and there was another couple there already, though there was room for us all; a place of young lovers. I told her how Janie had asked me to kiss the trees as I left. And it dawned on me then, sat on the hill in the sun, that perhaps as I was the last to leave them I had somehow been given or had soaked up part of their ancient energy. And the oaks of Stanworth were older than the oaks of elsewhere; old men among old men, left to grow wild in peace in a weathered valley out of the way of mankind. I wept in grief for those trees then, the first time since I had let out my emotion since the eviction. And as I cried it seemed that all the strange power I had been filled with flew out into the air and I was just a nineteen year old boy once again. Everything felt cleared out, a clarity and calm coming back into my mind at last, leaving me feeling thin and pleasantly hollow. I thought that was that.

"Come on 'old man'," said Sarah and led me back down to the town.

When we did make it back to Snelsmore, it seemed by the skin of our teeth. A couple in a red sports car had picked us up outside Brighton and dropped us off on the side of the motorway near the M25, not even near a sliproad. It dawned on us that this was very bad. Leaving the road altogether, we set off across some fields, through a copse and towards the random roofs of a nearby village. It turned out not to be a village at all, but a loose bundle of cul-de-sacs, dreary bag ends, an estate with no town to attach itself to. Bulldozers were working on a bank behind the houses – a narrow strip of land between the gardens and the motorway.

"Now we're going to have nowhere good to play" said a gang of kids when we caught up with them on the pavement. They seemed dismayed that we weren't staying, that we hadn't come especially to save the remains of their hill.

We climbed on a train, eventually being forced to pay through the nose for tickets, and got into Newbury late in the afternoon. A large flock of geese greeted us as we arrived, flying north over our heads in the early evening light us we made our way across the station carpark. Snelsmore was beautiful, leafy and cool in the summer heat. We played music and painted, sat in the net and quietly laughed at the bald heads of dog walkers traipsing through the path below us. The woods in the summer were another land entirely and the four of us; me and Sarah, Tami and Badger, revelled in it. Tami had become some kind of Queen Under the Beech, barefoot in a long beige dress, like hemp or like buckskin, a black haired princess of the woods. Badger and I levelled out a broad circle for a new firepit in front of the communal – we'd had enough of sitting on a slope. Badger began splitting staves of wood and hammering them into the ground – holding the banks of earth we'd created in place. It looked fantastic, just raw wood and fresh earth, the firepit itself and nothing else.

I wandered the bogs of the common barefoot, peat squelching between my toes, sunlight glinting off the moist greenness below. I felt as though I had returned to something like my childhood and was dissolving into a green and sunlit world of bliss.

Sarah and I had been going barefoot for some time now and our feet had formed thick, leathery pads. In the evenings, we'd check each other's soles for thorns. But our feet were already so hardened that even a bramble or a piece of sweet chestnut casing wouldn't be such a painful thing, and would usually stick in your foot unnoticed.

And it was good to feel the earth beneath your toes – whether it was the soft, shaded crumbs of leaf mould or yielding turf and grass. Somehow this had all been part of my dream of walking – a transformation of the world back into a state of primordial unity, some words like a half remembered prophecy forming in my mind,

"And where they walk across the asphalt, green grass shall spring forth, as though sown by the soles of their feet."

Then we went to Kent. After a night at the protest's main camp, during which I didn't sleep, I got a lift with Sarah to a large house and garden where a tree needed defending. As we arrived at the drive of the house, squatted and on route of the road, the strained relationship between the driver and a girl who'd come with us came to a sudden head. The woman at the wheel lost all patience and began to drive off. I climbed out spontaneously, feeling things were conspiring to stop me from saving the tree. Caught out by the rush and already nonplussed by my overly charismatic performance throughout the day, Sarah stayed in the car. She knew nothing of my not having slept the previous night. Thinking they'd found the perfect stand-in, the couple who were looking after the squat disappeared the next day, leaving me on my own in an overgrown garden and shadowy, derelict house.

Three or four days later found me sitting by the side of the forecourt of a garage across the road from the house. I hadn't slept or eaten since arriving at the house. Having sat there for some minutes it was a period of comparative inertia. I was feeling increasingly desperate as I thought every car crawling past was cutting off the lifeline to my girlfriend, who was also the embodiment of the land,

257

who'd been spirited away and could only communicate through birdsong. Sarah was in fact a few miles away down at the main camp, unaware of my troubles, surrounded by strangers and half annoyed at me not being there, not least because it was solstice and everyone was celebrating.

Unable to bear it any longer, I walked out in front of a slow moving car, draping myself across the bonnet and the shining metal grill of the radiator, shouting at the stunned looking occupants of the front seats, gesticulating my distress. At that very moment I got grabbed by half a dozen men in black and propelled swiftly, and strangely gracefully, towards the waiting interior of a white wagon. The owner of a garage across the road had phoned the police, thanks to my increasingly bizarre forays from the house. A night or two previously I'd been telling him who was going to arrive next and that he should send them over to me as I was planning a big party. Nobody had come. I sat on the floor of the van, compliant as we hurtled down green lanes. I thought they were taking me home.

Things went from bad to worse in hospital, but at least I had food to eat and water to drink and wasn't in physical danger. By all accounts, given my almost total lack of food and drink in the days at the derelict house, I was lucky to be alive. Badger received the news days later through a bizarre answer phone message at the Stoughton's that said "Jim's been found in Herne Bay." Whoever it was, the tone of voice spoke of the seriousness, making Badger think it was only my body that had turned up, after a disappearance he was unaware of, washed up on the shore of the Thames Estuary, floating head down in cold waters. In a sense, for a while, it was closer to the truth then people realised.

It was hard to say exactly what had led to this, but smoking hash had played its part and the pressure of living on squatted land, the impending sense of chaos, and the dramatic shift in lifestyle can't have been much help. The lack of proper food at Stanworth had taken its toll too. Perhaps overall it was just a result of being so thin skinned, that made taking mushrooms a very bad idea and the carnage at Stanworth all the more disturbing. And Stanworth was definitely carnage.

In hospital, time slipped by in a strange dream. Once I woke up and ran out into the corridor to see, printed clearly in the thick blue carpet, receding away from me towards a large window, a line of clear deer prints. It was dawn, and the bushes and the bank of earth through the window were grey and pensive, colour bleeding into them only very slowly. I felt like I should jump through the window, disappear into the bank to the country that waited beyond.

Besides the deer prints, all the other strangeness was in my head. And in the heads of those around me. When I recovered enough sense to realise that I was on a locked ward, and that I had very little choice about my stay here, I spent hours trying to covertly unscrew the security fittings to my window, which of course wouldn't move at all. Just outside, the birds sang a song of freedom, calling me to escape, speaking to me of a realm of beauty and joy that waited out in the world for me. I had to go soon, or my dreams would slip away.

Since my last time in Snelsmore, I had been wearing the thermal liners to a pair of mountaineering boots that someone had left behind. They had soft soles, which made them perfect for climbing trees without damaging the bark or your feet. Now I believed they had a life of their own and, squashing them out of the narrow gap in the window, told them to go and get help. They fell to the bushes outside and from there I saw them in my mind's eye, running off into the twilight across the wide lawns.

Days, maybe weeks later, Badger, Tami and Sarah turned up. They camped for the remainder of my stay in the hospital grounds. Though this didn't exactly please many of the staff, there was very little they could do, seeing as Sarah and the others had a net slung in one of the huge cedar trees, which they could retreat into if the need ever arose. For my part, I was glad beyond words to have my friends around me. It made a big difference.

Several indeterminate weeks after my arrival, I was discharged and driven back to my parents' house. One swift and grisly relapse later I was admitted to a hospital, this one much closer to home. I stayed there for the next three months. Sarah and Tami came to visit early on, though they weren't allowed to see me due to the state I was in. Slowly, I climbed back towards normality.

I got letters from Sarah and Badger and others I didn't know, telling me of life back in the woods. The population at Snelsmore had grown enormously by all accounts. One of Badger's letters ended:
"The Goddess is calling you so loud my ear is red...". I thought about Snelsmore all the time. Just to have been there would have been enough, but to be there now, in the height of summer, with people and music, would have been something else again. This ought to have been the summer of my life.

At the top of the building was an art room and I was left alone there to draw and paint. In the evening, the sound of local students playing baseball or cricket in a nearby park drifted up to the window and even this clean-cut fellowship was denied to me.

I grew worried that this isolation would become terminal, that from here on in I was set on a course to a lonely, cold, settling in of caution. I remembered the man

260

who'd given us a lift in his red sports car from Brighton only weeks ago. Grey before his time, saddened by life and somehow removed from the things that he should have been part of. Heavy and sensuous summer rains fell, full of longing and the songs of lost promise.

In the autumn, Sarah came to visit. She'd come down with Ed from Fairmile and another man from Snelsmore. I'd been pretty much given a free rein by this stage, so it was no problem when Sarah and the others drove me back to my folks'. I helped them set up a camp at the top of the woods and spent the evening up there, playing music and, later, watching as a lurid pink electric storm tore across the coast.

The next day, we went back to the clinic. The day after that, Sarah led me out to where the others had set up a new camp. They'd put the tarp up in a small piece of woodland on the edge of the Downs. The two of us talked for some time. All around us were gorse in flower, the smell of the dry summer turf, studded with hundreds of small flowers. Though she never quite said it outright, it was clear that Sarah had come to get me, that she wanted to take me back to the woods. She was confused that I didn't seem to want to come and somehow I wasn't quite able to tell her that I knew it was too soon, that they'd send people out looking for me, that my parents would be worried sick. As the others packed up the car, she had soft words for me. And then she was gone, walking away down the flint track, raising her arms above her head and letting something go. I knew I had lost her.

Weeks later, back at my folks, I wandered into the living room and switched the TV on. And there was Sarah;

261

beaming; talking to the camera. There'd been some kind of action, a first opening of hostilities in the coming battle and as such it had attracted a lot of attention. Brian Mawhinney had called short his year long suspension of the road, giving it his approval during the summer, in his last act as Secretary of State for Transport. As the reporter wound to a conclusion, the view cut to a still of Badger, sat on the roof of a cab of a digger. He was looking straight at the camera, calm enough, questioning. If I hadn't realised already, I now knew I was returning to Newbury.

V

The Third Battle of Newbury

Returning

I finally returned to Snelsmore in the middle of the following October; a year after my first arrival. A lift had dropped me off in the middle of town and I walked up the main road, catching another ride as I neared the woods with a dreadlocked chap in a yellow van. He had a big bag of skunk in the glove compartment and half a bag of potatoes on the floor. All at once, from getting picked up without effort on my way to site, and also from the van driver's excited chat, I knew there were a lot more people about.

The Common, when I got there, was dingy with the heavy mast still overhead. Benders were everywhere and the ground underfoot was churned to a thick pulp. The mud plastered the lower walls of the benders so that they seemed to be sinking into it. The impression was of some squalid, medieval hut village. I was dimly aware that the tree village I'd envisaged with Badger had now taken shape, though it was generally shrouded in leaves.

I sat down at the fire pit, which was crowded with people I didn't recognise. A group of men announced themselves as Druids, though they looked like they'd been sleeping in the mud for several months, and a circus troupe style round of introductions followed. They all had wildly straggling facial hair. The levelled circle of the firepit was now covered with a plastic tarp over a half bender and was full of cups and pans, seating logs, a sink and sideboard – which only seemed to crowd everything else out – and a general assortment of crates, reels of rope and other scattered detritus. Everyone was smoking and the smoke from the fire seemed to hang in the air before it made its way into the low canopy.

A man with a mohican stumbled out of the communal, swearing because he couldn't find one of his boots. He sat down by the fire anyway and proceeded to blag a rollie and fry up an egg. The communal looked suddenly decrepit, as though the frame was beginning to collapse into itself, worn out from a summer of excess and sinking into a shabby old age.

But walking down to the bank I met Sule; the girl who'd been making sandwiches in the treehouse at Stanworth. She and a brown dreaded girl called Sam were all smiles and took me over the valley to the original treehouses and a secondary camp, known as Skyward. The firepit for this was right under the oak I had lived in, the air was more open and not so hemmed in by tarps or low branches. A man appeared out of the bushes carrying a pair of water butts.

"Top of the morning!" he said to everyone at large and sat down to make chapattis out of flour and water. These were a kind of flat bread, which could be easily fried up on an open fire. You could do a lot worse than spend half the day eating chapattis and they lent themselves to a meditative and communalised grazing.

Sarah was there and after a while she led me out of the woods, away to a place further south, where Badger and Tami had set up a camp of their own. Badger and Tami had moved to get a little more peace and quiet, after Snelsmore's population explosion over the summer. We went over the ridge, down through the golf course and along under the giant beeches of Bagnor Lane. The trees were magnificent in full leaf, each of them towering way above us, the avenue leading away into the distance; ethereal in the sun and slight mist, fading into its own shade. The far end of Bagnor Lane was another land, and even when you walked the whole thing you still hadn't got there, because it was behind you now, up at the other end, near the mill which you couldn't quite see.

Having walked down the lane, we crossed through fields, past the woods that had been felled at one end, a ring of trees left at the edges. We had climbed up a hill again now and were on a level with the twin towers of Donnington Castle, away up behind us, rising out of the narrow Lambourn valley to the north east. Through another field, this one on the hilltop with a scattering of broad old oaks, over the A4 and down a hedged track and we were in the woods again. The ground dropped away sharply before us, running down to the Kennet valley. We branched off into the woods on our left and within twenty yards or so the rounded green frame of a bender appeared among the brambles. Badger and Tami emerged when we yipped and there were warm greetings all round.

We all clambered under the door tarp and into the thick warmth inside. This was the first bender I had been in since the spring and it felt like I had suddenly re-entered an old, strange world – a very different place to four cornered, electrically lit rooms. A couple of candles were burning and every spare space around the pallet bed was dotted with a familiar medley of tat; jars and mirrors, candles in bottles, blankets, clothing, books and legal paperwork, a pile of blue rope. There was quite a large open space near the door, about the size of the bed again – a seat on one side formed by a large, folded tarp. Tami was sat near the burner, digging into an orange, placing the peelings on the hotplate for incense. There was a faint dampness in the air outside the bender, the leaves only just on the turn and mingling with the woodsmoke – the smell of a woodland in autumn.

The bender was like a short, squat tunnel with a north facing doorway looking out onto a steep bank. The bank ran along the edge of the woods and was lined with mature trees and remains of a hedge. Below this, the trees had been felled, leaving only an outline much the same as the copse near the end of Bagnor Lane. But the trees here had been taken down maybe a couple of seasons ago, and a thick wall of new growth had sprung up; five or six feet high. I'd walked down this way on my own the previous winter, scouting things out a bit more and following the line of the road exactly. Sliding down the bank into the woods, I'd come face to face with a large adult deer, who'd looked at me squarely for a moment before bounding off into the impenetrable undergrowth. Deer usually seem intruded on when you stumble across them, as though you've walked in, unannounced, to another party altogether. Sometimes though, they're strangely nonplussed, like they were wondering what'd kept you so long.

The others took me down a tiny track along the top of the bank to see the tree that had given the camp its name – Granny Ash. The track was right on the edge of the bank, if not traversing the slope itself, and in places was already giving way to muddy landslides. Most of it seemed to be held together by roots.

Granny Ash was indeed a mother of a tree. Her trunk split in two early on – ten or fifteen feet up – and she was covered in a thick, venerable carpeting of ivy. Sarah pointed out an oval gap hidden in the ivy near the split – a wise and homely opening.

The camp only consisted of the bender, a big metal food chest and signs of a small firepit. Badger and Tami said they'd be up for my staying in their bender indefinitely – I'd managed to buy a good, green tarp after Stanworth, but this had somehow made it's way from Snelsmore to Fairmile over the summer and, somehow, I didn't seem to care. It was just good to be back in the woods with my friends.

270

Sarah left us to it and headed back the two or three miles to Snelsmore. I was considerably confused. Nothing at all had been said about where we stood with each other and, though I had an idea what might be going on, a little clarity would have gone a long way. Badger went off on a mission to town so I stayed in the bender with Tami, chainsmoking and playing cards and chopping food up with our penknives.

It got dark early and the evening seemed to drag on endlessly. There was little light, no television, nowhere else to go and nothing to do but sit there and carry on smoking. Even getting up and pacing around was impossible. Living back in the woods was obviously going to take some getting used to. And my medication was making me feel that something was missing, that some inner motor of my spirit and enthusiasm was damp and unable to start. Tami roasted sweet chestnuts on the burner and when Badger got back, we put the food on to stew. Burners are rarely the quickest way to cook food and I fell asleep long before it was ready, curled up on a pile of blankets, trying to disappear into myself.

We had various visitors over the next few days – people walking from camp to camp, stopping off on the way for cups of tea. We'd sit out in the pale sunlight by the bank, a faint ring of excitement in the air with all the newcomers and burgeoning camps. Autumn was like a second spring; a clean coldness defining things, etching out the woods all the clearer in the amber and mellower light of the sun. And to know that things were on the turn, to feel the year shift around you, to know that proper weather was coming in, even if it was likely to be harsh, was the cause of a strange inspiration. Just drinking tea seemed exciting, sat like we were out of doors.

The next camp along the route from us was the Kennet camp and, after a day or two, I headed down the track to

271

check it out. As the name made out, it sat right by the river Kennet, with the Kennet and Avon canal bordering it on its southern side, the two waterways not more than a hundred foot apart. It had been set up over the summer with the help of a working party from Fairmile – Richard and Ed amongst others. The Fairmile crew had also been largely responsible for kickstarting a camp at Selar in Wales – in woodland on the site of an open cast mine. Someone had given me a newspaper article about it while I was in hospital in Kent – 'Hearts of Oak Stage Protest in Rural Wales' ran the headline.

Everything had seemed at a zenith that summer, even from my remote point of view. A regional news programme ran an hour-long documentary, heavily slanted against roads, with plenty of footage of Fairmile. Both Richard and Ed appeared on the screen, smiling and enthusiastic in the sun. Somehow it felt like all my friends were being wheeled out especially for me, as I reminder of where I should be.

The Kennet lay on the far side of Speenham moor – first through the dense, boggy woodland and then the large, flat space of the meadows beyond. The fisherman's bridge across the main waterway in the woods had been repaired, though obviously only by hippies or kids – the newly replaced section formed from half a scaff plank and long, shaky poles and not far off from being submerged in the water. The meadows were also crisscrossed with waterways, cut to reclaim the whole place from marshland. But sedges still grew among the soft turf and the fields were utterly quiet, enclosed on most sides by dense woodland and still with an air of somewhere remote and removed from mankind. On the western side, the moor stretched away indefinitely, punctuated with an occasional pollarded willow, blanketed with an eerie and undisturbed sentience.

The Kennet itself was wide and clear and overhung thickly with trees. The final approach to the camp involved making a detour round to the east, to cross the water by a wide, concrete farmer's bridge. The land between the two main waterways was more or less covered in trees and there were already more than a few walkways and treehouses in evidence. The largest of these was built between a dozen or so small trees, just down the bank from the canal. It could sleep somewhere between twenty to thirty people and had a large porch at one end. The porch was reached by a rope ladder, was half covered in plastic sheeting and held a small kitchen, complete with an oil drum stove. The whole thing was known as the Mothership. It was dark inside and the air was rich with the ambience of sleeping bags and misplaced boots.

Down on the ground, round a firepit and its ubiquitous half bender and pallets, a couple of teenage, crusty girls were making chainsaw whips. These were lengths of polyprop with the last two to three feet unravelled, so the fibres flayed out like a horse's tail. These fibres, if bought into contact with a chainsaw bar, would get drawn into the mechanism, melting and clogging it up. It was a relatively safe way to sabotage a chainsaw and it took ages for them to clear the teeth of molten plastic. The chainsaw whips could be used from the ground – if you could get close enough. More likely though, they'd come into their own during clearance or an eviction – where'd you'd be in the tree above the chainsaw operator. It was a stark reminder of the impending confrontation. A few feet away, a man in a woolly hat was hacksawing through an old oil drum. It was taking him a while and it wasn't quiet.

The only camp between Granny Ash and Snelsmore was right on the banks of the Lambourn and not far from Bagnor village. It was known as Bagnor Camp and, later, Bog Camp and was in fact set on an island; a narrow

273

backwater rolling out from the riverside to cut the camp off from behind. Scaff planks took you over the mud. It had been set up for less than a week and consisted of only a three sided shelter, right on the water side. I sat there for a while with the only man there, the same who'd given me a lift up to Snelsmore in his yellow van. The river surged by at our feet; strong and swollen and powerfully impassive. Kenneth Grahame having lived in Bagnor village, I reckoned this was Pan Island. The far bank lay twenty foot away, rising up from the water in a thick crowd of brambles and trunks, as remote and as strange as a distant country; as though there were people there watching us, as though there were songs in the air that we couldn't quite catch. We were smoking good grass.

Once or twice, I went gathering sweet chestnuts with Tami. The place for these was further down the track past Granny Ash, where the felled area closed over again under a mature canopy. There were few paths here, until you hit the rutted tyre marks of a forester's track deep into the woods. That brought with it the thought of being found out, the old edginess that came from being on private land, however justified you felt about it – as though at any moment a landrover might come hurtling down on top of you, even though the tracks were old and mossy. The chestnut trees towered above us; majestic and graceful, the chestnuts themselves lying thick on the ground in a crazy green forest of spikes. There was very little cover in terms of brambles or bushes and the woods rolled away barrenly into the cold. The quiet was dense and empty at once, not short of a tangible thing.

Everyone had been busy harvesting. In Snelsmore, they'd been making hazelnut spread and crab apple jam, though someone hadn't boiled the crab apples first and very nearly poisoned everyone. Down in Fairmile - stories had already got back to me – Ed had become a manic brewer, knocking up gallons of cider and oak leaf wine.

Sarah came down from Snelsmore and we lit a fire outside near the bank. The moon was very nearly full, rising up through the trees like a watchful old ghost, throwing everything silver and shadowy blue. The ground sloped away before us, down to the moor and the river, the whole valley just visible over the tops of the woodland's new growth, when you stood up. Dark folds of trees were marked out by the moon, the hill of Wash Common rising up pale to the sky, two or three miles to the south. There was a young owl somewhere close by – its call not yet carried free from a startled and juvenile screech. It was almost Hallowe'en, Samhain: the Celtic New Year and the Feast of the Dead.

We went up to Snelsmore a night or two later, where there was going to be a big celebration. Young birch trees had been laid down along the paths, to help protect the ground habitat and to stop people getting snared in the blackthorns. Though half of these birches were beginning to rot, the bark was still there and it shone out bright in the darkness.

The fire was just where I left it when everyone was eating chapattis, though at night everything was different, so it could just as easily been anywhere else. It was a big enough fire, with something like forty people gathered round it, drinking cans of beer and passing round spliffs and ginger wine. People were playing music – fiddle and mandolin and somebody was fire breathing. I ended up sat next to Stewart - the man who'd come down to see me in hospital with Sarah. He had a lurcher called Sprout, was half hidden under a Moroccan hoody and was glad to see me back.

A little while later we were led to a clearing by a man in a white robe. His name was Kreb, Kreb Dragonrider as he called himself and he'd returned to Snelsmore over the summer after more than twenty years away. He'd gone to the Mary Hare Grammar School For The Deaf, just north of the orchard on the other side of the Wantage Road. It was a unique place, in that it offered a system of teaching and communication based on vibrations – something which the road would very probably disrupt.

Kreb directed us all into the circle, through a doorway formed by two trees. When a crowd of people piled over to us, late from the firepit, he shooed them all off and made them come back through the doorway.

Kreb was a true master of ceremonies and led us all deep into the ritual. At the very height of the ceremony, just as we were being led to meet the grey cloaked and nebulously powerful figure of Apollo himself, a lad to my left fell flat on his face. For a moment or two nobody moved, then people broke forward and rushed to his side. Turned out, he was off his face due to swigging paraffin for too long while fire breathing and the intensity of the ritual had gone to his head. Ceremonies can be powerful things and are usually best approached with a clear head, which is probably why masses are held in the morning, to catch all the Catholics early.

I walked back to Granny Ash that night with Sarah and a man called Doug. Doug had a wide brimmed hat, a long woollen scarf and, with his handlebar moustache and black beard, looked not unlike a hippy Doctor Who or skinny Rasputin.

A footpath led us under the trees of Castle Wood – on the other side of the ridge from Snelsmore and almost a part of the golf course. It was black as a cave under the trees – a great shroud of obscurity that folded around us, so we had to feel our way with our feet. Doug led us down through the disorientating gloom of the golf course and somehow we emerged on the other side, near the shadowy husk of the fallen and hollowed out beech.

Down Bagnor Lane and up on the hill with the solitary oaks, we all crouched down when someone noticed a couple of deer under one of the trees. They were quietly feeding; silhouetted against the horizon and the strange orange haze created by a thin, night time mist and the lights of the nearby A4. It was a good ten minutes before they caught wind of us and bounded off into the morning. We were covered in dew.

Stewart – he with the dog they called Sprout - had had my duck down army sleeping bag since the summer. I'd been sleeping in some spare thin thing in Granny Ash, piling blankets on top as the burner died in the early hours. Stewart was living in Reddings Copse now – the first camp south of the Kennet and I went down there one night, catching a lift with a shaven haired girl from Fairmile called Ruth. She'd been riding horses down at Fairmile and had funky, leather lined trousers to prove it.

I followed her into the woods in the dusk till we came to a huge man with thick, black dreads in a red, outdoors coat, huddled over a small, smoky fire. He'd just finished cooking a watery stew and Ruth offered me some in a Tupperware box. "Fodder" she said, grinning as usual. The cook was Scouse Mick, who was surly and friendly at once.

I explained to Ruth how I was getting wanderlust and thinking of returning to Fairmile. Though it was good to be back, nothing seemed quite right here. My heart wasn't in it somehow and I couldn't wander the camps forever. Either I was here and committed to help, or I'd be better off somewhere else. The evenings dragged out still, a creeping paralysis settling on my spirit, though I was getting used to it now and had stopped curling up in the corner. Ruth reckoned heading down to Fairmile wouldn't be a bad idea.

Stewart appeared and resignedly prussicked up to his treehouse to get my bag. Then Ruth drove back to Granny Ash, stopping on the way to salvage a load of wood that had been dumped near the entrance to some woods not far off. She wanted to build herself a treehouse and this stuff was just what we needed. I helped out with Stewart, though not with any great enthusiasm. Night time missions had lost their appeal and this was surely a sign of things to come if I stayed around much longer. We dragged out timbers and boards from amongst the rubble and bushes, finally breaking our backs with a couple of old doors. Nothing else would fit on the roof rack after that, though it all had to be unloaded the other end.

Ruth appeared back in Granny Ash very soon after, with the intention of building a treehouse in one of the solitary oaks across the A4. The one she chose was the same we'd seen the deer under and was part of a vague line of two or three oaks that stretched from the road to the far woods, whose end had been partially felled. The trees all fanned out in full crown; nothing short of giants in the mist. I admired Ruth for wanting to live here – it would be a lonely spot and close to the grinding noise of the A4, the tree being set back from the road by only a few hundred yards.

Ruth and a man we both knew set to work in the tree, tying on beams high in the branches. I helped them out up there at first, the platform taking shape between two horizontal outliers, fanning out from what was left of the main trunk, not far from the tip of the crown. As the floor progressed, there was no longer any need or room for three on the job and I hung around on the ground, waiting to tie things on. I was sat like this, with my back to the trunk,

278

when I noticed a man stood in front of me in a wax jacket. He was middle aged and solid looking and wasn't smiling.

"Hullo" I said languidly. He barely looked at me, obviously not finding me fit for his attention, lying about like I was in the grass.

"I take it you're building a treehouse?" he demanded, shouting up to the two in the tree and continuing to ignore me completely. It sounded like he was used to shouting, as though it was his preferred means of communication. People knew where they stood, he probably reasoned, if you shouted at them. The sound of hammering, which must have been echoing for miles around, suddenly stopped as Ruth shouted back down to him.

"Yes, we are!"

"Well, there's a pheasant shoot which takes place in the woods every Sunday – I'm sure they won't be happy about your presence – and don't use the woods as a toilet – they belong to me!"

He strode off towards a house in the corner of the field, bristling and indignant in his wellingtons. I sloped off to the woods around Granny Ash to scout out some decent bender poles. Sitting under the tree no longer felt like such a pleasant option. The respectable classes could strike without warning and I didn't want to present an easy target.

War with the Trolls

New people seemed to be appearing all the time and there was a definite sense of the whole campaign growing bigger – a momentum taking hold that was widening out every day, with no sign at all of tapering off. I slipped off amid the threshold of this heightened expectancy, giving my farewells to Sarah by the ducks and the swing bridge in town, before making my way up to the services, for a ritual pre-hitching shave, and then to the motorway itself.

The first lift I got was going all the way to Exeter and I found myself walking up the hill to Fairmile in the dark a few hours later. I yipped when I got near the oak, looming massively above me in the darkness. Nobody replied at first, until a girl shouted down from the branches,
"What's all that bloody noise? I'm trying to get some sleep!" Approaching the fence, I found it was shrouded by a massive trench. I'd heard about it, but hadn't expected it to be quite as big as this. It was easily four foot across and no telling how deep in this light, the walls sinking down into black wells of shadow. I almost fell in before I noticed it and made my way across a shaky narrow bridge to the arch of a side entrance – the main gate had the drawbridge pulled up.

There was no sign of life around the firepit, though the muffled sound of voices could just about be heard from the new giant bender. It was new to me at any rate, having only just got its tarp before I left for Stanworth in the spring. Inside, besides a couple of hairy faces I didn't recognise, I found Kit, Ceilidh and another old friend and found myself recounting pretty much everything that had happened since the spring. They'd heard half the story already of course, but not from my lips. It had been widely believed, at first, that my hospitalisation was part of some kind of conspiracy, the full extent of my sketchiness only dawning on people gradually.

Things had changed here since the spring – a tide of people having washed over the site during the summer. I'd been half expecting a huge fire and dozens of people and music and cider, as though the place had remained animated with the same high spirits I remembered it had when I left. But it was late in the year, the camp had been going awhile and people's enthusiasm was beginning to flag. Olly and Richard had moved into a house in the nearest village; Ottery St Mary. The house contained, besides the campaign office, a large part of Ed's brewery, a whole room almost entirely given over to bubbling demijohns. Richard was pretty tolerant about this, seeing as this was the room that he lived in.

There'd been a site cat turn up over the summer – a black cat who'd been found in a ditch and subsequently got named Snapgate. As the Fates would have it, a black cat had turned up at Snelsmore around the same time, waltzing onto site like a princess and getting called Twigloo, after the new kind of treehouses that had nets for floors. Both cats had since gone pretty much feral again and were only to be seen now and then, by those with the right kind of nose.

The oak now harboured a good half dozen treehouses, while the new bender had been dubbed a communal blender – half of it was full of a pile of unclaimed tat several feet high; stuff that people had left and never come back for. I'd left a rucksack here myself, though Ceilidh had to admit that,

"You, of all people Jim, had an excuse." I decided that night to take myself off my medication; I just couldn't handle the feeling of disconnection any more. Maybe here I could begin to human again. I'd been warned that I shouldn't, and in time that advice would prove to be pretty well founded, but the nature of the drugs was so overwhelming that I felt like I had no option at the time besides coming off them. Life was for living after all, and if I couldn't feel remotely engaged in a place such as this, then there didn't seem much point in living at all.

Over the valley from Fairmile, sat on the opposite hill, was Trollheim – punk fortress. It had been set up after the Beltaine celebrations in May, to accommodate and make use of the ridiculous numbers of people floating about. It was in the shadow of a large pine wood that straddled the ridge. Much of this had already been felled, though most of the trees had been left where they were. Trollheim's defences had been built from the pine – not just a barricade, but a full on fortress with pallet floored battlements ten foot up. You got in through a cobbled gatehouse – a sharp toothed, steel plate portcullis hovering uncertainly somewhere above. All the men had shaved heads and piercings and the air seemed thick with rollie smoke, though it was probably just the damp pine on the fire. Half grown, black dogs were running and rolling around everywhere, barking and getting shouted at by just about everyone. A couple of people were sat round the fire on sun chairs, ripping the piss out of anyone nearby. They were friendly enough to me though and seemed pretty surprised that anyone had come to visit them from over the valley. Things had got pretty polarised over the summer, the two camps attracting different crowds. At one point – just after people at Fairmile had started collecting garden gnomes – the situation rapidly degenerated into all out war. Trollheim sent out squads to kidnap the gnomes, ritually decapitating them before putting the heads on display. A banner gave their variant on the DBFO acronym:

'DON'T BOTHER, FUCK OFF.'

No more motivated than before, I still knew it was out of order to sit around and do nothing all day. Doing nothing, being a lazy arse, was lunching out and when everything got lunched out, things began to fall apart. Being out to lunch, being a lunch out therefore put you among the lowest of the low, though lunching out for a while was a very necessary part of every day. Days were very often not defined by what you did, but by the periods in between when you lunched out to have a fag, or lunched out to get your breath round the fire. Though spending too long round the fire, especially if you were prone to mild catatonia or an inability to stoke the fire up, meant you might get called a kettle watcher and that was dangerously close to becoming an energy vampire, which was about as bad as it got.

Everyone was being a bit of a lunch out at Fairmile at the moment though, but that was alright, so long as everyone did their bit. I interspersed my cups of tea with trips to get water and wooding. But because Fairmile had been going for over a year now, and because there were no huge tracts of woodland that close, all the good wood now lay on the other side of Trollheim – something they were well aware of when you tried to sneak past with a saw,

"OI!" came the shout from the battlements "Leave our wood alone you dirty thieving hippy scumbag!"

But there were punks at Fairmile as well – two of them now occupying the old communal, which they'd decorated inside with camouflage netting. One of them was none other than the mohawked geezer from Stanworth, still wearing a face like he'd been chewing on something nasty. Wearing a World War Two American helmet, he told me round the fire one day how he'd come out from London to 'fight the system.' I didn't see it so clearly as that at the time and felt like we could be from different planets. He just seemed to want to tear everything down. Though perhaps, in the end, he was just more realistic than me. Perhaps he had a better idea of what we were up against, once we began to be effective. But I couldn't help feeling that his aggression and divisiveness was as much a part of the problem as everything he professed to be against. It wasn't so much to do with what he stood for. It was how he chose to go about it.

I soon learned that playing the whistle round the fire had become a political decision – attracting mutters or shouts of,

"Fuckin' yoghurt weaving." It was a phrase I'd heard at the Kennet too – a surly criticism of anything overtly resembling creativity. But more specifically any displays of particularly hippified expressions of art. Yoghurt weaving was the poorly played whistle, the bad drumming going on too long into the night, dewy eyed chants, an overfondness for anything floral, the half baked poetry séance round the fire. Weavers had a weakness for verbal tapestries, wore woolly jumpers and had wayward memories, like goat bells in the breeze. Yoghurt had a lot to do with muesli.

People were falling over each other to distance themselves from the stigma of this new brand. On one hand, this probably prevented a general subsistence into a mire of new-agey daftness and self indulgence. But it threatened to reduce site life to a world of quasi militaristic posturing, where any respect was only earned by the distance you could spit and where music wasn't allowed. Unless it came from a sound system, or tinny stereo. I decided pretty early on that I'd rather be a blatant herald of Yoghurt than a vassal of the uber punks and, after a while, I found I could say and play what I liked unmolested.

"Thing about you," a part time fire spitter finally admitted "…is you do good yoghurt." Though it was likely the others had simply got sick of my persistence.

Fairmile had grown famous over the summer for the frenetic trench digging. People told me how the whole camp would get up early, dig with pickaxes and shovels for several hours, knock off for a while around noon and then do another shift late in the day. Somewhere along the line, a firm work ethic had taken hold, as though the whole campaign now rested on the depth and width of some holes. An extreme example of the kind of pressure that existed came when a friend got up in the morning to find one of the camp's sketchier residents - who'd slept round the fire in a vest – already trudging off towards the trenches, dragging a pick axe, without any breakfast and not even willing to stop for some tea.

A couple who'd been at Stanworth and who'd made a twigloo from a boat suspended in the copse, arrived back on site and very soon after corralled the few of us around into a spot of trench extension.

"I don't know about you lot," the woman had said to us, "but personally I want to get this finished so I don't get woken up by a bailiff's boot on my head." It seemed a fair point and, in any case, we weren't doing much else besides drinking tea so there wasn't much scope for argument.

After several hours stood in the orange earth, which was glowing with the thin sunlight, passing a bucket over my head, we'd hardly made a scratch on what still needed doing, to bring the trench up to the fence line. It seemed pretty mad that the trench only covered two sides of the camp – one of which we were working on now. The plan had been to make approach impossible from the front by machine, though it occurred to us later that they could just back fill easily enough with a digger. But it might have better to dig a triangular ditch that could have been easily enlarged, rather than a full on, fat trench we were struggling to finish. People later had dreams that we shouldn't be doing this, digging so deep into the ground like this without good reason, and concentrated on building more properly thought out defences instead. Even then though, I wasn't convinced by the trench. It didn't seem worth getting in a sweat over. But I was probably just being lazy as well.

Though the size and the effort put into the trenches was questionable, the barricades they were a part of had its uses. They would slow down any baillifs, giving people time to get in the trees and the tunnels, and they added to a very necessary sense of security. Sometimes though, a bit too much of a fort mentality came to the fore – some people found it intimidating to come inside, if they didn't encounter someone friendly, and I met several people later on who had gone up on good faith and been turned away by an ingrained indifference to outsiders from whoever was on site at the time. Big sites could be sometimes be off putting even when you'd been there before and making people feel welcome was always one of the best things you could do, even if it meant drinking tea for hours, and not accomplishing anything physical.

But the trench hadn't been the only digging going on over the summer. Fairmile had spawned a huge underground network of tunnels. I'd heard plenty of people back at Newbury talk about them. Some were worried that if people at Fairmile carried on digging much longer, the whole hill might collapse. Kit reckoned most of the tunnels were currently waterlogged and too dangerous to go down, though there was one separate system that should be alright. Borrowing a head torch, and letting someone know where I was going, in case I didn't re-emerge, I headed towards the entrance in the copse.

The tunnel mouth was surrounded by rhododendrums and marked by a large heap of orange earth and a sign with the words 'Here Be Dragons.' I stooped along a short, narrow passage and turned on the torch as I rounded a corner to my left. Here was a large chamber, maybe ten foot square, with the dark mouth of another tunnel leading off on the opposite side. It ought to have been big enough to stand up in, but a large plywood board that seemed to form the best bit of the roof was bowing to such an extent that I'd have to stoop to get under it. It formed a full, rounded curve. There was no way I was going any further in.

Shortly after this, while I was still wondering whether to return to Newbury or not, preparations began for a play down in Ottery. Tucked away behind the village's pint sized industrial estate was RIO – Recycling in Ottery. This was manned by a fair few people from site plus one or two more bona fide locals. RIO were putting on the play, Ceilidh acting as director and every willing spare hand dragged in to help. I decided to stick around for the duration of the play, to help out and maybe sort my head out a little in the process.

The play we'd be putting on was one of Dr Zeus's – The Lorax. The central theme was that you shouldn't cut down trees to fuel an illusory industrial monster and that ultimately, even in the most wasted of landscapes, there is always hope. We set to work, making costumes and building props out of recycled tat – a set of gold, velvet curtains for the Barbaloop Bears, huge cardboard cylinders and crepe paper for the Trufular Trees. An outside observer may have had their doubts but nevertheless, after a week of painstaking rehearsals, the show was ready to go on.

I led the main cast down the aisle of the community hall – our temporary theatre – playing a good Irish tune on the whistle. As one of the Barbaloop Bears, I rolled around on stage half the play, the Swammy Swans had learnt to cry eerily like sad peacocks while Percy, for his part, did a fine impression of a Humming Fish; flapping around on the floor with a turquoise bar strapped to his head.

It was a fantastic success, with a large part of the local community turning out to watch. Afterwards, we held a huge party in one of the upstairs rooms. Everyone drank beer and cider and wine, just about everything in fact, while I played the whistle and Ceilidh and Ruth danced on the tables. Although it was my last performance in that particular play, the others kept it going for a long time afterwards, touring the country with it, visiting schools and festivals.

There was a particularly lethargic mood on site for a while after that. The only people in evidence were the handful of punks, who had taken it upon themselves to sort out the rat problem. There had been an exponential rise in rodents on site during my time away – thanks to not only the influx of people but also the extensive tunnel network, which was a bit of a rat highway. Having a secret entrance to the tunnels in the new communal meant that sleeping there was an unsettling experience. Several times I was woken in the middle of the night, sure something had just clambered over my legs.

Now the punks, including one whith a large Union Jill inside his bender, had decided that enough was enough. The Union Jill is a subversion of the traditional Union Jack, being composed of many composite psychedelic colours. Some say it portrays a form of national pride based on the diversity of British cultures rather than old attitudes tied up with empire and the rest. But it had to be said too that the punks just like to screw with people's minds.

They set to work, stripping down and removing the Union Jill bender entirely, hunting down the scattering creatures with the flat end of shovels and garden forks. Dispatched vermin were thrown on the fire, some of their cremated remains later being retrieved to be placed in jam jars. These were then used as totems to ward off the others – rats hate the smell of their own dead brethren – placed in strategic positions around the new communal. Bits of charred, dead rat in glass jars dotted around the place were only very slightly better than live ones.

It was definitely time to be going. With the play finished, there didn't seem to be much worth hanging around for. And I was finding it hard getting back into the swing of being outdoors. My days at Fairmile had become a kind of half medicated no time, where enthusiasm was elusive and the fire was the sole source of vague comfort. I was becoming a kettle watcher, on the road to an energy vampire, and I didn't like it.

On my last night I slept outside the communal, in a temporarily empty bender whose burner I couldn't be arsed to light. When I woke up, it was snowing. The snow settled down, leaving a covering like a heavy frost so the ground was brown and white – half mooned craters in old bootprints in the mud. I caught a lift straight to Newbury with a man in a bus – 'just people' Jerry. Months later, he'd become a victim of a vigilante attack, waking up one night on a quiet road near Reddings Copse to the sound of something hitting the side of the vehicle. He went straight to the wheel and accelerated away, a ball of flames in his rear view. The molotov had landed right where his young son was still sleeping, above the fuel tank.

I got out of the bus in an empty carpark in the middle of town. It was evening but long dark and a sharp inland coldness was waiting for me, giving me warning that winter was getting its teeth out.

The Third Battle Begins

Back at Granny Ash, everyone was huddled in the bender, which had moved over the last few weeks by as much as twenty or thirty feet. If anyone else had noticed, they didn't let on.

Sarah was there, as was Balin, who I hadn't seen in a long while. The most startling of the new arrivals was a man called Mark, togged up in a combination of cycling and outdoor shop gear, fresh out from London and making intelligent conversation about the benefits of modern technology. Like bikes, for instance. This was new hat to us, almost heretical. Not that we disapproved of bikes, or didn't use them, but that for some of us, a stone age aesthetic was beginning to take hold; aspiring to a purity of being in the world that might have been legendary and was certainly hard to get across to characters like Mark. Living in the woods taught you that everything had a value, a resonance, and the closer a thing was to its natural state, the better it was to have around. Things had got a little entrenched in our fundamentals over the months, though we were only trying to follow our better instincts. And wearing a synthetic cycling top in the middle of the woods just seemed downright suspicious behaviour.

"You've come back!" Sarah was surprised to see me. "Just as things are getting hectic as well." I had spent the last few weeks being soft with myself, but now I was back on the brink of the thick of it, it seemed almost a relief. Notices to vacate had been served, strewn around the place, pinned to trees or chucked in the mud, posted on the barbed wire fence at the top of the ridge. They had all been signed by someone called GP Rainbow. He was probably only a

290

cleaner at the police station, but his name had been too good not to use.

Soon we would go to court, more of a formality than anything else, as winning the case was pretty unlikely. But the court procedures were a major delaying tactic in themselves, another holding action in what I was beginning to believe would be one long drawn out defeat. Fortunately our horizons were spread a little further than just Newbury. And more and more camps were springing up along the route all the time, each of which would have to be dealt with from scratch.

It would all cost time and money and make them think long and hard about doing something similar later on. And as the saying still went: "If they put a price on our environment, then we will raise than price." Maybe one day it will be a price they could no longer afford, which is what is has been all along, when you look at the world without money. Without money, or obsessions with economies that have to be fed at all costs; a fire in an ever expanding furnace that becomes like a god in itself, never mind that every sweet thing has to be swept up and shovelled into it, just to keep the flame burning.

The field between Granny Ash and the A4 was full of throaty sounding sheep and the farmer who looked after them was no less keenly aware of the state of play than we were.
"I'll have to be moving them off soon" he told us one evening, sighing as he fed them all cake.

Another new and conspicuous arrival on site was Big Pete. Big Pete was fresh out of the green movement in London too, though a world away from Mark and his cycling shirts. Being out in the country again was, for Pete, more of a return to an old, former life. He was a giant of a man, wore a big overcoat and seemed mildly amazed by everything that happened around him. As the communal was full, I slept in his tent. He'd put it up in a coppice covered hollow the other side of the track. It was like sharing a cave with a bear. But it was warm.

Badger had hitched off to Ireland for reasons unknown and returned a while later with a hand made, low D whistle – a present to welcome me home. It was silver and tapered and sounded beautiful, though I only played it tentatively; the spacing of the holes being something to get used to. I was terrified it would get trashed and kept it reverently in its plastic box, safe in the back of Pete's van.

Once back in England, Badger kept up his habit of disappearing for large portions of the night, sometimes to see people in town, quite often to visit other camps. He'd appear back after we'd already crashed out, heralded by the rustling of the stiff folds of tarp and invariably we'd all wake up again to welcome him back, not least because he might have bought biscuits.

I stayed around Granny Ash for another week or so, getting up late and sitting round the fire. Pete, or Balin, would get up with first light and get the fire going, usually grabbing dry kindling from the raised coppice stools. People with climbing gear were busy putting up walkways and Sarah was making a home of her own in Granny Ash. The adjacent tree – Grandfather Oak – was now the sight of much activity as a multilevel tree dwelling began to take shape. Someone had found a huge rope lying in the grass just the other side of the barbed wire on the bank. It can't have been there that long, because it was damp and not rotten and soon it was hanging down from the platform in Grandfather Oak. It was grey and as thick as your wrist and could have been a gym rope if it wasn't as long as it was. I found I could just about climb up it unaided. Balin used to abseil down it, using his biker's jacket like a kind of figure of eight, wrapping the rope round his arms, wearing gloves. There was a mild smell of burning when he reached the ground. People reckoned it was a ship's rope, and that seemed fitting enough.

I took the train home for Christmas and didn't emerge once from the house into the cold. It was probably the first time in my life I'd ever appreciated central heating. When I got back to Granny Ash, Mark and Big Pete had stories of long nights round the fire, where they'd stayed up as long as possible so as to put off the return to the freezing cold bender.

Two new arrivals were another Doug and a man who called himself Hawk, who paid large sums of money to do shamanism workshops. They had a good spirit though, were up for the whole thing and picked things up pretty quickly, so they were welcome additions to the site. The new Doug later got the nickname Twig, as he always had twigs in his dreads when walking into a local's kitchen. It saved confusion with Doug number one. Twig had brought with him a smooth, pink shelled conch, though we refused to use it like a talking stick, things getting a bit close to Lord of the Flies all of a sudden and Twig carried it around with him instead, like a kind of wartrumpet.

We now knew that clearance work was due to start very soon. The security had been hired, all the contracts had been tied up. Work on the road was due to start the next day. "It's Defcon One Jim!" said Badger, putting on an expression of horror that wasn't really a joke.

We'd been tipped off that the field across the road, the one where I'd helped Ruth build the treehouse, was likely to have a compound put in it. It'd obviously need watching, though no one was overly enthusiastic about sitting in a windswept field for hours on end. When the subject came up, everybody sat and stared at the fire. I could see that, if somebody didn't do something very soon, in a day or two we'd be living with the compound on our doorstep. I said I'd get up early and keep watch from the tarpless treehouse, not much looking forward to the prospect of either an early start or the elemental exposure. Ruth had never come back to live in the treehouse and it had sat there forlornly in the wind and rain ever since. Badger pointed out that, seeing as there was a spare plastic tarp, and the treehouse already had a bender frame, I might as well spend the night up there. Although I expressed my hopes that the tree would become a kind of lookout tower, manned by a rota of people from Granny Ash, I could see already that it looked like I'd end up living there. The current of events was drawing me ever closer to the middle of things.

I remembered the dream I'd had in Snelsmore, of being in a lone oak in the middle of a field with the world's press looking on. With the feeling once again of stepping off the edge of known territory, I agreed to Badger's plan and a party of us set off across the road in the dark.

Badger, myself and another man climbed the tree and tied the tarp at the corners. The platform was completely soaked so we put a few layers of blankets down, topped with foam roll mats. Most of the folks of Granny Ash had come over now for the tree warming and Sarah sat against the trunk below us, playing her fiddle. Twig left me the conch, so I'd be able to summon help at a moment's notice.

The wind whipped through the bare tree, which was on the very top of the hill; on a level with Donnington Castle to the north east and far above the few scattered lights of the Kennet valley and Wash Common to the south. With the tarp only fastened at the corners, and with nothing over the entrance hole, the inside of the treehouse wasn't exactly as snug as it could have been. I wrapped my head in a plaid blanket Balin had given me, which also helped dull the sound of the tarp; whipping and cracking in the continual wind.

With the platform built on just two heavy branches, and with it being so high in the crown there was more movement here than I was used to and I'd been dozing, rather than properly asleep, when the beeping of a vehicle reversing brought me fully awake. Lifting up one side of the tarp, I was just in time to see a lorry out on a small road branching from the A4, tipping a load of aggregate onto one of the entrances to the field. I grabbed the conch, with visions of the whole crew from Granny Ash springing up over the road within minutes. But, putting the shell to my lips, I remembered I'd never thought to try blowing if before and realised now it was virtually useless – a thin squeak emerging from the other end in a feeble sound of panic. Even at the top of my lungs, I'd never be able to shout loud enough for the others to hear me, especially with the traffic on the A4 winding up to a rush hour crescendo. I'd have to run for it. I dropped through the hole by my feet – the cold from the wind was stunning – and hurried across the fields to Granny Ash.

I scrambled down the slope to find Balin lighting a fire, as placid as could be. After quickly gabbling to him what was happening, I stuck my head into the communal to wake everyone up before jogging on my own back to the tree. By the time the others had begun to arrive, the lorry was long gone, but the pile of aggregates, presumably there to make an entrance into the field, was plain to see. After an hour or so, as word got out, a few people from other parts of the route started to appear along with two men in a landrover. They were from Bray's Detective Agency – contracted out by the Department of Transport to spy and collect information on protestors. Nine tenths of it was a tactic of intimidation. They started filming everyone in sight, which in a way was confirmation that our presence here was pissing somebody off. A solitary security guard was dropped off, presumably to guard the aggregate. He stood by the junction to the A4 for hours, forlorn and obviously hoping that the other guards would turn up really, really soon.

Then we heard that the security had been blocked in their compound by a tripod set up in the early hours. The security guards had been hired in their thousands and were mainly being put up in the hangers of an old airforce base – a place called Abbots Farm near Reading. The tripod had been built from three fifteen foot lengths of scaffolding bars, connected by clips, with polyprop rungs at the top for people to stand on. Doug was one of the two up there, grinning under his moustache and in a hard hat of his own. It was too dangerous for the police to try and move them – if the tripod was interfered with it could fold up like a pair of scissors and topple over.

This meant our field was the scene of all the action on route for the day. Somebody – quick as you like – had organised a press conference under the tree. It was wearing into the afternoon by then and James from Snelsmore, the one who'd been making chapattis, had appeared. Feeling mutually bemused by developments, we climbed up together to hang a huge banner somebody had made; 'BULLDOZING 'R' FUTURE' it said, along with a cartoonesque bulldozer toppling a tree. After the conference, which took place at a safe distance below us, James and his girlfriend, the brown dreaded Sam, went into town to get me provisions for my upcoming siege. They returned with a couple of bags of packaged food – instant meals and powdered soups. I hadn't told them I didn't have anything to cook them on.

That night there was a big turn out from Granny Ash to have a go at the pile of aggregate. Though if anyone asked, nocturnal missions like this were always attributed to the pixies. The pixies did this or the pixies did that – pulled up some fences, moved some surveying pins, disabled a digger or dug up a road. Nobody knew who the pixies were and, as with knowledge of things like real elves, if they knew much at all it was wise not to let on.

Seeing as there hadn't been much time for organisation, there was a conspicuous lack of proper digging implements. All but one of the cooking pots from the camp had been commissioned and got thoroughly trashed as the night progressed. Mark the cyclist was worrying that this might all be a bit rash, that we had a long campaign ahead of us and we might not be able to keep up a pace like this, working half the night. But there was no stopping most people – this was the first chance they'd had to do something proactive.

"Come on! No pain, no gain!" somebody grunted. Bits of gravel went flying into the night air behind us, landing in a succession of snakey dull thuds. Everytime a car came down the side road, a man from Newbury made us all duck down behind the hedge.

"Out of sight, out of mind!" he told us "Out of sight, out of mind!" Adversity was obviously breeding bad catchphrases. It was already shaping up to be a long campaign.

The mound of aggregate was eventually reduced to a strip too narrow to drive on. Now we set about putting up a tripod of our own. Once the scaff poles were clipped together, while somebody stood at the base of the two legs, a bunch of us grabbed the third, hauling the whole thing up with it, like we were raising a flag in a warzone. Once it had been manouvered over the gravel, blocking the entranceway, Balin volunteered to stay up it. He rigged up some polyprop so he could get some sleep up there, clipped onto the scaff poles, wrapped up in his bag, a cunning loop or two to support his head and his legs. As we left him to it, he claimed he was very comfortable. There were several other entrances to the field, but they were all along the A4 and this was obviously the one they wanted. And the tripod was a grand symbol of defiance in its own right.

The next day a couple of makeshift benders were built by the hedge, next to Balin and his tripod. He was still in a cheerful mood and said he'd passed the night very well. The word today was that the security had managed to get out of their compound and were now working somewhere on route, protecting the chainsaw operators and other contractors. A posse from Granny Ash waited around Balin for a vehicle to appear and transport them to the action.

Two massive lads in their twenties had come down from Bog Camp. They were twins; both had long, blond dreads and formed part of the guard when the others had all climbed into a van and evaporated. The twins had a lot to say for themselves and were very glad to be here. A young chap called Richie with dreads and shaved sides of his head had appeared overnight, straight out from clubland in London. He was glad to be here too and set himself up in one of the new, plastic tarped benders by the side of the hedge. Balin's guard of honour also took in a man in a black woollen hat whose name I never remembered and a man out from the nearest village, Speen, bringing up the rear, having seen us on TV. He wore a white striped red tracksuit and filled us in, intermittently, on what the world was watching. We were all very glad to be here, we said, and there was certainly no denying the excitement in the air. But even with so much in the offing and Balin waving at the hooting motorists and attracting visitors and journalists for us to talk to, and some of them bringing food and one or two even some hash (though not the journalists), even then it was hard to get overly enthusiastic when it was so bloody cold. Mostly, people brought us soup.

Balin was rapidly adopting the mantle of a truly iconic figure. Though he didn't do particularly much to court it, he was hard to miss in the first place and stuck fifteen up by the side of an A road, the sudden turn of events was only to be expected. If anyone hurtled by shouting what sounded like abuse, he'd wave back, beaming and shout, "...and I hope you have a nice day too!" Balin was a truly nice bloke. And he toked like a trooper, which must have helped his position no end.

Late in the overcast afternoon, we heard that work had been stopped after protestors had pushed the security line back so far that the diggers didn't have room to move. One or two people were beginning to actually say out loud that there was a chance we could stop this road.

I awoke early the next morning, I didn't need any lorries or alarm calls to wake me up now; I shot out of the depths of sleep like a polystyrene float, my blood pounding clear in my ears as the dawn came in. After several hours of listening out for any signs of approaching doom, I went down to see Richie and Balin. The field we were in was roughly rectangular, with the oak straight in the middle and the A4 forming one of the two longer lengths, the far woods the other, with Balin out on the end in the west. I was beginning to get to know the field very well, recognising the ruts and rough dips where the water collected. The ground was of grass grown through old, brown stubble and you developed a long lope to move across it at any speed.

Late in the morning, I went over to Granny Ash. I'd been calling in in the evenings, to get some food and get warm for a while. Today, now that work had been declared somewhere else, I reckoned it was safe to leave my tree unguarded. Returning to the camp that evening, after an afternoon back at the oak, I was followed down the track by the posh voiced enquiries of a news crew, who wanted to know if they could film our camp. I thought it would be harmless enough, though thinking about it later, it would have been better if they'd not known where we were. Not that they wouldn't have found us in the end. They followed me through the woods and, when it emerged that nearly everyone in the bender was already asleep, they ended up filming just two of us, my friend being directed when to look at the postcard he was faking interest in, me playing my whistle like a performing monkey, quietly swearing that the next time a news crew asked to see where I lived, I'd leave them alone in the dark.

The next day, somebody told me that Sarah had a surprise but I already had a clue as to what it might be. A man had appeared from Liverpool, who was studying in the same place as Clare. Clare, the girl in the green dress who I'd met on an Easter Sunday that was already a long way away. She appeared late that night, along with her boyfriend Shaun, who built a small shelter for them both under my tree. Shaun was a man of many piercings and Clare's dreads were full grown, some of them dyed orange, some of them wrapped round with spirals of metal. It was a bittersweet thing to see her, though I was glad she was here. It was good to have a familiar face around.

The weekend arrived along with a consignment of teenagers from the Isle of Wight. Following Shaun and Clare's example, they all pitched their tents under the oak, so there was now a little ring of nylon domes round the trunk. The teenagers were slightly eerie reflections of myself two years before, except they drank more cheap cider. Like my former self, they had a serious pot noodle habit, which their parents ought to have warned them about.

A bunch of people were sat by the hedge below Balin on Saturday night, when someone appeared with a demi-john of homemade raspberry wine. I ended up necking a fair quantity before staggering off across the field in the direction of the oak. After performing a trailing arch from my true course, I eventually collapsed altogether and was left to reflect on how high the grass had grown, half amused by the distant shouts of everyone looking for me. It was Clare who finally found me, after first performing some kind of prayer for the purpose, though she could just have easily followed the trail of raspberry smelling patches of sick.

I woke up on Sunday morning in one of the teenager's tents, Clare having had to pull me back from my attempts at climbing the tree the night before. The news was that Balin and Richie had come under attack from vigilantes. Some lads had come by after closing time, had shouted abuse at Balin and thrown the remains of their Happy Meals into the bender at Richie. They probably weren't meaning to cause any serious damage, but with McDonalds food involved, you couldn't be too sure. Richie moved his bender to the safety of the oak after that. Balin continued his stand.

One of the girls from the Isle of Wight wandered off to have a piss in the nearest woods a little later on. Unfortunately, her bladder guided her by a star of ill fate and she managed to wander right over to the corner of the field and choose a spot that turned out to be the front of somebody's garden. It was the only house for a long way around, so it was pretty impressive, in a way. And sure enough, entertaining a guest inside his conservatory was barbour jacket man, he who had so thoroughly ignored me that day under the oak.

"Good god!" cried his esteemed friend, spluttering over his tea "… is this the sort of thing you have to put up with?" The girl from the Island came strolling back towards us, relieved and carefree and completely unaware of the gathering storm behind her. Barbour jacket man swept in around us only a few paces after the girl. It was fair to say that what ensued involved us getting a piece of his mind. Shaun wasn't having any of it; the girl was one of us after all and we should be standing up for her. He was probably right, even if the girl had been a bit daft, but looking at the two men squaring up to each other, I found it hard to see much besides the relationship with the only nearby locals going straight down the pan.

But other locals came constantly over the weekend to Granny Ash, conveniently directed by Balin and his entourage, whose stocks of donated food had been overflowing from the outset. Soup was everywhere. It was a pretty good call in the circumstances, though we did begin to wonder if some people hadn't used it as an excuse to get rid of the old thermos that had been sat in the back of their cupboards since the days of their kids lunchboxes, or their old mother's trips to the sea. Hardly anyone came back to pick up their thermoses.

For a few folks, donating food to us seemed to be a lot like feeding the lions, though we appreciated it all the same. We tried to be as friendly as possible to the locals and anyone else who turned up to say hello, but there were a fair few gaps to be bridged. A lot of the visitors were involved in the local campaign, though this was usually the first time they'd been out to the camps. And there were always a few who had just seen us on the news, or had driven by a few times and wanted to do something to help. And some of these even came back again, and some of them ended up friends. Those who got involved were to become part of something bigger than any of us were expecting. But for countless more, who drove past and never stopped to talk, it remains unseen how their lives might have been changed and what it might have led to. Too many people couldn't see beyond the way we looked.

We didn't look bad, by the way, just a bit weird, by and large.

By the Newbury standard though, we'd gone through weird and come out the other side. If we weren't positively strange in many eyes, then we were verging on disgusting. We were all togged up to the limit to fend off the cold, trying to outdo each other for the Michelin Man awards. Some folks were wearing home made ponchos – blankets with holes cut in the middle, but for most of us it was just layers. Upon layers. Upon layers. And life in the woods lent itself to a bit of stubble. It went with the mud and the woodsmoke. I'd stopped shaving altogether and was already sprouting a gingery beard. You got used to getting stared at on the High Street. Some people even got spat at. Then again, some people liked to dance around on street corners in their climbing harnesses, listening to loud techno from the van they'd just piled out of. But spitting was still a bit harsh.

Settling in

Monday came round again and clearance work started once more. I awoke with the light and lay there, listening for ominous signs. Balin was still up his tripod; a small figure at the edge of the stony, rutted field, about a hundred and fifty yards from me. Nearly everyone around the tree got a lift to where felling was being attempted, somewhere in Penwood. Once it seemed sure that that was where they were working, with no one running with the news that there'd been a sudden change of plan, or about turn, I headed over to Granny Ash for my morning rituals.

A trip to the woods with a spade was one of the best bits of the day. For once you could wander off site, without having to worry about looking for firewood, taking in the woodland, free from all hassle. Then a quiet squat, which was almost a prayer; a moment's communion between you and the thick silence of the trees all around.

Coming back to the firepit, I'd heat up one of the donated tins of meat soup on the fire. No one else would touch the meat soup besides Balin, so I thought I was doing everyone a favour and, seeing as it was donated and I hadn't paid any money for it, I reckoned it was karma free.

Later in the week, after ensuring there was someone to guard my tree for the day, I took one of the lifts to where work was going on. Today it was at Swithy's Copse – just the other side of the Wantage road from Snelsmore. I'd been here quite a few times before, traipsing around on a hunt for sawn out bat roosts, when I'd been living at Snelsmore. There'd been a few of us out on the hunt – me and Badger and possibly Tami and Olly as well. The woods seemed to go on forever in every direction – not ranks of young plantation but old, mature woodland;

304

dignified statues of beech and oak towering out from the patchy scrub and the tracts of bare leafmould.

This is where we found the orchard. Acres of it, unclothed in the winter besides lichen and moss, untended and seemingly lost among the hawthorn and hazel. Today, on the action, piling out of the car by The Hare and Hounds pub, I hoped the orchard would still be untouched, that it would be off route and survive long after this.

It was cold and overcast and strangely silent despite the roar of the traffic, which could have been from another dimension. The Hare and Hounds was near the main road, the A34 - bare slopes pulling up on the other side from us, pale and spartan with the winter. We started to walk uphill, in the other direction and away from the road. Across the fields from us sat the woods, spreading down from the slope, their edge maybe quarter of a mile away. A line of old trees on our right had already been cut into, a bender now sitting squat between some of those remaining. This camp was Mary Hare. I was glad not to be living here – the main road, the A34, was bigger and gnarlier than the A4, and the camp was pretty close to it.

The field to the woods was full of people; a wide, scattered throng tapering thickly towards where the sound of chainsaws was drifting out from the woods. It was almost like a festival, familiar faces appearing from under their hoods, except this wasn't just a celebration of unity. This was a fight and the enemy could be seen all the more clearly here; a line of neon yellow emerging through the mist near the treeline.

I fell in with a crew from Skyward and, once in the woods, we sat on a log to smoke a quick rollie. People moved swiftly past us to the action, half shrouded with the heavier mist under the trees, the sound of chainsaws all the more cutting close up. People were shouting at the security, shouting from the heart, sounding urgent and

305

distressed. Someone played half a tune on the whistle. The branches were silhouetted in the mist and you knew that on a midwinter day like this, everything ought to be still here. The security were only a little way in and I was geared to run, in either direction, my nerves strung tight and my belly somewhere in my ribs. My lungs were trying to climb up my throat.

Behind the line of security could be seen the dark forms of protestors in the low trees, huddled and squat in the branches, or laid out thinly, stood on one leg, their body against the trunk of the large, outgrown fruit trees. They'd come for the orchard. I started to walk around the cordon, trying to ignore the guards, who mostly seemed passive and stared at their feet or something far off in embarrassment. Others were puffy eyed and disinterested, or stared back wired up, chewing gum.

There were no gaps in the cordon and with no way in to join those in the trees, or to disrupt the chainsaws directly, I climbed a beech just to the west of the line, in case they wanted to extend the felling area.

I stood for hours on a thin branch just above a rhododendron, looking out for any signs of action and exchanging rough pleasantries with the lads in the next tree along. The only real action back here though was a man in a neon jump suit, running around handing protestors bundles of things to munch on. Turned out, this was Julian Cope, the psychedelic rock singer more usually seen in tight trousers. There was nothing to do except sit it out, listening to the shouts and the chainsaws, and try not to think about what was left of the orchard.

After a long time the security moved off, the line of yellow jackets and white hats tramping out towards the field like a receding nightmare. People started climbing down from the trees and hugging each other. I hadn't been long down and was wandering among the survivors when somebody started shouting – they were cutting down by the Hare and Hounds. Everybody started running.

We jolted through the field from the woods, overtaking most of the security on the way. A dozen or so guards were ranged thinly in front of a straggling line of young aspens. They were grabbing one or two of us as we bundled past but loads of people were getting through. I was aware of more security closing in as I started to clamber up a trunk. The trees weren't big, so you could only fit two to three people to each one. People were running along the line of them, trying to find one to climb up, like musical chairs. I think some security were trying to pull someone out, to loads of accompanied shouting. We were like starlings, shouting across to each other in the twilight, happy because we knew we'd got these trees covered. A girl in the next tree from me fished out a recorder from her poncho and one or two others took up the tune. Realising it was too late to try anything else that day, the security waddled down to their fleet of white coaches, waiting in the wings of the A34 to cart them all back to internment. A few of us began the long walk back to Granny Ash in the dark, getting lost for a while in the dark tracts of rhododendron forest surrounding Mary Hare school.

A local woman called Fran, who I'd met shortly after returning in October, invited a load of us down to her house, to watch videos and hang out and get out of the cold for a bit. Mostly it was Skyward crew, plus a few of us from Granny Ash and a few more besides. We were all crammed into her huge living room, watching a video about the eviction at Claremont, as if people weren't already up to their eyeballs with mayhem and security and police. But it seemed like a good idea at the time and it

307

was good just to watch a flickering screen for a bit. But in the strange environment of a centrally heated house, people began to show each other sides of themselves that they normally never would – like t-shirts and shirts and bare arms. Piles of empty wool were mounting up all over the place, the air filling with a hum that was never noticed outdoors with all the layers and the superior ventilation. There were more than a few adherents among us to the theory that a good layer of dirt held the heat in and there might have been something in that. Fran had made us all a huge batch of vegan flapjack, which helped take our minds off the hum.

The days began to fall into a steady pattern. I'd wake early, listening out, lifting up the tarp every ten minutes or so, poking my head out for a look round to make sure there'd been no sudden appearance of hordes of white vehicles. This was done simply by wriggling a little closer to the edge by my head and lifting up the tarp. There was only ever one vehicle – a medium sized white van parked near the ornate gates of some nearby big house, a few hundred yards down to the east – the only thing visible along the A4 besides hedges and trees and the lampposts. Maybe it was nothing, but I had a few doubts. White vans were classic surveillance vehicles; it was certainly always a white van watching us at Fairmile and this one would be there consistently every morning, presumably to see if my tree was occupied every night or not.

I'd keep my lookout up for an hour or two until the danger had passed, then I'd doze or listen to the radio. Quite often the radio was my first way of knowing where work was taking place. A man who called himself Snow Leopard, a London green activist who wore a black barge cap and appeared in the field from time to time, had gotten the radio for me. It only worked when I held a fork in the back as an aerial and it only picked up one station – Talk Radio. For too many mornings, while I waited for news bulletins, I listened in to Tommy Boyd holding phone-ins about sports cars or the devil.

Around eleven, when I'd had enough of the radio and felt sure they wouldn't be coming for me that day, I'd cross the road to Granny Ash for breakfast and a chance to see some people. There was always a reasonable crew shifting about; a fair few people opting to stay on site rather than catch a lift to the mayhem. Besides the work on the trees there were visitors to receive, wood to be collected and sawn and washing up to do. The plates and bowls were normally frozen from the night before, congealed food and ice meaning the job was almost always getting put off till late in the day.

Just to sit by a fire out of the wind was a huge relief. There were often reporters and almost always someone lurking around with a fat camera. We were beginning to grow used to being under an almost constant scrutiny, from some member of the press if not police or detectives. It led to the increased sense of being inside a film, where your every movement could be getting relayed to an audience. Life was turning into a performance, which is what it had been all along, only now there was no getting round it.

To court the press's attention intentionally, or to play up to them too much made you a media tart, or as Badger spoonerised it; a tedia mart. Rose, who probably deserves a book of her own, was the biggest tart of them all and would pose side on whenever a camera was pointed at her, flicking her eyes up now and then to see if they'd finished, playing the game perfectly.

After a couple of hours doing a bit of sawing and chewing the cud I'd scoot up the track to see how Balin was doing, though he was rarely without company for any part of the day. The tide of visitors to Balin was only set to continue and, as the day wore on there was scarcely a moment when he wasn't talking to some new face. He'd only come down in the evenings for a quick trip to Granny Ash to eat and visit the woods. Articles were beginning to appear about him in the papers. People who drove past him in the morning and still saw him on their way home were beginning to stop and talk. People were calling him a knight, or a saint, or comparing him to literary heroes. At the moment he was reading Cervantes, after an article had compared him to Don Quixote – a knight on a quest to confront the mills of the modern world, in this case the grinding expansion of a deviant infrastructure. Don Quixote – half blind and half mad – was a curious figure to live up to though and Balin wasn't finding much assurance in the comparison.

After a few hours wrapped up in my treehouse, reading the only book I could find - a Mills and Boon novellette about fox hunting - I'd return to Granny Ash as the dark gathered, joining the swelling firepit in the smoky wait for stew.

The firepit was right at the beginning of the slope and was covered over with a tunnel like bender, open at both ends. A large log formed the base of the southern entrance, with pallets ranged around the inside; ranks of kitchen tat lurking in the shadows behind people's backs, safely removed from the mud. If anyone wanted something, like a wooden spoon or the tomato puree, the trick was to plunge your hand into the medley behind you without looking back, to see if you could pluck out the right thing. Some people got quite good at it and some people were downright uncanny.

In the mornings, Rose would haul herself up onto the log, balancing her way along to the empty pallets, in a ginger effort to stay free of the mud. The mud was thickening by the day, creeping in along the path from the track and culminating in a complete mire a foot deep infront of the firepit, completely liquidesquent, like childhood jelly squished through the teeth. Tami, determined not to let her boots rot, was following Rose's tack, sat up on the pallets in the mornings, dubbing her boots, resolute in the face of a brown tide of chaos lapping at every attempt at some order.

The back of the firepit bender was only a fairly shallow opening, the bank rising up steeply behind it. The smoke was always funnelled through the back here, making the back pallet pretty impossible to sit on. It looked like this might have been solved when someone unearthed a pair of World War One flying goggles, but even then, you still had to breathe.

It was always a crowd in the evenings, people arriving back in random small groups, usually with special guests they'd met along the way. Some of them had walked back from where work was going on, usually in the south of the route. They stumbled up the track hours after sunset, knackered and elated, or just fried. Slop, or actual stew on a good day, would be served with a weird ceremony where the bowls would get handed around the entire circle of twenty or more people, the first fishing up by the server.

Eventually the time would come when the effect of the company no longer counteracted the soreness of sitting on pallets or the smoke, which managed to swirl around enough to get a good look in at everyone's eyes before disappearing out the back. Badger came down the bank one evening and told us all we led very sheltered lives down here. Even with the night leaking breezes all around us, and our feet growing cold despite our boots being in danger of melting, even then he wasn't wrong. Up past the bank the wind would be howling – a raw, black wind like knives of ice, the kind you only found in places of extremity, or in books.

And over the bank was my route to bed. I'd take it at a run, so that halfway across the first field I'd hardly notice the wind and, by the time I'd clambered up the oak, I'd have warmed up nicely, and only needed to take my boots and harness off and maybe a jumper or two before climbing in my sleeping bag and carefully covering myself up with a thick layer of blankets. The plaid blanket, which I'd now taken to wearing as a kind of shawl to help ward off the worst of the wind, I still wrapped round my head every night, with just a hole to breathe out of.

The water bottles next to my face would be frozen come the morning and all the treehouse was full of a through draught, blowing up round the loose sides; flapping and tearing at themselves in the wind, the thick plastic a constant cracking and the whole tree winding back and forth in an old circumscription of the wind. And somewhere out there, with not much else besides a sleeping bag and a few sheets of plastic, Balin was up in his tripod, resolute and solidly stuck to his post, sleeping the sleep of the just, or battling with monsters.

Naming

The Isle of Wight crew had long moved off, back to college or pot den conspiracies, but they promised they'd come again soon. Clare and Shaun had only stayed a few nights before moving their shelter to the nearby woods, the end where the trees had been cut, leaving the exposed semicircular rim. It was sheltered down there and they'd soon built themselves a proper bender, lagged with blankets and everything. They called it Seaview, because the trees on the rim were all beeches and because they thought that suburbia had to be laughed at.

It was truly peaceful where they were, out of the wind with the light streaming in through the ring of the beeches, the cleared open space somehow adding to the serenity, even though you knew it must have been better with all the trees still in it.

Richie moved down not long after and could often be found swinging in a hammock, beaming madly while listening to a walkman, breaking into song like spontaneous combustion. Richie was younger than any of us and took ecstasy at the weekend, when he had it. He'd blat back to London for a few days and come back raving about some club, where there was some kind of semi evangelical open mike thing. Instead of music, people would be given a chance to rant or more peacefully spout forth about anything they felt need saying. And Richie talked about Newbury. The folks in the clubs were obviously like family to Richie, just as he was fast becoming part of ours and you got the impression that, if he had his way, the whole of the London underground scene would troop out in his wake, step out from their tribal narcissism for a while and put the world to rights.

I was hanging out down in Seaview one evening, for a change from Granny Ash, when a man called Mark appeared, long haired from Norwich and on fire with excitement at being here. He was a boat builder, but was growing tired of it now, tired of fibreglass and it getting under his skin. We talked about adventures and boats for what seemed like half the night, alive with the mutual recognition of a kindred spirit and with being in the woods on a still night, half in the dark by the bender but miles away from any real obscurity.

And all the time Granny Ash was growing, spreading its sentient maw to accommodate an ever wider community. A monster of a bender was under construction, on the other side of the fire from the first one, and under the band of trees that ran to the track – tall ashes mostly that divided high up, where more walkways were appearing daily, linking the row that ran along the bank. My sister's boyfriend had given me a Tibetan prayer flag for Christmas – a row of primary coloured patches of blessings that hung on the air. I tied it to the bottom rung of the walkway directly over the firepit.

Down the track from Granny Ash, the woods fell away on both sides, leaving a slope that ran down to a long run of meadows. The first woods of Speenham moor were only a hundred yards from the bottom of the track, which ended by a wooden gate and a sprawling, low, pollarded willow. The woods rose up in a continuous, dark rank that ran with the meadows to either side as far as you could make out. The track did a right-angle by the gate, becoming a footpath that ran the two miles into town; under a railway bridge, along by the grimy wasteground of a waterworks and through a broad park where the bank Granny Ash lay on seemed to continue – bright and bare with green grass in the watery sunlight. The path followed some back roads before a final channelling down a narrow, old passage, that bought you out right on the High Street by the bridge, throwing you – after a hour or so's walk of calm – straight into a garish tide of humanity and steel. The distance always dragged on the way back, which was always after dark and when we were usually stoned.

The short distance between the gate and the woods of the moor was marked by a straight line of trees – aspens, most likely – possibly the remains of an old field boundary. The trees followed a shallow bank to the woods, their roots protruding in the few exposed feet, the surrounding ground sunken in softness. Here was another tree, another willow, but taller this time and split down the middle, right down to the ground so the two sides had gnarled round into themselves, forming a narrow, forked gateway.

The way into the woods lay just beyond that, a gap between the barbed wire and a gate that was chained shut. This led alongside a waterway that turned a rightangle just inside the treeline. It did the same thing further down, enclosing a rectangle of woodland on at least three sides – the fourth tapering off into marsh and mangrove-like root displays. No one seemed to know what lay out that way. No one had bothered to find out or, if they had, they'd never told anyone where they were going and they'd never come back.

This was the way to the Kennet and the site of the weirdly repaired fisherman's bridge. The waterway it spanned was wider than any old stream – twenty foot or so of cold, clear water that ran on a table we couldn't quite fathom – starting somewhere, finishing up somewhere else, but never a place that we knew of. Further down, where the water turned again, there was actually a waterborne crossroads – four channels converging, or wandering off; a heady meeting place of conflicting currents, whirlpools and

315

undertows eddying at your feet as you watched them, mesmerised by the movement and the sound – the only sound here, except birds.

Even here though, a new camp had been founded – a blue plastic tarp strung between the meshed bulks of fallen, ivy covered trees, a firepit in the middle of the trunks. Three women had set up here, eyeing up the trees even as they settled in – looking for places for platforms and places to string up some rope. Bea was a climber from London, somewhere in her forties or fifties but stupidly fit for all that. At Stanworth, alone in the very tops of a tree, she'd held out against climbers for days. Rachel the Red was another one out from the M11; long red dreads and laughing at stuff, somewhere in her twenties and satisfyingly mad. Alex had come out from London, or Guildford, probably both at different times. Shaved temples and dyed ginger dreads, a lip ring, striped tights somewhere between her layers and her boots. A pretty amusing cackling trio, who I liked to drink tea with when everything else had gone quiet.

We were about to paint post boxes for Granny Ash and the waterways camp, which meant that it needed a name. It was early evening, dark, and a bunch of us were sat round the fire discussing it. Having a post box and getting stuff sent to it meant you were an officially recognized address and a legal dwelling place, which would help with the court proceedings when they tried to evict us. Up in Pixie Village at Snelsmore – site of the original ground camp and over the valley from Skyward – they'd painted a pallet red and done the name of each treehouse on the separate planks.

Badger suggested 'Wolfsbridge' as a name for the new camp. He'd looked up the meaning of Speen, the nearest village, in the library and it had apparently meant 'the people of Wolf' – a Saxon settler and chief. A floor-level

316

walkway had just been strung up next to the bridge, as a more sorted way of getting across. But the bridge meant dogs were not excluded, so 'Wolfsbridge' was doubly appropriate. Most people reckoned Rickety Bridge was a far better name and we finally settled on 'Rickety Wolfsbridge,' though it became Rickety Bridge in the end anyway, which was probably all for the best.

Since Granny Ash had been started, we'd been getting water from a trough up the track. This was safe enough if you took the water straight where it came out of the inflow pipe, holding the ballcock down to get a flow and keeping the bottleneck clear of the rest of the water. You could fill up a butt like this, one bottle at time, but it meant keeping most of the bottle underwater and one of your hands with it. In a winter like this, it bore all the masochistic hallmarks of a Japanese gameshow.

Fortunately for us and in no small part due to Balin's heroics, we'd somehow managed to befriend the people who lived in the corner of the field – Barbour Jacket Man and his wife – Peter and Caroline Bartley. It was an unlikely turnaround, but a surprisingly pleasant one. Now everyone wanted to get the water. These days, the water in the trough was literally frozen most of the time and we were getting through a lot more water anyway, so access to a proper tap was nothing short of a godsend. Not only that but Mrs B was a maestro with tea and toast. I never thought toast could taste so good. Their kitchen quickly became a kind of sanctuary, from the cold if nothing else.

New faces on the constant crew at Granny Ash included John the Cook, who had come out from a squat in London, and who had been followed by Richie. John was pretty clear about his contribution to the camp, and it made a big difference to have the cooking taken care of, with no

317

need for constant negotiations or half begrudged volunteering from people who cooked too much and would rather do something else once in a while. With glasses and shaved black hair that ran into dreads somewhere behind him and a welcoming, grubbily stubbled face, John was nearly always by the firepit, chopping up veg and quietly clocking everything going on. Scottish Clare and Tara were two more veterans from the M11, who formed a trio with Sarah, cackling in a corner, singing 'In the Ghetto,' doing Elvis voices, which they always thought was hilarious.

The new bender had been completed, using two big, green tarps and sleeping up to twenty, potentially. Only trouble was, it was heated by Puff, who was finding it hard going to warm up such a large space. But the evenings in there were a welcome change from nights round the firepit. And emerging for a piss after hours inside with the spliffs going round always held its own magic; the moon riding up gracefully through the branches, a blue forest floor, slightly silvered with the frost, a sudden stillness and hush of the woods in the winter.

Badger was coming and going as much as ever, often away for half the night on midnight walkwaying missions somewhere else on route. Where clearance work was at its most intense, mostly in Penwood, the night was a time when territory could be reclaimed, walkways that had been cut getting restrung. Badger and the others would work almost feverishly, their headtorches lighting the way, the buzz of the climb and the height they were up keeping them at it.

Balin had been up in his tripod for about two weeks and a few of us were beginning to get worried. Not that he was showing any signs of the pressure, only we wondered if he still needed to be up there. There were other entrances after all, so his stand was becoming increasingly symbolic.

But perhaps that was the point, and the reason why he was so reluctant to quit the field.

Perhaps everything we were doing here was nine tenths symbolic – making our voices heard, making a point, showing that there were still people who cared about the future, a rising generation who couldn't hide any longer from the tide of the times and who weren't prepared to bury their heads in a world of parties and drugs or shopping or debt induced, dead ended work. The whole modern world, once you tried to step outside it, was revealing itself as an ever more elaborate lie, Babylon that lay at the borders of the woods, larger than either governments or corporations, though they could be its tools, a lie of comfort and self service that sought to seduce, or otherwise bludgeon us all into subservience and a state of thinly veiled bondage. All very well if you were happy to live the lie, perhaps, only it was defiling the world, encouraging us all to draw more to ourselves, to turn the blind eye, until there were no more morals, no conviction, sick spirits and very little hope.

This was what we were fighting – not just a road, or a network of roads, but everything they stood for; the grip of a mill that would pull us all under before grinding us up. And Balin was there right at the front, further out now than any of us; out on a limb from the out on a limb, a signpost of courage and hope. But it was getting hard to see him hanging there day after day and we wondered how long he could stand it.

We didn't have to wonder very much longer. Balin was seemingly impervious to shouts of abuse and was even nonchalant about the shots fired from passing cars, which after all might have been fireworks. But when a load of lads piled out of a car, late on an otherwise quiet Wednesday night, and pulled his tripod to the ground, he didn't get up again. He was unhurt in the fall, but too entangled in his webbing to take on his attackers, or at least to defend himself. He told them instead, calmly enough considering the circumstances, that he'd remember their registration number.

"If you tell the police," they told him "we'll come and stick a pickaxe through your head."

He did tell the police, though they took an hour to turn up and had him waiting another three and a half in the station before he could make a ten minute statement. He didn't go up in the tripod after that. He'd been up there for two and a half weeks by then though, and it was good to see him round the fire in the evenings again.

On an afternoon not long after, I was clearing up the remains of Balin's camp when a camera crew and reporter appeared out of nowhere. They were doing a piece on the cold and wanted to know how we were coping with it. Had it been the winter before, I could have told them we were doing very well, that we were models of endurance and fitness. But this winter that clearly wasn't the case, a constant bout of heavy colds were doing the rounds – something that probably had a lot to do with the amount of people coming and going, bringing all the germs of the cities out with them and never staying long enough to properly get used to the cold. And this winter the cold took some getting used to by anyone's standards.

The amount of nicotine being smoked can't have helped much either, especially the habit of sparking up rollies right after a meal; a practice that was said to destroy a large amount of the nutrients just eaten. And the food wasn't exactly packed full of goodness at the best of times. Most nights hippy slop – the watery stew that made it relatively easy to feed a large mob – ruled the roost. Lentils were the chief source of protein and, while there was nothing wrong with that, you sometimes wondered if there was enough to go round. Lentils, for the most part, instead fulfilled the function of brightening up the woodland floor, being the most frequent victim of high profile spillages; large patches of orange split peas decorating the doorway of every bender and caravan at some point or other, slowly sinking into the mud as the days drew on; a submerging promise of adequate sustenance.

I was hungry enough at the most plentiful of times at that point in my life and that winter I seemed to burn food off just from being out in the cold. So when the reporter asked me whether the cold was making us ill, my mind wandered over all this until I came back with a murmuring answer, the first of a classic bad interview. The reporter told me the story of a man who'd fought on the Somme in the winter, who said he'd never been cold since. Obviously, this was the kind of gem of gritty anecdotage he'd been after and he shortly wandered off with his crew, in search of a better subject, or despairing of hippies altogether.

Interviews were a bit of a hit and miss process with me. When it worked they were great but now and again I transformed to the Boy With No Brains, when questions seemed overly taxing, or when I was thinking of food.

The Isle of Wight crew reappeared that weekend and, gathered under the oak with them, with Clare and Shaun and a few up from Granny, we decided it was time the tree got a name. My first idea was 'The Elfin Alamo,' influenced in no small way by the Tim Burton masterpiece – Pee Wee Herman's Big Adventure. Everyone else was a bit unsure about this – wouldn't 'the Alamo' be tempting fate, and where did Davy Crocket come into it anyway?

Centre Oak would be a good name they all thought. It was in the centre of the field after all, and sort of central to the whole route. It sounded a bit too much like Centreparcs to me though, and 'centre' had a kind of clinical and dead ring to it. Middle Oak would be better, I reckoned, and suddenly everything fell into place.

Lines of Defiance

The night everyone left the bottom of Middle Oak for the shelter of Seaview I had a strange and terrifying dream. It culminated in my walking up the curving steps of an old house. Everything was dark, the boards of the stairs were bare and wooden and wallpaper was coming off the walls all around me. The way up the steps was almost blocked with old women, skinny old women with long, lank hair and no clothes, their skin diseased and mottled, or covered with sores. As I passed they uttered their names; all of them names of the camps on route, but slightly twisted.

"I'm Mary Whore" one woman told me, her eyes imploring and accusatory at the same time. At the top of the stairs I turned to find a room with a large bath in the centre. A girl rose up out of it as I watched; she was white and skeletal and had rusted metal dreadlocks running down between her protruding shoulder blades.

"They're going to get me anyway" she said and pointed to the window. Rushing in from the blues and blacks of a shadowy garden came the nightmarish sound of a chainsaw starting up, like a woken, antagonised child.

I woke up panting, I could still hear chainsaws, coming from a tree by the A4. Somewhere in between waking and poking my head out from the tarp, the noise stopped. There was nobody in sight near the road, which was itself dead quiet, eerie and still in the sodium. This must have been the tree I was in talking to me, the girl in the bath a manifestation of her spirit. And were these old women the spirits of trees who knew they were doomed to die? Or was this merely a dark dream, the flipside of beauty, territory not to be dwelt on? Certainly there was a sense sometimes, in old trees like these in the winter, that the tree

323

just wanted to be left alone to sleep and that our arrival brought with it an awakening they could do without. But usually this phase passed, some harmony coming into the two sleepers, the tree welcoming you in, a wider world opening out in the vision of your dreaming mind. But perhaps I wasn't there with Middle Oak yet and with this dream I lost all hope that she could be saved. It was a bitter thought.

On January 26th Badger and Doug, amongst others, trooped off to the High Court in London to help defend the Kennet, Granny Ash, Rickety Bridge and several other sites besides. The case had come up several weeks earlier but we'd got an adjournment on the grounds that we hadn't had enough time to prepare a case between the eviction notices being served and the hearing.

Later that day, I joined John the Cook on a water mission to the Bartley's. We had a butt each and a wheelbarrow to carry one in. Carrying one butt was worse than carrying two, as it left you off balance, though at least you had a chance to move it around to stop the handle digging into your fingers. Sometimes you'd try and carry it against your chest, with your hands beneath it, but if it was leaking then the water would go down your front and maybe your legs. And in weather like this, that was definitely not good.

The tap in the Bartley's back garden was frozen when we got there and we had to fill the butts from the bath. I'd shared a spliff with John a little earlier and now we sat enjoying Mrs B's tea while we stared out at the snow that had just started. John wasn't the most overtly talkative bloke going and, with my brains beginning to drift with the snow, I was aware we probably looked as stoned as we felt. But if she thought we were acting strange, Mrs B had the heart not to mention it and we carried on staring out at the snow, which was really drifting now, settling on the neat grass of the garden and flurrying all the more thickly in silent but visible howls. It was suddenly very good to be indoors and when Mrs B offered us more tea and toast we knew what the answer was immediately, even though we pretended to have to make our minds up, for appearances sake.

On the way back, the sky thick and weirdly defined with the inverted depths of random flakes, we could just about make out a group of protestors under Middle Oak, all huddled around something. When I got there myself I found Tami and Richie, staring at the brown and orange mess of a giant flysheet. The man who'd left it was still standing by, having just unloaded it from the back of a rusty coloured Volvo estate. He had a moustache and beard, a greying ponytail and very wide eyes.

"Look after it man" he told me, presumably talking about the tent, "this one's been through the Isle of Wight." It was old enough to have witnessed Jimi Hendrix, in so far as nylon and metal poles and plastic windows can witness anything. All the same it seemed a prestigious inheritance.

As we began to set it up, in what was rapidly becoming a blizzard, the Jimi Hendrix tent unveiled itself to be large, rectangular and family sized; the kind you can find on large, all amenities campsites. It had curtains with brown and yellow flowers. The framework took a while to figure out, metal poles being the last thing you want to be handling with bare hands on a hill in a snowstorm. It became a battle between us and the wind driven snow, but we got it up in the end, curtains and all. Richie moved in straight away, which pleased him no end. He spun around with his arms outstretched, then did a little dance.

Back at the firepit just after dark and an owl flew low over the camp, its wings outstretched and silhouetted against the last of the fading light. It was a big owl too, with a wingspan of maybe a metre or more. Just after that Potty Phil turned up, with the bad news that we'd lost the case in the High Court and that evictions could start at any time. I'd been expecting the case to be adjourned again, for maybe another few weeks, so this was gutting news.

As Potty Phil stopped talking a horn blew repeatedly from somewhere down in the valley. The notes hung in the air, the trees ringing round with it, like we were being called awake, alerted to the news, like the whole place was being called to stir up and defend itself against what was coming. It was stirring, but it was also sad, because everything was suddenly inevitable. It turned out to be Twig with his conch, walking back from the campaign office with Rachel the Red. He'd heard the result of the hearing from Channel Four News, when he'd picked up a phone and they'd asked,

"You've lost the Court Case, how do you feel?" A little while later an American news group had called up asking,

"You've been evicted, how do you feel?"

The snow didn't settle that night but the temperature fell to minus seven, apparently, and that was before windchill. The packets of soup stared me in the face like never before, and I wished I'd got it together to get a trangia from somewhere. Just going out and buying one hadn't seemed like an option for some reason. But Mrs B had been moved to give me an eiderdown duvet, which made an amazing amount of difference and meant I didn't need to be so precious about any of my bedding falling off in the night. I awoke to a heavy ongoing snowfall and while - from my vantage point - I could see that it wasn't settling too much, when I got down on the ground it looked like a thick carpeting.

A girl arrived at Granny Ash one day, someone who'd we'd heard about through osmosis from the camps to the north. Acid Kath was a casualty of the highest order, sleeping all day and laughing or singing to herself for much of the rest of the time. She'd been tolerated for a long time at Snelsmore, even though she seemed to be enveloped in a cloud of bad luck. No one really thought much of it when she gave a kind of rag doll she had as a present to a couple who lived in a yellow van. They'd been planning to leave site the next day, but found their normally healthy engine wouldn't start. People only started to make the connection when somebody burnt the doll on impulse weeks later, a clandestine ceremonial huddle forming round the fire. The van started fine after that. She was finally booted off site altogether after she lunged for another girl with a pair of scissors. And now she was with us.

But she wasn't alone. Augmenting her armada of weirdness was Keith. Keith slept half the day too and when he did emerge from the communal, it would only be to sit round the fire and smoke rollies. Keith must have needed some help, but this wasn't the time or place for anyone to give it. It was ironic that I hadn't been in much of a better state myself before Christmas, only I knew the territory and knew enough to help out where I could. If he'd been around before the papers were served, perhaps he'd have been treated more gently but as it was, people took the piss fairly pitilessly, in an effort to get him to do some work. But heavy handed hints just seemed to bounce off his defence mechanisms.

It was a Saturday and I'd been told a big event had been planned for around Middle Oak the next day. There'd be morris dancers for a start, plus a big fort building, enclosing the space around the trunk. It'd be a chance for loads of people who couldn't make it to the action during the week to make a solid, physical contribution.

Only thing was, the Jimi Hendrix tent needed moving outside the planned fort's perimeter, and Acid Kath was asleep inside. I managed to infiltrate her mutterings until I could just make out that she couldn't get up because she only had one boot. Another bout of wading through the fog of half coherencies threw up the fact that Keith had taken it.

It wasn't hard to find Keith, given that he was only ever in one of two places. He told me, from his ongoing residence in the communal, that he'd only taken Kath's boot because she'd taken one of his. Sure enough, back in the tent two fields away, Keith's boot was lurking, captive in Kath's fractal lair. Soon though, they were both restored to the realms of the fully shoed. We managed to hassle Kath enough to get her out of her sleeping bag and she rose up staggering and mumbling grievances before leering off to find some unspecified firepit, which was suddenly down on its luck.

In the evening Potty Phil appeared in the Pig Magnet – the campaign's flatbed truck. It was loaded up with lengths of fat birch from Penwood, eight foot to twelve foot long. I helped him unload and then carried them over to the tree, laying them round the trunk in a wide circle. It took the Pig Magnet two or three runs to get all the logs and I ended up working long into the night, carrying them the couple of hundred yards from the road to the tree.

Just as I was falling into an exhausted sleep, a weirdly familiar sound came creeping into my consciousness. It sounded like something impossible. Like a boat rattling and chugging across the field, some tug come to tow me away somewhere sane. I stuck my head out to see two headlights bouncing towards me. Someone was mad enough to drive their car across the ruts and stones of the field - and they were coming towards me. The car stopped abruptly outside the Jimi Hendrix tent (now moved to its new location) and beeped its horn, like some kind of bizarre, impatient alien. Fortunately for me, Richie had appeared back since I'd gone to bed and he staggered out of the tent to the men in the car, who'd heard there was some kind of party going on. Once he'd put them straight they turned around and drove off again, driving *through* the hedge and onto the A4.

By the time I woke up the next day, loads of people were milling around on the ground below me. When I arrived on the ground myself I found plenty of people I knew; folks from Snelsmore and people from town I'd come to know over the last year and a half. The Bartleys were around, as were the Stoughtons with their two young girls. Karen, a friend from town, was shocked to find out I didn't have any gloves and gave me the ones she was wearing. They'd been her dad's.

"He won't need them anymore" she told me. They were good gloves.

When sixty or more people had gathered, all wrapped up against a bitter north easterly that was coming over from Donnington, we formed a huge circle round the tree. After a minute's communion with the tree, I realised everyone was looking to me, as if I had a plan. I started to measure out a length of polyprop so we could have the stakes at the same distance from the trunk all the way round. But everyone clearly didn't have time to wait around in the freezing cold for this and started sticking posts in the ground there and then. I contented myself with making sure people were putting the stakes in outside the perimeter marked by the tree's crown, which ought to have ensured they'd then be clear of most of the roots.

People had bought tools and before long everyone was busy digging holes. I climbed up the tree as everyone worked and tried to re-string the 'Bulldozing 'R' Future banner, which had got wrapped round the branches in the high winds. I was hoping I'd be able to climb up to the platform without generating too much attention, for a sneaky bit of breakfast.

Once all the stakes were in place, people began nailing bits of plywood and pallets to them. I'd been envisioning some kind of wattle or dead wood screen, but it was too late for that now and I watched with sudden disinterest as bits of chipboard and crap wood were driven into the posts in a random mash up of enthusiasm. Quite where the good wood for my fancy plans would have come from was another matter, never mind who would have done it, but it was getting hard not to think big.

Most people had started digging a big ditch round the fence. There was a lot of digging to do though – the crown's hemisphere defined a pretty big space after all. It was all a bit bemusing, in a way, and I couldn't help thinking of the Fairmile defences, about all the time and effort that went into them and whether they'd be much use in the end anyway. But as a symbolic act and an opportunity for people to make a physical contribution, it was hard to deny a trench's appeal. It was also a chance to create a space – a zone that security or police couldn't just wander into at the drop of a hat, a place that was ours and ours alone, where each shovelful was an act of consecration. It might not hold them out for very long, but it felt good doing it.

A small gang of radio journalists had been knocking about, heading off only after extracting another classically bad interview from me, during which I remembered I hadn't had any lunch. Richie appeared and dropped a tab of acid, grinning, and dancing a bit too with the whole buzz

330

of everything. Four morris dancers eventually pitched up, bells and all, down from Oxford, livening things up while everyone shovelled and pickaxed. They were in fact dancers from 'the Tribe of Doris' and instead of wooden clubs used feather dusters. I think it had something to do with spring cleaning.

It was suddenly amazing to see so many people here, all my cynicism faded away with the tunes. They'd all come here for this tree, it was coming to mean so much for so many whereas I had just begrudgingly and fatalistically climbed up to look after it, for want of anything better to do. People downed tools and joined hands and danced round to the music. Against all the odds, I was feeling inspired.

The families drifted off, leaving a dwindling hardcore that consisted, ultimately, only of Balin, who carried on working till eight, while we all went off to get dinner.
"I like to work past the point where it hurts" said Balin "otherwise, it doesn't feel like I've done anything."

One of the last men to depart gave me a CB. Middle Oak wasn't just a tree any more. It was a camp. I held the responsibility in my hands for a while before giving it a go. There were a set of instructions with it, giving all the camps' radio names – which were pretty obvious like Tango Bravo for the Third Battle office and Gamma Alpha for Granny Ash. The instructions also gave what channels were in use from day to day and which ones to hop to if you thought you were being listened in to. As it turned out, the aerial on my CB was broken, so I could hear everyone else, but no one could hear me. The conch would have been more use, though slightly less amusing. At least this way I didn't have to bring myself to say 'Mike Oscar' over and over again.

I spent the evening in the communal; there'd been plans to have some kind of party round Middle Oak but the wind put a stop to that – it was too cold to stand around in the dark and the fire that'd been lit was dangerous to go near, spouting horizontal flames that eddied around at a moment's notice. Someone let a camera crew from GMTV stick their lens in the communal, capturing us all looking knackered, or sleeping, or stoned. I hadn't noticed the camera and had no idea that the very next morning, people round the country would be eating their cornflakes to the image of my toking on a huge, fat bifta. I could have done with some cornflakes myself, a little while later.

Back in the oak, I woke up with the distinctive sensation that something rat sized was crawling over my ankles. It was still dark and before I had time to reach for a light, the thing had scampered up to my face. It was a kitten! I stuck my head out from the tarp to see a huge, black limbed, medieval siege tower up against Granny Ash, smoke billowing up into the air.

I climbed down and rushed over to find Badger. He was on the green field at the base of the tree, a vague impression of something like a town under siege shaping up behind him, where the ground was dropping away to the Kennet valley.

"They're coming for your tree Jim!" he told me and I turned round to run but was suddenly being surrounded by policemen. I tried to outrun them but one had grabbed hold of the back of my top, slowing me down so it was like moving through mud, half swamped by shadows. They had hold of my legs as I started to climb Middle Oak, I was halfway up when they caught me completely and I woke up, panting.

I stuck my head out from under the tarp again. There was a siege tower by Granny Ash... I had two or three dreams like this; that started with my waking up in the treehouse. When I finally did wake up, I wasn't sure whether to believe it, the dreams had been so real.

Tree dreams could be particularly powerful. Someone at Seaview woke up and looked out from the treehouse to find the whole field on fire. Somebody else got the nickname Moses after he dreamt his treehouse was burning. He woke up on the ground, still in one piece, with the treehouse above him in flames. Somebody else had a sleepwalking dream and awoke to find themselves, horizontal, but clinging onto a branch, with only their feet on the platform. The friend who'd inherited my original treehouse in Snelsmore, which was now topped with a bender on the roof, dreamt one night that something like pixies were all around the treehouse in the night, shouting and laughing, tapping on the walls and pulling at the tarp and having a great time. She began to get scared with the intensity of it, a chorus of noise that was as alive as the woods around her. She shouted for them to stop and woke up with the abruptness of the calm. The wind had been blowing a gale all night and had suddenly dropped altogether, as though on command.

333

Back in Penwood

On Monday I thought it was about time I went on another action. I took the risk of leaving Middle Oak on its own and got a lift into town with Big Pete and another geezer from Granny Ash. I'd tried to avoid the office and had only ventured in here once before, to try and sort out the legal paperwork that all the other camps had been concerning themselves with. I'd been put off by the hecticness though; I was pretty unclear what I'd needed to get sorted and there was no one around with any better idea, at least no one who wasn't already busy answering phones, or charging around with forms. A girl with dreads in a big coat was screwing up her face over an affidavit, like it was an overdue homework assignment, which it probably more or less was. Maybe I'd come back when I knew what I needed, I thought. But that had been more than a week ago. And here I was again, still none the wiser.

The office was on a floor of an industrial unit, on an estate somewhere around where the old railway yard had been, in the days when they used to move freight on the tracks, before we took to clogging the roads up with lorries, carting bananas from Southampton to Liverpool for storage, then down to Southampton again for distribution. Or fish from Scotland for smoking in Cornwall, before the return trip to stores in Scotland again. Most of Newbury's rail freight yard had been built over by the new Sainsbury's, which had also involved putting traffic lights on the existing A34, which must have helped the congestion loads.

If the office had been chaotic before, it was now something else again. Two large rooms full of people led off a corridor, where people with dogs were waiting to see the new quartermaster, or just waiting around. Someone was rocking back and forth half way down the corridor, chanting mantras. The door to the only toilet wouldn't close properly due to a large cable that was running out through its window, presumably for the CB mast. 'Sing, or have no modesty' said the sign. This was truly a place without sanctuary.

Somebody took us aside to a stairwell to discuss our plan. It was a secret plan and there was less chance of it being discovered if we talked about it somewhere unbugged. Which the office certainly was. Pete, myself, a smallish, dark haired, northern girl called Cath and one other had been brought together as none of us had been arrested yet. If we all got arrested at the same time, there was a chance someone might be able to put a good case for our defence and in doing so, make a good case against all the arrests taking place under the Criminal Justice Bill.

So that was our mission – to get arrested, though preferably not for anything more than Aggravated Trespass. Not GBH, for example, and presumaby not for resisting arrest. We piled into another car and headed down to Great Penwood. The car dropped us off by the brick bridge on the small road that ran through the middle of the wood. As we set off into the woods a man was shouting from the doorway of a coach,
"Warwick people, back at the coach by five o'clock please!" which made the whole thing seem like a school trip, for a moment or two.

After an expanse of muddy ground, half firm with the frost still in places, we hit the first camp. A few small benders and tents were scattered around, a few people sat half listless by a smoking pine fire. Every few hundred yards or so there was another camp like this, sometimes with the beginnings of wooden defences, usually with a few treehouses somewhere up in the pines above us, trails of blue polyprop hanging down everywhere from the untrimmed ends of the walkways. Gaps were opening up in the trees between camps and the people by the fires looked like they knew all about the ongoing sound of chainsaws. The path we were following took us, for the most part, right by the firepits. The two or three people manning each one looked up at us half friendly, half weary, like they'd seen more than enough people walk by them that morning, like they'd seen more than enough altogether.

The sound of chainsaws got nearer and nearer and eventually we could see the line of neon yellow through the trees. The security were out in their hundreds, blocking the path we'd been following and enclosing an area of two or three acres. Chainsaw crews were busy in the centre and every so often a long, thin pine would fall to the ground, smashing through the spindly branches of the trees all around it on the way down.

Then I realised I recognised this place – we were stood on the bank, looking down over the trees to our right, a square clearing just infront, full of rotting old stumps and a swathe of brown bracken. This was where I had camped on one of first nights out from home, just after I'd left the potato famine, Somerset lads. I remembered it as it had been then for a moment; a tranquil place, the air full of darting birds. There were no birds here now.

People were up in the trees above us, stood on the crazy pathways of polyprop, or looking out from plastic covered twigloos. Someone was having a piss from a walkway, forming an arc between him and the ground.
"That's disgusting," said the guard infront of me, craning his neck for a better view. "But I suppose" he continued, clocking my unbothered look, "he doesn't have anywhere else to go does he?"

Pissing from on high was actually one of the secret pleasures of living in a tree, if you were a chap, though you generally didn't do it when people could see you. In Middle Oak, due to the proximity of the A4, I'd thought it prudent to piss in a bottle instead and empty this out into the wind. Provided there wasn't anyone below the tree at the time. Other times though, it was a minor highlight of the day, leaning against a branch, with a huge span between you and the floor. At night it was particularly satisfying, a eerie silence for several seconds before you heard contact with the ground, the interval giving an indication of your height, like dropping a stone down a well.

We were right up against the line of security now and they were proving to be pretty friendly, even amusing. Half of them wanted to make friends with us – it was better than just listening to our abuse and they were usually bored more than anything else, stood in a line doing nothing. A lot of them had been signing on prior to coming out here, but had been told they'd get their benefits stopped if they didn't sign up, whatever their ethics might be. Right now though, Cath was talking to a team leader, a red hat, a sassy black Londoner, trying to get him to hand over a load of polyprop that had been pulled from the trees.

"That rope belongs to us, it's our property!" she'd told him.

"All property is theft" said the Londoner, pleased with his joke, grinning his petty hypocrisy.

Just afterwards, the cordon began to move. The redhats, who'd been in a kind of huddle for a short while, emerged to shout at the white hats to start moving. The white hats dutifully slumped into gear, slowly at first as they were cold to the bone. The younger ones looked suddenly wild eyed with the commotion, some of the older ones swearing under their breath at the red hats, not liking getting shouted at. Soon they were all running in a rough medley along the footpath and we were running with them, trying to get past to steal the initiative on the next site, mingling with their ranks so we might end up inside the next cordon. Eventually they came to a halt and formed an abrupt wall infront of us.

The path had bought us to a place where we weren't on a bank any longer, the ground rising up either side to bring us on a level. I realised that they hadn't got anyone guarding a pile of felled pines on our right and made a break for it, clambering over the toppled trees. A shout went up behind me as I jumped from log to log; alarm from the guards, cheers from protestors, adrenaline in my blood, propelling me forward. It was hard to move too quickly though – holes underfoot all around me – and I hadn't gone more than twenty or thirty foot when I heard Cath cry out, "Jim! Look out behind you!" The next moment a white hat had jumped at my legs, sending us both crashing against the dead wood. Two of them led me back to the path, laughing, telling me not to do it again.

I headed round to the other side of the cordon, to try my luck there. There was more open space here and the security were packed together less densely. A large space mostly free of trees lay invitingly on the other side, the chainsaw workers a good way off in the distance. It was easy enough to walk along the line and, finding a small gap, barge through it. There were other security behind the front - a thinly scattered second line of defence, laying in wait for breaches like mine. I ran zigzagging past them, a guard dived to tackle me but I span off him, like this was rugby. Another guard went for my legs and again I spun free, guards closing round in the space infront of me even as it opened up, the third or fourth finally bringing me down.

I was dragged out, with less civility this time, and hauled up infront of a white haired policeman. He gave me an official warning, trying to sound authorative but obviously getting rattled. I had just commited Aggravated Tresspass under the Criminal Justice Act and if I breached the cordon again I would be arrested. Aggravated Tresspass was a clause aimed specifically against road protestors and hunt sabs. I had a rant, telling him I didn't recognise the legitimacy of the Criminal Justice Act. He looked back blankly for a moment before telling me that wasn't a matter for him. Even if he was the one enforcing it, I thought, though I realised there wasn't much point pursuing the conversation any further.

I should have tried to break the cordon again there and then but the truth was I bottled it and drifted instead towards a large knot of protestors at the corner of the cordon. People's clothing stood out in contrast to the security's neon; a rough swathe of ponchos and wax jackets and woollen jumpers, green and brown and dark blue or grey. Or bright pink, or altogether multicoloured; beaded with wet from a thin, gathering mist. People were mobbed up against the security, pushing against them when suddenly, under the barking command of a half dozen red hats, the security began to push back. Everyone was now giving ground, foot over foot, scrabbling in the mud, getting driven into a small band of young pines.

"Get in the trees!" a girl screamed, half hysterical and suddenly I saw what the whole thing was about. I jumped up the nearest tree without thinking, shinnying up it, wrapping my legs round the trunk. People were cheering and yipping again, pushing my feet and I'd totally forgotten I was meant to be getting arrested. Adrenaline kicked in familiarly; a white heat in my bloodstream, all the shouting suddenly roaring in my head and my chest.

Then a nearby policeman turned round and grabbed my ankle. They were meant to be here, I thought, as impartial observers. He looked youngish and scared and had obviously grabbed at me in a panic, forgetting in the heat just what his part was in this strange and heady game. I managed to break free of his grip though and climbed a few feet higher, but couldn't get a proper hold as there were no branches, only the rotten and breakable stubs that told where the branches had been. I kept on slipping down, cutting the backs of my legs on the bark and the stubs, trying to free the tapes on my harness that would let me just hang from the tree.

After only a very short couple of minutes, during which another couple of people had managed to climb trees, the cordon moved off.

"If he wants to play up there, leave him to it" said one red hat, dismissive in the face of defeat. I stayed in the tree for a little while longer, talking to the guy in the next tree along, unsure if they were calling our bluff and about to come back. Half and hour later, the coast looked clear enough and I climbed back down to the ground.

A friend from town was carrying around an urn of tea on a set of granny shopping basket wheels, a strange gleam in his eyes. There was a huge crowd of people. Everyone was milling around everywhere. It suddenly seemed sane in the treetops.

The security had moved north to the railway line, which this far east in the woods was in a wide, totally overgrown cutting, like a small valley. After a while sat on a log with Pete and some others, not far from the white hats, I thought it might be a good idea to climb a tree, in case they tried to expand the cordon. All thoughts of breaking through it again were now far away. The line looked impenetrable for one thing and besides, I was secretly scared of getting arrested. The thought of it was one thing, but actually doing it, deliberately, was another altogether.

Instead, as discreetly as possible, I undid my tapes and got them ready to climb a tree. The tree was only yards away from the white hats. No one was defending the trees here and I thought it would be too easy for them just to barge everyone on the ground out of the way again if they wanted them cut. The principle to climbing trees with tapes is a lot like prussiking; two loops round the tree like it was the rope, you hanging from your waist one step, then standing on your foot loop the next. I slowly inched my way up and had got three or four foot off the ground before the security realised what I was up to. Within moments I was surrounded by senior guards, all of them trying to pull me down. But, hanging from my waist loop, I wasn't going anywhere. The guards hadn't all figured this out though and carried on trying to pull me down.

"Careful" said a yellow hat in his forties "or we're going to end up hurting this one."

"Hurt him..." called a red hat from out by the line "...it's the only way to get him down!" The red hat looked stressed and aggressive, eyes bulging from a puffy red face, the sort of man you'd stay clear of on the street on a Saturday night.

The yellow hat gave him a dirty look for a moment before trying to undo my main carabina. My main crab was a large loop of metal fastening my harness together and was also what I was hanging from, the loop around the tree fastened to it. The yellow hat started to undo the carabina's screwgate and, though I tried to stop him, other guards had grabbed my hands. But even with the gate undone, the loop was caught in the top hook of the carabina. He tried to get the other guards to push me up, releasing the tension on the tape so I could be unhooked, but I sat back with all my weight, freeing a hand to hold my tape tight to the crab. They soon gave up, leaving me free to climb the tree. This was better than if they'd just left me alone in the first place, because now we all knew that they wanted this tree today, and all the ones round it.

"Another tree saved for England!" someone shouted, and we all pretended for a moment that it'd still be here next week.

I passed the time up there counting security. A book I'd read when I was younger, set among Napoleonics, had taught me to count ten men at a time. I reckoned there were about five hundred security that I could see, and I had enough time for a second and a third count. Apparently though, there were as many as 1600 security guards being used on route, so while it looked like I was right in the middle of everything, they were probably also working somewhere else, and this was just part of the action.

Before I'd been up in the tree any great time, the working day was over – something signified by the security breaking rank and then swarming past under me, wave after wave of neon, white hatted hordes.

I walked the rest of the embankment path with Pete and Cath and the other bloke, not alone in not having been nicked. The path was overhung with deciduous trees – low and dense and brown leaved and wet – the first dark waves of a winter evening gathering round us as we walked towards the A34 to hitch back to town. We got a lift almost immediately with a man returning from work who'd been at the fort building. We waved triumphantly at the horde of security, still waiting for their coaches like left behind children.

The next day I spent at Middle Oak, busying myself with a tat shelf in the treehouse so as not to feel bad about not going out to the action. It had been good for a day, but I knew if I kept at it any longer it would probably get a bit much. For hundreds of others though, the madness and carnage in Penwood and elsewhere was a daily reality; a place they'd put themselves in without question, dawn to dusk, day after day. For most people, that was their defining experience of Newbury; running around in the mist and the cold, dealing with a media circus and endless police and security and surveillance teams, and sitting up spindly pines all day long, freezing their tits off, watching the woods getting trashed. And then they'd get up and do it again.

I hauled up a spare piece of laminated chipboard and started to tie it into place above where I slept – two rungs of spare polyprop keeping it in place, or trying to. There was now just room to belly crawl from the door hatch – which still had neither a hatch or a door, making it just a hole – to the space where you could sit up on your elbows, roll a fag and listen to the radio. But while the rope held the shelf up, it never held it in place and if you nudged it by mistake tins of food would fall off, sometimes on your back, sometimes rolling out of the treehouse altogether, bouncing painfully off the branches on the way down.

The sides of my treehouse had still not been sorted, draughts spewing up all over the place. Most people had a nice canvas tarp, tied down securely and a carpet, and sometimes a little wood border to stop any possible breezes and make it properly snug. Some people even had burners. I had a hole in the plastic – a great seaming tear in the side where the wind had driven and flapped to the point of no return. I'd stuck another piece of plastic behind the tear, fastened with gaffa tape, and hoped it wouldn't get any bigger. The split was right next to my head as I slept, the new plastic an added percussion in the wind, so I had to have faith it would hold out. Otherwise I'd have to get an entirely new tarp from somewhere and that would be far too much bother, at this stage in the game. It seemed daft to be spending loads of time and energy making my home better to live in when it might only be here another few weeks. Living like this I had less to lose.

My treehouse stood out as a little blue dome, silhouetted against the skyline among the skeletal crown like a weirdly levitated tent. It looked homely from a distance and truly it was, only threadbare and breezeleaky, a short term affair that never seemed worth making nice. One solitary line of polyprop stretched all the way from near the base of the platform to another oak right by the A4. I'd forgotten who'd put it up – maybe it was Ruth and that geezer, maybe it was Badger. It had been meant as the start of a walkway, but it drooped so much in the middle it was clear it'd never work. You'd need steel cable for a distance like that, and even then you'd be pushing it. Somebody asked me early on if it was a telegraph wire to Granny Ash and that was what I told everyone afterwards, if it looked like there was a half a chance they'd believe me, which they usually did.

I gave up on perfecting my rope slung shelf system – gone were the days when I'd rabidly pursue a project to within an inch of perfection – and sat at the base of the trunk for a while. I could swear I could hear the faint sound of tinwhistles being played – snatches of tunes drifting as though from underwater, at the corner of hearing, off behind your shoulder or behind you, from the depths of the tree itself. Just a bit of stillness was all it took, and peace, and the tree would replay its memories; echoes and songs that could only be caught in the murmuring glimpses of music.

When it came to getting arrested, Pete wasn't so faint hearted, had no shelves to put up and no pressing appointments with ethereal music. He went out on actions all through the week, before finally getting arrested one day up at Mary Hare. He gave Granny Ash as his address but Granny Ash was under an eviction order so he was bailed off route. He'd been given the Newbury Sausage. If he was found breaking bail, he could be put in prison.

The exclusion zone looked like a sausage on a map, spreading a kilometre in all directions from the line of the route; a big, flatulent curve over the countryside. Maybe it was just as well that I hadn't got arrested, given the less than fanatic rota to man Middle Oak. A butcher in town had a sign over his window that said 'Home of the Famous Newbury Sausage' but he can't have known what he was saying.

I got told the next day, or the day after that, that everything north east of the Wantage road, besides the camps, had been cleared. That meant a huge chunk of woodland, the same area of trees that Snelsmore was a part of; old beeches and oaks. And the orchard. It brought it home to me everything around us would soon be gone. Not just the trees, but even the very hill I stood on would be torn apart – a huge series of cuttings ripped out of it to make way for an interchange.

It was impossible to live out on the land and not become attached to it. I'd get wistful on my way to and from Middle Oak – looking over to Granny Ash and her cousin as they stood out proud over the brow of the hill; green towers of ivy. And as far as the hill went, as the prospect of destruction grew ever more imminent, it started to feel like I was walking on air, like the landscape under me was becoming more insubstantial. Other times it felt pensive and heavy with the anticipation of what was to come. Maybe I was becoming numb with the prospect of it all, the numbness you get if you've just been hit by something larger than you, something too big to understand at first, pain only seeping in as an afterthought, if you ever woke up at all. I later heard the thought that it was an honour to be among the last to live on a piece of land before it was taken. But it was far from a sweet kind of privilege.

Sarah, I knew, was feeling equally fried and we hatched a plan to hitch down to Fairmile and chill out for a bit. But not before the next Sunday. Though people had tried to keep it a surprise, I'd nonetheless heard that a huge ceremony was planned for around Middle Oak, with a crowd of Druids due to turn up. It was something to look forward to, though it was still a week away and that seemed a very long time.

The next night I got woken by the sound of clinking bottles and muffled lad's laughter far below me. I looked out but couldn't see or hear a thing. A strong wind was blowing, probably a gale, though most nights were windy up here and any sound was now being carried far off. Perhaps it was another weird dream, another trick of the tree, a party underneath the branches in some land halfway to sleep. I contemplated climbing down to investigate but the thought of getting out of my sleeping bag and out into the wind was not tempting. Better by far just to ignore it all and drift back into the waiting chambers of sleep, which wasn't a difficult thing to do. My ability to sleep remained almost legendary throughout this part of the campaign and though it came from a sense of despondency rather than any innate security, it was nonetheless a great saviour. Possibly this night more than any other.

Richie and a few others had made a new bender inside the enclosure of the fort – a well measured, even looking construction with a sound, pallet floor. The man who'd given us a lift from Penwood appeared with his kids not long after and asked if he could use the bender during the day as a kind of workshop space for the kids – somewhere to go on a Saturday that involved being out of a house.

Looking out the next morning I could see the bender had been trashed; the tarp torn off and the frame half mangled. I put it down to the wind, but when I got down I realised the pallets had been thrown around. These were heavy, solid pallets, twice as big as normal ones and topped with thick boards of plywood, rather than thin slats. There was no way they could have been picked up by anything other than people. A dull pulse of rage rose up from somewhere just below my ribs. What if someone had been sleeping in there? My anger wasn't helped when I saw where they'd tried to tear down the barricade and when I remembered that I'd been lain idle in bed. I should have climbed down and cracked all their heads together, jumped out at them in the dark from the first fork in the trunk and sent them all packing. But there were bricks among the wreckage and when I found the bottles in the trench – gaffa tape round their tops and still stinking of petrol – the full seriousness of it all began to sink in.

Mr Bartley, the Columbo of Whittle Copse, reckoned the only reason they hadn't managed to get the molotovs alight was the high wind. Finally persuaded to tell the police by Mr and Mrs B, I was driven into the station later that day by Mrs Bartley herself. I'd never been inside a police station before, having thwarted my own destiny as one of the CJA four. It was ironic that I'd failed to get arrested in a place where people were getting pigged right, left and centre, without that much effort on their parts. Though it had transpired that the day I was down in Penwood, there'd been no arrests made at all, so perhaps they'd got wind of our plan.

I sat in an empty and dingy carpeted foyer, on one of a row of brown plastic chairs. Sat there waiting for a detective inspector to come over from Reading, I suddenly remembered the blim of dope someone had given me that still lurked in the fluffy depths of my trouser pocket.

Paranoid scenarios trooped out in front of me one by one, led by rabid sniffer dogs and underpinned by all-knowing inspectors who'd see the look in my eye, or would search me as a matter of course, just for the audacity of my coming to their cop shop unbidden. Finally, surreptitiously, I wrapped the blim – smaller than my thumbnail – up in a rizla, and dropped it into the bin in relief.

The detective inspector, when he turned up, turned out to be entirely unthreatening, only a bit overworked and with a mildly alarming moustache. The futility of the entire trip became apparent when I unveiled the bottle, which by that time had been handled by me and just about everyone else. The inspector raised a tired eyebrow. It had obviously been a very long day.

Back in Middle Oak that night I still felt safe enough, despite the attacks. If anyone tried to climb up I'd know about it – the whole tree lurching in response to their movements. And it was highly unlikely that any meatheaded lad would be able to climb the tree in the dark, however tanked up they there. The inspector had been surprised I hadn't realised there'd been storms blowing all week. I'd thought it was only a little more windy than usual.

False Alarms, Coppers and Rope in the Dark

A friend from town, who supplied a fair share of the alternative population with skunk and hash, came up a few nights later with his small dog and his fat dreads. He was thinking the time might have come for him to get properly involved with this whole malarkey, things getting as they were. I'd spent several happy nights with him in a pub the winter before, while I was chasing a townie girl and on the run from ill lit, windblown nights of solitude at Snelsmore. The girl was a barmaid in the Catherine Wheel, had clean black hair and wore tight, sleeveless tops. Pubs named after grisly martyrdoms are probably best avoided, by and large, particularly where women are concerned.

I'd got to know her after striking up a conversation with a dreadlocked man sat by the window. I'd just got back off the train after a trip to see my brother off to Australia and had convinced myself the man must be part of the campaign, maybe even a resident of the nebulous camp in Penwood. The journey back to my parents had been a bit of a nightmare, as I'd decided to try jumping the train and the same guard had appeared on three separate trains. I'd ended up having to sleep in a station lift somewhere near Reading. The journey back had been better.

The dreadlocked bloke had turned out to be a motorcycle courier, but I'd really needed a pint, and he knew this gang of girls so it hardly seemed to matter. Later, on the way to Newbury's only nightclub, herded with a throng of the Saturday night, just-out-from-the-pub pretty munted, a lad confided at the top of his voice that this was Newbury, this was what Newbury was about if you lived here, some mad night of chaos twice a week, everyone howling in release as we got swept round the wide corner from the blank, open square of the market place.

Crossing over the road to Granny Ash one evening, a man in his forties pulled over to hand me twenty quid.
"I just wanted to say thanks for what you're doing" he told me, before launching into an unbidden expounding of his viewpoint. "Newbury's not like it was. Nowhere is anymore really. They used to still herd the cattle up the High Street from the market place not so long back, in the Seventies. Now it's all cars and offices. Everything's changing. But nice one for fighting it." I nodded in agreement and we looked at each in a moment of recognition before he drove off. Profound things could strike without warning these days. All I'd been doing was crossing the road.

The nightclub, when we got to it, wouldn't let me in for having no shirt or clean, black boots. I sat by the fountain in the courtyard instead, talking to a bloke who turned out to be from a busking ska band, who'd I'd seen in my home town. The girl with clean hair came out to see me, but not for too long, this being Saturday night and all and this being Newbury's only nightclub.

But in subsequent nights in the pub with Fat Dread the drugs dealer - who wasn't the courier, but who I'd got to know anyway - he tried to indoctrinate me with his Rastafarianism, telling me stories of how young American Indians were growing dreads and turning their backs on their elders and their teachings. The sound system and the fat love of one world was the new religion now, according to Fat Dread. I wasn't entirely convinced by this apparent washing away of old wisdom, though one love was a thing I could believe in.

As for the girl with clean hair, though she'd been giving out leaflets about the campaign, she continued to show no real signs of wanting to visit the woods in winter and soon I gave up on townies altogether. It didn't help that I'd given her what I called a piece of 'magic wood', which was actually impregnated with luminous fungi. I'd told her to look at it with the lights off. I hadn't realised that the fungi died off once removed from the woods.

I sat up late into the night with Fat Dread and with Ceri; a friend of Sarah's who'd just materialised from the depths of Wales. Fat Dread was talking about maybe building a treehouse in Rickety Bridge. It was a fine night, with the stars out and all the trees blue and just for now, everything seemed assured and peaceful. Ceri sat wrapped in a black cloak, stately and friendly at once and when Fat Dread went home with his dog, we stayed up talking a good while longer.

The news was the contractors were starting to venture out of Penwood more and more. As most of the camps were in larger or smaller areas of woodland, they were felling everything around a given camp, taking all the trees that weren't already defended. They'd been working on Reddings Copse the last few days, the biggest area of woodland outside Penwood, besides Snelsmore. I'd envisaged things as a long wait, then mayhem, then it all being over; not some drawn out, piecemeal bloodbath we'd be forced to witness, them taking the trees bit by bit.

I woke up to the sound of Ceri calling me from the ground and stuck my head out of the hatch that wasn't a hatch. There'd been a thick frost and from here the ground looked like a million crystals, Ceri stood out in her cloak, looking up clear faced, like a rock among water. She shouted up that there were diversion signs on the roads nearby, making a good chance of there being an eviction here or at Granny Ash. Teams of spotters would go out each morning, cold and unsung, keeping a look out on the major road junctions for security and police. The main convoy would never be too hard to spot, consisting as it did of several large coaches, besides scores of police wagons and conspicuous landrovers.

I let down the rope and Ceri prussicked up, joining me in a bout of rollies till Badger rolled up to give us the all clear. The convoy had landed elsewhere.

Later that day I was given a big box of eviction stash food. A quick rummage revealed loads of instantly edible stuff – things that could be eaten without the stove I didn't have. The box was a good development and I strapped it securely to a branch near the hatch, not having room for it inside, even with the shelf.

Badger appeared again not long after and we discussed a plan we'd been hatching. A good few poles were left over from the fort building – poles that were either too long or too heavy to be lifted over to the tree, and which now sat halfway there in the field, waiting for inspiration. Badger's plan was to build a tripod tower, exactly halfway between Middle Oak and the tree by the road, which would allow a proper, working walkway. It would take some pretty serious work, would require the help of a fair few people and need a load more poles to boot, but we were sure it was do-able. For now though, we just stood in the middle of the field gesticulating wildly with our arms, glad to have some semi-imaginary escape from our impending doom.

Back at the fort we rummaged through the accumulating pile of tat that people had seen fit to drop off; piles of rope and fencing wire for the most part. This random stock taking was suddenly intruded on by two policemen, all done up in commando gear; woollen hats and multi pocketed waistcoats and trousers, all in black. They bounded up to us with Judge Dread jaws and stuck a photo of an innocuous looking couple under our noses. The couple had apparently absconded with a toddler they were looking after but didn't have full legal rights to. Now the bobby commandos were going from camp to camp, demanding whether people had seen the abductors. It was hard not to feel like you should comply without question where a missing child was concerned, but somehow the whole story seemed a bit tenuous. And the police, who seemed overly edgy and more than a little disingenuous, were taking a keen note of everything on site. It was all a bit convenient for them, having to tour the camps like this, right on the eve of evictions.

"Is there anyone staying in that tent?" Copper number one asked me, pointing at the Jimi Hendrix pavilion.

"Yeah, four people" I lied "They're away on an action at the moment." The copper's cogs whirred almost audibly for a moment, his face maintaining an impassive blank as he computed the likelihood of me telling the truth and the near impossibility of him ever corroborating it with any certainty. Badger commented they weren't very clear photos and was told they were photocopies of photocopies. The couple looked out at us; grainy and pleading their innocence.

"What..." said Badger "...you mean they stuck their heads in a photocopier?" said Badger. The coppers weren't impressed and very soon waddled off altogether, stiff with self-importance and very much none the wiser.

As a crowning finish to an already over eventful day, I managed to get stuck in the Bartley's while Scottish Clare and Mr B had a hour long barney about fox hunting.

Considering Clare was an ex hunt sab and Mr B was an ex hunter, it was pretty impressive they managed to draw short of spitting. Mr B was magnanimous in his opinions and Scottish Clare was clever enough to know better than shout her head off, rattling out narrowly controlled interjections, only really venting her spleen as we walked back to the camp.

They'd got onto meat and vegetarianism in the end, predictably enough, with Mr B's quantum leaps of common logic. Scottish Clare simmered now, out in the dark, half muttering opinions like the lid of a pan on low heat. Meat eaters were all a bunch of frigging hypocrites, she told me, they'd probably all get bowel cancer and die slow deaths, if they got was what coming to them. This wasn't the time to mention the tins of meat soup. Even if they had been donated.

As far as I was concerned, the problem lay in the amount of meat most Westerners eat, and the modern industry that supports, where animals are subjected to a wide variety of unnecessary cruelties, where vast areas of land are given over to growing their fodder and chemicals and hormones are applied with an almost religious zeal. Scottish Clare had good reason to be angry.

I reckoned that it was all a bit fucked up, in one way or another, as soon as people were removed from the things that they made, or consumed. That was half the reason they were building these roads, to transport more stuff ever further away from their original place, one huge dance of disruption that had started before anyone could remember, being fuelled now by expediency and profiteers into a cyclone that was sucking everything into it, larger than anyone now, faster and greedier, like it was a living thing. And who'd rein it in?

After eating some stew, I went for a long walk on my own in the dark. I needed the exercise, though I was fairly toned up from climbing up and down the tree all day long. I'd got it down to a fine art – a jump for the first, fine branches, then a swing to hook my legs over – up to the fork after that, ten foot or so up, a twist round the main fork on several fat side branches, then the hairiest bit where you had to let yourself fall, your feet still on the same branch, until your arms could reach the next climbable limb. It was only a span of a foot or two, while your upper torso was airborne, but it had taken a bit of getting used to. Bridging the gap meant stretching your leg up – something that had taken getting used to as well – sticking your knee in the crook of the branch. Knees got used a lot in tree climbing, some people knackering them up completely, usually in combination with heavy walkway use.

It was an easy climb after the hairy bit – ten or fifteen foot up to the hatch via branches that could have been made for clambering around on. The hairy bit - or the branch after it - were most people's baulking point, a kind of safety measure in a sense, for me. It was responsible in the end for a large hole in the left knee of my trousers. I might have got knee pads, but that would have been daft.

I walked out to the west, where the hill plateaued out in a flat series of roads and fields, made all the flatter and vaster by the continual wind and the black night. But it was good to stretch my legs, get away from the camps for a while and walk in a place that wasn't due to be completely annihilated. I made the decision that if I did nothing else that summer, I'd do lots of walking, tramping the land. It was the only thing that made sense any more.

When I got back I went to check out a newly completed bender across the track from Granny Ash, near where Pete's tent had been. The earth bank folded in on itself here in humps and curves, forming hollows in the moonlit coppice. The bender had been built by a guy called Simon, who'd been kicking around site for a while. He wore a thick overcoat and stripy woollen hat and was cynical and enthusiastic about things by even measure. He had a good burner, with a biscuit tin lid curved into shape for the door. The bender was up to a really good heat when I got there with Sarah and Ceri curled up inside, just back from a blat to Reading to get climbing supplies. Taking my jumpers off, I realised I'd forgotten what it was like to be warm. The only other burner was the diminutive Puff; just taking the worst of the chill from the air in the new monster communal.

The cold had been seeping into our bones – constantly around us and, until now, inescapable until you were wrapped up for the night. Sawing wood became an end in itself – just to keep you warm. Wood is said to warm you three times – once when you collect it, once when you saw it and once when you finally burn it.

As well as this sanctuary, Simon was also to be thanked for creating the mud pusher – half a split log on the end of a stick. Every morning, the mud pusher would be wheeled out to clear the quag infront of the firepit. It was a sign of how our spirits were getting on site that something so simple could bring us such joy. The mud pusher probably should have been consecrated and Simon canonised, though we contented ourselves with just pushing mud off the path.

Simon's bender became a regular refuge over the next few weeks. It wasn't very big, but there always seemed to be enough room for a few of us. We crammed in there on the coldest nights, actually sweating after a while, so you could go out in your t-shirt afterwards and not feel the cold, for a few precious seconds at least.

On an evening soon after, I came down to Granny Ash to be told most people were stringing up walkways in a group of aspens down the track. The aspens were tall and thin and had to be tape climbed. Though it was an effort climbing forty feet like this, I was eventually hung neck and neck, so to speak, with everyone else. Doug, Tami and Badger were all up here, along with some others, headtorches flickering about. Keith - fully booted still and unearthed from his communal obscurity - lent moral support, far on the ground below us, waving a luminous camping stick.

When it came to doing the walkways, we found the trees were so elastic you could just keep on tightening and tightening the lines as the trees got closer and closer together. It also meant that when you stood on a walkway, it could go slack, the two trees to which it was tied bending towards each other. We had to tighten several at a time, pulling a tree in several directions before the walkways were safe to travel on.

The trees were all so thin and so close together it felt like we were on some kind of stage backdrop – people's hunched silhouettes crawling up the black trees against the faintest of background light. It could have been a nautical opera, all the trees swaying back and forth with us on the end, except none of us were singing. Though there was a kind of music in my head.

The next afternoon I was up in my treehouse, reading, when I heard someone shout up from below. This was happening more and more now, more people finding a reason to tramp across the field and pay me a visit. The trouble was, it was impossible to see the whole camp from any position in the treehouse and people shouting up to you would invariably stand exactly where you couldn't see them.

Today it was a few maturish students down from Cambridge, including Paddy, who was Scottish. They were looking to set up a camp and the office had pointed them in the direction of Bagnor Lane. They just needed a final steer. We piled in Paddy's van, and set off to find the Lane; a challenge for me too as I'd never tried to get to it by road from here and it involved a circuitous route through the village of Speen. The fact that I kept on thinking about it as 'spleen' was sad, if a little inevitable. The road through wound round like an obscure tract of intestine, the very occasional pedestrian giving us bilious looks.

Paddy had just come back from Bosnia, as part of an aid convoy, where things were very different, not least because a lot of the places there didn't have any decent roads at all, unless you counted potholed tracks over the mountains. They sounded good enough to me, but then I wanted to travel the country with a packhorse and wasn't trying to drive a van full of food over them.

I'd been in Bagnor Lane only the week before, helping to put up walkways with Badger and a bloke from Snelsmore called Reuben. Reuben had messy brown hair, a proper outdoor coat, and was always manifesting things out of thin air like thermoses of hot coffee, or biscuits. He could turn the most windblown, rainsoaked field into a model of English propriety. He'd develop a glint in his eyes as we talked about walkways, call us both chaps and rub his hands together in happy anticipation. He was mad like Brunel; bridging the impossible, or like a lion tamer, only more cunning and without the moustache.

We'd just finished working on the second walkway and were sat on the ground drinking coffee when Potty Phil's head appeared through a gap in the hedge, attached to the

Pig Magnet. He dropped us off some snacks, including skipped bags of crisps - which seemed somehow bizarre - before speeding off, a thousand missions to accomplish on the enigmatic path of a blatting campaign flatbed.

I spent much of the next few days walking to Bog Camp as the other two worked, to try and rustle up people to help us connect the last few trees. I'd never been scared of heights before but here, unlike being in the middle of a wood, there were no surrounding trees to baffle our sense of altitude. On the last afternoon, as I was trying to climb a hairy stretch in the fading light, eighty foot up, my nerve went completely. I was suddenly trembling, my knees felt weak and I when I called down to Badger I even sounded scared. I was standing on a broad branch, unclipped, leaning against the smooth skin of the trunk, the next branch up too high to hold onto. I'd reached my limit and climbed down in the dark, waves of relief coming up as the ground grew closer.

When I got to the Lane with Paddy, having passed undigested through Speen, I helped him and his friends construct a tent like structure with some rope and a blue plastic tarp. I left them to it as they made the finishing touches, brewing up tea and contemplating with excitement the prospect of a night out in February, practically under a hedge. The camp was soon up and running, manned by a rota of people down from the University. It helped show that the campaign, always one of national significance, had somehow moved up a few notches, that it was now not just the concern of the few thousand directly involved, but that we acted on behalf of a growing multitude, who'd seen enough roads being built, who held out some hope that their children could walk in a country still fit to be lived in.

Around the Old Oak

The day before the Druid ceremony having finally arrived, I spent a few hours trying to tidy up the tat around Middle Oak. Besides the fencing wire and the rope, which had already been taken to other places, there were loads of fortification materials – bits of random wood; poles and pallets and chip board. The Jimi Hendrix tent now needed dismantling – Richie had disappeared again in to the bowels of London and I'd woken up one morning to see it mangled in on itself, never having been meant to survive for so long on such a windy hill. The poles joined the tat round the rim of the fort while the flysheet ended up at Seaview, forming another layer over the plastic tarp on their snug communal.

Ceri came and built a new bender out of the wreckage of the one trashed by the vigilantes. It was a graceful piece of work, finely rounded and topped with a white tarp and blue door, reminiscent somehow of something holy.

The resonation with Mother Mary was fairly pertinent. Imbolc, the Celtic festival that the ceremony would be celebrating, had been adopted by the Christian church under the guise of Candlemas – a typical continuation of older currents of believe. The Christian Church did this a lot, as a means of assuming the older currents within these islands, and therefore assuring their place in the continuing order of things. A continuation that only met with trouble with the coming to power of Henry the Eighth, after the untimely death of his elder brother, the young prince Arthur.

The habit of assumption adopted by the early Christian church, a story repeated worldwide, wasn't restricted to festivals; figureheads and goddesses had a part to play too.

In the Catholic calendar, Candlemas is officially the Feast of the Purification of the Virgin Mary, where candles are carried in procession; most likely adopted from a Roman festival, where the lights are a welcome blessing at that time of year. Imbolc is also the feast of St Brigit, who, though a historical figure, assumed much of the mantle of an older Goddess. A perpetual fire was kept in her honour at a monastery in Kildare until the reign of Henry.

The tragedy is that for far too long, people have been unaware, or have chosen to ignore or suppress these original roots, religions of the book compounding the difference with a difficult legacy of theological doctrine, which has more to do with the mechanics of a politicised organisation than with teachings of the prophets. It'd be a far better world if people chose to act from the heart a little more often rather than following things that are laid down in writing.

With Henry's ascendance and the break from Rome, the subsequent authority of word based religion in this country had as much to do with the ascendant power of the individual, fairly refreshing after some of the crooked machinations of the Roman church, as with theological shifts. In this country at least, this tension between individual power and higher authority reached a kind of resolution with the restoration of Charles the Second – the 'Divine Right of Kings' having been successfully challenged, but a king still found to be needed. I reckon if we were a little more honest about the sacred function of monarchy, for England at least, safely removed from an overtly pragmatic domain, we'd go a long way to understanding why it continues to have such emotive appeal. The question is whether our current heads of state, built as they are on foundations on conquest, can have any relevance to the times we now face.

With the day of the ceremony upon me, I made sure I was up, for at least once in my life, to greet people as they arrived. The first was a guy called Andy, down from Skyward, who'd apparently organised the whole thing. He had a pointy black beard and moustache and wore a purple robe but seemed strangely earthy all the same, like he'd just popped out of the earth infact, or slept there at night. He asked me if I minded that my home was about to be invaded by loads of people, which of course I didn't, though it was nice to be asked, even if it was too late to do anything about it.

More people began to arrive, including handfuls of Druids. They were pretty easy to spot, wearing white or off-white robes with individual touches like animal skins or shawls over their shoulders, giving them the appearance of a handful of ancestors. One or two of them stopped to pull out knobbly staffs from the boots of estate wagons, looking wild eyed.

People began to mill in from all directions and Tara from Granny Ash came over to thrust something into my hand. It was a necklace she'd got in India, that she'd had blessed by the Dalai Lama and was formed in the image of many carved, white skulls.

"You should wear it today Jim" she told me. "This is your day." I put it on and watched as more people flooded into the fort.

All the Druids had arrived before long, about two dozen of them, having come from all corners of the country. As they formed a circle round the tree, a hundred others from town and different parts of the route were stood in the fort all around them. It was impressive how many people the fort could hold – a sea of shoulders and faces looking expectantly in from every direction. It was the first full moon in Febuary – the festival of Candlemass, or Imbolc, the first seeds of spring and the return of the

Goddess's maiden aspects, after the dark days of the Hag of Winter.

Afterwards, though I'd been stood in one place all along, I remembered the ceremony from different directions, as though it had been us dancing around the Druids and the Druids stood still, not the other way round. As they danced, clockwise, some of them spinning around on the spot, some of them banging drums, there was a tremendous feeling of energy rising up from the ground and funnelling down from the sky through the branches of the oak, which was suddenly thunderous and alive.

The dancing white figures seemed to be at the centre of a chorus of energy – the earth seemed to sing and then... noticeably wobble. At least a few times, like a pulse that came rising up from behind the scenes of things, expanding everything it touched for a moment, which lasted a very long time.

The ceremony ended with everyone chanting 'Awen' the Druid's word and mantra for power and magical inspiration. It was a powerful experience, with so many people gathered together like that. These were proper Druids, no doubt about it.

A Druid woman with raven black hair had helped lead the ceremony along with a man with a wolfskin round his shoulders. She located me across the circle and asked everyone to bless me for protecting the tree. As everyone chorused "Bless you Jim!" I probably should have said something mighty and inspired, but the moment had taken me completely by surprise and I looked around, dumbfounded and awestruck before hugging a friend stood close by.

Andy from Skyward walked into the centre then, drawing our attention to a young oak sapling that had been placed by Middle Oak's trunk for the duration of the ceremony. It would be taken away and planted elsewhere, we were told, where it could grow to maturity in safety. He said that not one of us knew whether Middle Oak would live or fall, that there was still every chance of stopping the road.

His conviction was persuasive and I tried to take his words to heart, but I'd had the dream where the tree herself had told me she was going to go. I couldn't tell anyone here that, especially not today, with everyone looking so inspired and hopeful. It was a load I'd have to bear in secret.

The ceremonies and speeches (or non-speeches) over, everyone rushed forwards to the tree. We'd been given out ribbons to tie to the branches – clouties – that showed our reverence and good wishes. Middle Oak had some branches just right for this, a bushy protuberance of twiggy strands stuck out all the way round at chest level. People clustered in bunches, tying on cloth with raw, exposed fingers. Very soon the branches were full of colour. Some people had even tied on one of their dreads.

I began to realise just what a symbol Middle Oak was becoming to many people. The only tree that was gaining similar attention was the Pine in Reddings Copse – one hundred and twenty foot high and just visible from the Granny Ash firepit. The Pine was developing a cult of reverence not just for its height but also because it would be hard to evict – it was visually and actually a bastion of resistance and it cheered people up to think about it.

Middle Oak was relatively vulnerable but it was also much more visible – in a field near the road and inherently a symbol in its own right; a rounded crown of an oak on a hilltop in England. A lot of people had given their time and energy to the tree now; my concern and affections stood only as those of one among many. The clouties – a hundred prayers on the wind - stood in testament to that.

Clare and Shaun had returned from a week away to find their bender in the middle of a stream, the damp earth in the midst of the half ring having given ground to the intermittent rain. If I'd have known, or been a little less preoccupied, I might have kept an eye on it for them, but they'd seemed to disappear into a land of their own for a while and I hadn't even realised they'd been away. Ruefully, they wrung out their bedding and set up again at the edge of the trees. They were back in the field now, just about, on the high side of the woods, where the slope rose up from the meadows at the end of Bagnor Lane.

After the ceremony, perhaps still harbouring memories of the flood, they moved away from Seaview altogether, down to the apparent sanctuary of Rickety Bridge. Though that was no less likely to be prone to unreasonable wet. By now Seaview had a steady, but rapidly changing population. Mark who built boats had become a constant figure, together with one or two of the Isle of Wight crew. If anything, Seaview was more exposed than Middle Oak, the north easterlies from Donnington doing their worst. The Seaview fire would normally move about seven foot during the course of a night, embers and everything blown steadily towards their communal, a dark streak of ash in the grass come the morning. I'd go over and visit most evenings now – another round to the day to break up the waiting, another excuse to walk somewhere and try and get warm in the process.

There was a guy from Seaview who was always coming and going to Wales, where the opencast mine protest that had started in the summer was still going. It was in its final stages now, one of the sites already having been evicted, where the climbers had later admitted to getting stuffed. Wales seemed a long way away and darker and colder, a huge mass of wildness somewhere outside the light of the firepit, somewhere off past the B road, if you kept going a bit. There was a sense too of things kicking off everywhere, of more going on than you could possibly get your head around. There was no getting round it; this was a height of our tide.

On a day when a pale, winter sun had come out, shedding a weak but welcome warmth, I went on a walk to visit Snelsmore. There was now an even greater sense of time running out and I thought I ought to take any opportunity to see the old woods again. The sun gave a faint amber glow to the fringes of twigs in the hedgerows and frost whitened grass and the countryside echoed to the sound of hammering. Hammering from Seaview and Bagnor Lane and over the fields from Bog Camp and the new nearby sites of Castle Wood and Elephant Tree. Everyone was building platforms and the sound of the hammers, warped and echoing weirdly with the cold, bit into the winter silence, muffled only mildly by their distance. There was a distinct impression of an army hidden in the woods all around me, undeniable though out of sight, knocking together defences, or engines of war. Only the occasional treehouse stood out in view; up in the tips of a tree higher than those all around it, another domed sentinel stood out in the skyline. All I saw of the people though were the folks on the ground at Bagnor Lane, surrounded by organised straw bales, doing the washing up.

I hung out at Skyward, where the firepit had such a flux of people it was being referred to by some as a café. The Womble Café infact, Wombles being the posse from Skyward; bimbling on the Common. I shared a few spliffs for my part and took in the gigantic trunks of the oaks. For girth and height they were still like nothing I'd ever seen. Even in Stanworth, which had felt ancient and wild, the oaks weren't so massive and towering as this. These were true English standards, columns hidden away in the heartland, as solid as any cathedral and more lively.

There was a tunnel somewhere on Snelsmore now, the entrances kept a close secret. People had been working on it for months and when the contractors came in, it would stop them using heavy machinery for fear of collapse. It would be the first ever tunnel eviction and nobody knew how long it would take, or whether it might manage to stop work altogether. There was a quiet air of excitement and triumph about the tunnel and people looked pleased whenever you asked about it.

A party of yellow jackets appeared as we sat there, their coats glinting ominously as they entered the woods, the complete contrast between the bare and brown woodland saying it all, as it always did. They came closer into the woods and began to wander around, still in a huddle, probably surveying. A party of people went to face up to them while others round the firepit took to their drums. It was a sudden inversion of the stillness – the invasion and the coats, the drums and the oaks and the adrenaline that came with the prospect of confrontation all conspired to send my blood pounding in my chest and my temples. The enemy was already on our borders and the relative peace seemed suddenly more transient than ever.

I went back to the office, unable to fend off any longer the need to sort out Middle Oak's paperwork. This time I had the good fortune to run into someone I knew and, miraculously, they had time to help me out. All the other camps round me seemed to have sorted this out by now – sending in legal details to the Treasury Solicitor – and I was getting worried that my name would go down blackly in history, for having lunched something so fundamental out, letting my camp be swept away for want of legal protection. But when my friend phoned up a solicitor that worked for the campaign, he was told there was no point in my sending anything off, as it would only be doing their work for them. I was confused, but relieved that I hadn't done something that could have been detrimental and relieved that I'd nothing to do.

What had probably happened was that all the other camps had already received eviction orders and been compelled to respond in order to have any chance of a court case. It looked like Middle Oak had somehow escaped the net, so there was no point in my drawing attention to myself. It was the best result I could have hoped for.

On the way down the stairwell I saw a girl from Stanworth I knew, descending the flight below me in a hooded coat, trimmed with fake fur. I called out to her and we got talking. I liked this girl a lot – she'd been part of a tin whistling posse from the East End, who'd always been trying to drag me up to a treehouse so I could teach them my tunes. It felt like a miracle to be talking to her again, me being single and her remembering who I was. She had bright, almond shaped eyes and auburn dreads and asked me back to her camp. I thought about it for a bit, about leaving Middle Oak unguarded for the night, about how it was unlikely that anyone would see fit to look after it the next morning and how it would be just my luck if something kicked off the one time I'd left it alone. We said our goodbyes and went back to our separate trees, miles apart. I didn't see her again. The last I heard she was somewhere in Europe, as part of a travelling circus. I'm fairly sure she never grew a beard.

That night I dreamt of a huge procession through London like a massive funeral, or trooping of the colour, with black and ornate carriages, hung with silver and pulled by scores of black horses. And in the carriages sat Russian princesses, returned from the depths of obscurity like Anastasia, their noses hooked a little with age, silver hair flowing down to their shoulders, benign and knowledgable smiles in their eyes. One of them pointed behind me, where a zebra crossing led to the mouth of an underground station, a score of lost children stood by the gates. They'd been there for ages, as long as the princesses perhaps and somehow I had to lead them all out, a role that had fallen to me from my sleeping in the vantage point of this tree.

Dreams like this got under my skin, ebbed away the border lines between my mind and the world around me, images coming suddenly and vivid as soon as I closed my eyes for the night; Ceri looking up from the ground, then another face, my own, as though I was the tree now, my younger self waiting on tamer foundations, looking up into the wilds.

Not long after, a group of rock climbers appeared at Middle Oak, just down from North Wales. They'd come to put up their new invention – a fifty foot, single pole, metal tower. They worked through the night to erect it, about thirty foot east from the oak. I helped out for a few hours but my fingers soon froze and I left them to it; they seemed enthusiastic and knew what they were doing and I sensed I was beginning to get in the way. The morning revealed it as comprised of four separate sections, one on top of the other, each held in place with three or four steel cable guy ropes, bunting strung along them to prevent nasty accidents. At the very top was space for a rectangular, steel plate – where one or two people could rest come the eviction.

It was a fantastic piece of engineering, though most of us looked at it slightly bemused; a strange aberration of steel and wire on an otherwise pristine hill. Certainly there was no one to be found with much enthusiasm for climbing up it. It quickly became known as 'the robo tree' and was originally topped with a large purple flag, painted with a white, winter oak. When this got blown down I stashed it with the other tat in the fort before stringing it up in the topmost branches of Middle Oak itself. It was a goodsized, square flag, nothing short of a standard infact, and people took to it immediately. This was difficult because I'd realised it cracked in the wind something chronic, the tops of the branches only being ten foot or so above my sleeping head. It made the whip cracking of the tarp around me seem like the rustling of a plastic bag. But there was no choice of taking it down, people's response being so enthusiastic.

Flags and towers or not, things were still hung very finely - the outcome of our endeavours were far from clear and the world hung around us as heavy as ever. Only a thin hope remained, a certain bloody mindedness and a determination to see this all through to the end.

The next weekend, a big march had been prepared – from Snelsmore going south along the route. It was a national rally, with much coverage in the press and a chance for everyone in the country to show their opposition to the bypass and to road schemes in general. There still seemed to be some chance that, with enough pressure, the government might back down and scrap the road. An article had appeared in 'Construction News' saying that the bidders for the main contract were getting worried about the cost of the protest and bad publicity, with

370

subcontractors wary of getting involved as they couldn't afford not to get paid if the road got scrapped.

An impassioned plea appeared in the Telegraph, written by a Marchioness, urging 'barbours and tweed hats' along with other 'titled folk' to join the march. A sympathetic civil servant had told her that the government would only reconsider the scheme if Middle England was seen to be against it.

It looked like the march would come down as far as the Visitor's Camp – an off route reception site that had been set up just below the Kennet. On the morning itself, expecting a horde of respectable visitors to come flocking by, I thought I'd better make myself busy and started to work strengthening the fortifications. Several semi-dovetailed railings later, Ruth from Fairmile appeared, bounding across the field with a big grin. A big Fairmile posse had come up to perform the Lorax and were now down at the Granny Ash firepit, getting in costume and putting on makeup, much to the consternation of everyone else on site, who sat looking gingerly at the manifestation of this bunch of apparent theatrical types. They wanted me to be a Barbaloop Bear.

On many levels it was to be a monumental day, a day fit for listening to speeches or standing silently in your harness and receiving heartfelt accolades. Brave Sir Robin was given medals by a World War Two veteran. I ran around in a stitched up set of old curtains, with a black nose and whiskers painted on my face.

The veteran, Fred Gibson, had been carrying the Union Jack upside down, as a symbol of the nation in distress. Robin had tried to give the medals back but Fred wasn't having any of it,

"I didn't really deserve medals just because I was born at that time, an accident of birth. Now you guys are carrying on that struggle. Bloody marvellous. I wish I was young again. I'd be there."

The march – 7,000 strong – didn't make it so far as the Visitor's Camp, a last minute alteration having been made to cut down on miles. It finished instead in the field by Bagnor Lane, a flood of barbours and mountaineering jackets and acrylic hats. An army marquee had been set up and some people were giving speeches somewhere, far off in the crowd from me. After we did the Lorax, Ceilidh threw acorns from the Fairmile oak into the crowd. As twilight set in, Badger and some others were still working away above everyone; walkwaying high in the beeches. It gave me a feeling of desperation to see them up there. It felt like the last hour.

There turned out to be no work on Monday, the following day. They knew there'd still be loads of people down from the march and had decided to cut their losses and declare a 'training day' instead. A big meeting was held under Middle Oak to decide what to do. Several dozen people turned up, fired up though white faced from the cold. This was obviously a valuable chance for us to go on the offensive and an office action was declared. Our target would be Tarmac – the main contractors for the building of the road, who also happened to have a big office in Newbury – a dark, stony, blocky building, just across a mini roundabout from the job centre. I stayed by my tree, once again glad for an excuse to cop out, a rising tide of adrenaline already going to my head with the prospect of the thing.

The news got back to me that evening – the office had got trashed, files were thrown around and rearranged, computers had water poured on them or were otherwise deactivated, staff evacuated or locked themselves into rooms until police turned up. It drew a lot of bad press, was seen by many as the unacceptable face of protest, as though stood in a field and shaking your fist was all well and good, but damage to property, even that owned by those acting against the public interest, was over stepping the boundaries of propriety. As if it wasn't anything less than criminal damage to carve up nine miles of countryside for the sakes of profits and dubious political manoeuvres.

The protest movement, in some quarters, had developed an image of harmless, pacifistic and loveable characters who put themselves in the way of action, looked very admirable in front of the camera but never really put a step out of line. But we were far from harmless – that would have meant we were ineffective and behind even the cutest of activists was the recognition that while non-violence was always to be upheld, the whole idea was to get in the way and make their life difficult. We were there to cost them time and to cost them money and anything that could help this was to be encouraged. To think anything else would be to assume that all we were up to was a kind of glorified publicity stunt.

However gratifying and useful favourable reporting might have been, even in the face of complete demonising by the media, most of the people here would have still carried on, sure enough of their convictions. We wanted to stop them. Physically. That's what gave the movement its sense of purpose and power. Sabotage was a part of that.

It would never be talked about, unless you were part of the plan; criminal damage held a heavy sentence and it was best to assume that very few could be trusted. And if you didn't have a need to know, if you weren't immediately involved, you knew not to ask questions if people were muttering conspiratorially at the edge of the firepit, or wandering off into the night without explanation. Apart from anything else, it excused you from suspicion, not showing undue and dangerous curiosity.

Tears for the Heartland

We weren't quite prepared when they came for Granny Ash the first time, only a few people were up in the trees and no one made it to the aspens down the track. It wasn't an eviction, merely clearance work but it was a shock to the system to have so many security around the camp. They strung out in a loop infront of the firepit and benders, with nothing for us to do but watch as the chainsaws got to work.

I stayed by Middle Oak for most of the day, sat with my back to the trunk, trying to block out the noise that was drifting across. Tami came over later on, looking distressed. She'd been walking back and forth down the security line for hours, trying to make them feel uncomfortable, but had finally had her head done in by the invasion. I went across in the evening, once the security and police had left. A couple of big trees on the edge of the bank had been felled. They'd been walkwayed up but there weren't enough people up there to defend them. And all the thick growth below and around the camp had been trashed. There was now an eerie view over to Wash Common and the west of the town from the kitchen bender, the sodium lights burning harsh and odd in the dark. The line the security had stood in was still visible from a string of white, polystyrene cups, half of them crushed underfoot or thrown into the foliage, semi luminous in the twilight like plutonium. Everyone was dazed, but dinner happened regardless. We ate in near silence.

The day they came for Snelsmore I was being interviewed by a man from the BBC. He was part of a team doing a pilot youth TV programme and, this being their second day around the oak, I was beginning to wonder what I'd let myself in for. Sat by the foot of the trunk now, the man in question with his radio recording gear all set up and we could just hear the sounds of chainsaws coming down on the faint north easterly, down from the direction of Donnington. A dawning nightmare was creeping in around my ears now, the thought of that place, of all places, being removed. A helicopter was flying round and round in the air above us, the last traces of any kind of peace being steadily scrubbed out.

Snelsmore was the first proper eviction. The clearance work was over. They'd come in around four in the morning and told the only person down the tunnel that they'd send dogs down if they didn't come out. It was a bluff, apparently, but it worked. They knew exactly where the tunnel was.

I had an appointment to keep with a doctor in Sussex and had asked a lad called Julian from Granny Ash to look after Middle Oak for the few days I'd be away. Julian was German and was part of a crew who had been at Granny Ash for a while. They were friendly and hard working, though only a few of them spoke much English. Apart from supporting us by their presence, they'd come over to pick up a few tricks, wanting to stage a protest of their own to save a wood from development. With the worldwide attention we seemed to be getting, it was good to think what we might be inspiring elsewhere.

The BBC crew, which, with the cameramen gone, now only consisted of an affable man and woman in their early thirties, spotted Badger walking across the field in a blue blanket; wrapped over his shoulders against the cold like a cloak. They hadn't been working in the media long which is probably why I quite liked them. They came back fuming about what their editor had asked them to do, though they wouldn't tell me what and didn't do it anyway. They were mesmerised by the whole thing – the tree, the music I'd played, being outside, being outside of London. They reckoned Badger looked like a King. The tides were growing stronger and stronger around us, more attention was being heaped on our shoulders as things came to a head. It was unthinkable to consider leaving now, it was impossible to think how we could have ever not been here. Everything had led to this and now we just had to ride it out. I was dreaming of the summer already, sat on a hill a long way away, somewhere peaceful, as if things would be the same after this.

For all that, I knew it was important for me to keep the appointment with the doctor, if only to avoid further hassle and keep the authorities off my back. I knew Julian could be trusted, and it would only be for a few days. Although it seemed mad to be going with everything at such a height, my appointment seemed unshakable and when I got into the BBC couple's car and we wheeled onto the A4, it was not without a profound sense of relief. For a day or two I'd be out of the wind and the cold and far away from the sound of chainsaws.

When we got to London, I was invited into the BBC building, to look at the stuff they'd filmed so far. We were stopped by the famous red and white barred checkpoint, a strange feeling of the boundaries between the everyday and the semi mythical dropping away from me as I stared up at the main building and its studded concrete. The prospect of looking at myself on a screen seemed suddenly indulgent though, and there was no telling what might happen if I stepped through those doors. Feeling less than completely together and wary of being manipulated, with a scenario of spilling Bruce Forsyth's tea in the canteen flashing unbidden into my mind, I declined their offer and climbed out of the car. I made my way across the road to a waiting tube subway, which suddenly seemed identical to the one in my dream, where all the children had been waiting.

I made my way back up to Newbury a day or two later, catching a minibus up from Brighton. I stood waiting for it in the evening dark by the side of St Peter's church, traffic thundering by blackly on all sides. A friend appeared, who'd been part of the mushroom picking posse under Beacon Hill. She'd recently moved to Brighton from Glastonbury, swapping her woolly jumper for a bomber jacket. Now she was wearing a green army jumpsuit. The mini bus was full of anarcho types animatedly discussing the revolution. Not having much to add to the conversation, and the rest of them mutually indifferent to my presence, I sat at the back staring at the verges go by in the dark, happily alone with my thoughts, lost in the momentum that had taken hold of everything for months and which would tonight put me back in the oak.

When I got back to Granny Ash, Badger filled me in on the news from Snelsmore. The security hadn't guarded the site properly at night so people had been able to sneak in. They reoccupied trees that had been cleared of protestors though not felled yet. The spiral beech was still standing, which cheered me up a lot. And as it was now Sunday, people had had two days to consolidate losses, put up new walkways, put up a barricade on the ground from cut wood. There'd been a strong turnout of people on the ground – a swelling of anger from the locals. A lot of people in Newbury had a long standing connection with Snelsmore, and they weren't going to see it go without a fight. Police horses had driven the local gentry into the brambles.

A lot of police made a point of saying they didn't agree with what was happening, the destruction they were being asked to protect. Some of them had known Snelsmore since they were kids, some of them were in tears, their backs to the screams and the carnage. They'd come for

Snelsmore first as it was one of the oldest and strongest camps and seen as a spiritual headquarters. Good friends of mine were up there, going through the mill, all hell breaking lose in the heartland.

This had been my home, the first place I'd come to live as an independent adult. Arguably, it makes no sense to get attached to a place you know is in such a precarious position, but doing otherwise was practically impossible. The place was alive, and Snelsmore was more than just a habitat – she had a character all of her own, and living there had been a profound blessing.

And, up and down the route, up and down the camps throughout the country, it had been this way for many others. People were able to live close to nature in a way that, in other times, is virtually impossible. The protests had given this opportunity to people who had precious few means of living on the land, having been coerced into urban living ever since the mechanisation of agriculture and the rise of the mills.

And to be out here again on the earth gave us strength, and our common purpose bound us together as a true tribe – not merely making the right noises, but acting together with our hearts. With the evictions, all that was now looking in danger.

It felt like a hole had been cut in me to know Snelsmore was half gone, a cold vacuum somewhere in my chest, phantom limbs flailing around in my mind.

I retrieved my low whistle from Pete's van and talked to a few new arrivals – Ralph and Demelsa. Ralph was ginger bearded and rough faced, like he'd been in the woods a long time. Demelsa was young and black haired and up from Devon, full of the understated soundness that many Devonshire teenagers have. There was a lad with Demelsa and they said they had a feeling in their guts that we'd get evicted the next day. I didn't take them too seriously, having lost faith in gut feelings somewhere down the line, and tucked my whistle high in the poles of the kitchen bender, to keep it out of harm's way.

On my way back across to Middle Oak, I found Badger and another guy working on a platform in a tree right by the A4. I stayed with them, by the foot of the tree, tying things on when they needed them. Badger had dubbed it the DNA Oak as the trunk was one long, fat twist. After a few hours I left them to it, cold to the bone myself and well ready for sleep.

I was woken by the voice of Mr Bartley, sounding only slightly more agitated and commanding than usual. He was shouting up at me from the ground, demanding to know whether I was awake, whether I was in the tree at all. I lifted up the tarp by my head and drew in my breath. A long and unsettling line of white vehicles were strewn along the side of the A4 and the smaller B road. The field on the other side of the A4 was full of neon jackets. It was cold and early and none of it seemed quite real.

"You were supposed to be keeping a look out!" Mr B shouted, unpleased. Fortunately, Badger and the other man had only just finished work on the DNA platform when the hordes had begun to roll up, so the alarm had been raised in the end after all.

I watched as the main bulk of security slipped over the bank, into the woods and out of sight. Somebody climbed up Middle Oak to help guard it; we were certainly close enough to be under threat. Before very long a huge crowd of protestors was gathered in the field over the A4, trying to stop a couple of cherrypickers make their way to the trees. The whole field was a blur of people from here, the crowd only defined by the scattering of figures at the ragged edges. The cherrypickers loomed over the shoulders of the security surrounding them, their cranes folded back over their tracks, the cabs standing proud at the back; temporarily thwarted and trundling engines of doom.

Right up to the last hour, many people's hopes stayed alive that the road could still be stopped, that even this far down the line it might be called off. The latest big thing was that, if they hadn't cut all the trees before March, it'd officially be bird nesting season, and they'd be prevented from cutting by law. It was a new directive that had come into effect the last year. Some people spouted about this almost evangelically, all their faith in it. But the day they came for Granny Ash was already the fourth of March, and they clearly weren't worried about birds.

If the cherrypickers could be kept from the trees, there might still be some chance, but all people could do was watch and shove as they drew across the field, uncheckable, slowly closing the gap of people's last hope. And what would follow was so certain, was still so hard to picture, that people were crying out in horror and anger – I could hear it from the oak; a rising cry from a field full of people, who now knew the way things were going to go, but who weren't willing to let them go quietly. A steady stream of people were being led out to the meat wagons waiting on the roadside, getting photographed and then bundled into the back.

The man who'd climbed up Middle Oak sat on a branch, resolute in the cold, next to the single 'telegraph wire' line of polyprop to the next tree. If they came for us he said he'd clip onto it. After a while sitting up in my treehouse I tried to take over from him but he wouldn't have it, so I gave him a thick blanket instead.

The day wore on while we waited, I couldn't see much from here but every so often someone would be led by the police to a waiting wagon. It was intensely cold – a thin wind driving up from the Kennet valley, meeting your face full on as you looked over the road. I looked up at Granny Ash and Grandfather Oak – the twin trees that defined the camp and stood proud from all the others on the ridge. They weren't there. I hadn't heard them fall, hadn't even heard the chainsaws. A strange new gap hung in the air. There was something very wrong about it.

Sarah came across with a blurred face and red eyes, her cheeks splayed out with dry tears. She'd been pulled out of Granny Ash not long before it'd been felled and been de-arrested by a senior policeman who'd walked past as she'd been sat in a puddle, weeping.

Soon after they came for the DNA Oak. I could hear people shouting Badger's name over and over and knew he must be struggling with the bailiffs, though I couldn't make anything out. Security surrounded the tree this side of the A4, the tree the line was attached to. No one was up it. God knows why I didn't climb on the line myself, or why the man in the blanket didn't. I can only say we must have had our reasons, that maybe it looked like the belly on the line was so deep that we'd just end up on the ground in the middle, or else go unnoticed while the tree was cut. No one had hung from that line before. It was more than three hundred and fifty yards long.

As it happened, the crowd that had come over the road took things in their own hands, throwing a rope over the middle of the line and pulling it down to the ground. When they let go and the line sprang back up, a man was attached to it, clipped on. He pulled himself up on top of the line and began to shinny his way up to the tree. As he got closer, the angle on the rope became steeper and steeper but somehow he managed to pull himself up it, a huge cheer going up as he reached the tree's branches. It later turned out to be Shaun, Shaun the multiply pierced from Seaview.

Meanwhile, the DNA Oak had been felled, pushed to the ground with the help of a digger. Someone hurried across to us, a few of us in the branches and near to the trunk on the ground now. They'd run to tell us they'd overheard someone senior looking say they'd come for us next.

The word went round and people began jogging across the field to us. Soon there were forty or fifty people stood or sat in the fan of Middle Oak's branches. A group of purple hatted surveyors walked in through the ground defences to have a nose round. As the rest of the security crossed the A4, it looked as though our time had come. It was strange to think it'd soon all be over – so many months of waiting and then everything happening in the course of one day. We waited tensely for them to surround the tree. People were calling out to their mates in other parts of the tree, to see how they were doing, to check they were doing alright.

The security began to jog down the field along the hedge line, surrounding an avenue of trees which I'd always thought were off route. There'd been no time for any protestors to get to them and we watched, powerless, as the chainsaws kicked in. When the trees were all down and lying uncrowned in the field, the security began to break up; shuffling their way in twos and threes back to their coaches. It was late in the day and it must have seemed too tall an order to get us all out of one tree. We were safe, for a while.

I went over to the remains of Granny Ash. The ground camp had been totally destroyed. Poking out of the mesh of felled branches were bits of smashed up treehouse; broken boards and beams, mangled tarps, people's belongings; sleeping bags, blankets, a bashed in primus, a book with the cover ripped off. Someone's bag of oils was in there too, half the bottles inside broken. Blue polyprop, snagged in every conceivable place, disappeared into the mounds and looped out again. Climbing rope did the same, now as good as useless, even if you could pull it out.

It was strange to see the tops of the trees on the ground, the thin ends of the branches crowded together with the weight of the crown, somehow still seeming alive, as though the sap wouldn't leave them just yet.

The stumps of the trees were fat and raw and seemed to cry out to me in shock. Hours ago they'd been the root of an incredible, living thing and now they stood there; white and garish, testament to fresh amputation. This place had been beautiful last night and now it was a swamp of carnage. People clambered round the wreckage, picking their way among the branches looking for stuff, looking listless. No one was really talking to anyone else. There wasn't much to be said. We just looked at each other. Everyone seemed to have a weird black rim round their eyes.

I couldn't find the low whistle I'd left in the kitchen bender. Richie appeared with it later – he'd found it under a log. It was bent almost in an L shape but I managed to bend it back, so it looked almost like its old self; a kink in the middle the only remaining sign of what had happened. People had had the insight to move the communal bender off route a few days before – across the track in the hollow by Simon's bender, so no one was homeless. Though most people didn't want to hang around, even if they hadn't got bailed off route.

We watched the news that night in the Bartley's kitchen. Julian appeared on the screen, on the platform of Grandfather Oak – which had developed two or three storeys in its last days. He was being hit repeatedly with a riot shield by a bailiff still in the cherrypicker cab, doubling up under the blows.

Balin had avoided being pinned down for a long while, emptying tin after tin of soup and beans on the approaching bailiffs. When they finally got him and he was being lowered to the ground in the cab, they turned him away from the crowd and punched his face repeatedly. He was in handcuffs. Everyone in the field still saw it, apart from the numerous police, who'd all been looking away.

Ralph appeared a few days later with a heavily bruised face. He'd climbed a small tree at the last minute and ended up there all day. They came for him last, finally felling the tree with him still in, felling it down the bank so he had further to fall. A group of security had then given him a beating.

Some of the reporting from the eviction didn't make us look great. "Police condemn Newbury protestors' dangerous weapons," blared the newsreader in the Bartley's. A police chief appeared holding up a spiked, hazel ball. It was a pretty evil looking thing sure enough; a load of sticks about a foot long tied together with the ends sharpened up. A geezer who'd been into his re-enactments had made it and people just let him have his fun, not giving it much thought, it being just another thing in a day full of goings on. He'd hung it from a tree where it had stayed, inert, until the police found it. It was all a bit stupid, but it was certainly never intended to be used as a weapon, at the most just a device for making the tree look off putting to the climbers and men in the cherrypickers, who probably never even noticed it.

The police were also holding up a caltrop they'd found – a medieval style three pointed piece of iron that was designed to always have one point upright when thrown on the ground. Though these were originally devised as an anti-cavalry weapon, and though there were mounted police in the field that day, it'd most likely been put down in an attempt to stop the cherrypickers reaching the trees. The use of caltrops was a new one on me, and they didn't seem a brilliant idea, in a field where people were getting pushed and dragged around. The police certainly loved it as it made us all look conveniently demonic, even if there had probably only been one person responsible, who'd undoubtedly dropped it very much on the sly. And it hadn't stopped the cherrypickers anyway.

The communal across the track at Granny Ash was tatted down and everyone moved off to other camps, or left the campaign altogether. The Germans moved down en masse to Rickety. A crowd of people helped me build a long kitchen bender under Middle Oak, out of one of the communal tarps. Balin moved into it. It was open at both ends and the nights were still frosty but he seemed to like it that way. Life became strangely tranquil for me after that, for a while. All around me, camps were falling to bailiffs and while I knew my turn couldn't be far off, I seemed to be at the quiet eye of the storm and was grateful for whatever peace each day brought. I concerned myself with the camp; cooking in the evenings, strengthening the barricade and helping Balin build a new monster platform underneath my treehouse.

One stupidly windy day myself and Balin, for want of anything better to do, decided to make a hanglider out of a spare tarp, with a bender pole frame. The wind had dropped by the time we'd finished but the whole thing fell neatly into a half bender shape. It became the covering for a new shit pit, which was about as far away as possible from what we'd intended, but probably the only useful thing it could have ever become.

Around this time I got taken off for dinner by a local family who lived somewhere out the other end of Speenham estate. They didn't know me particularly well, so it was a generous thing to do. I spent the evening talking across a fireplace to a man with a big moustache, as he smoked from a old fashioned pipe. It was a good night and I felt myself drawn into some quiet homeliness that could have been the spirit of Berkshire itself; the tranquillity of the flats and waterways of the moors creeping in around us still, but with some sense of strange order; something drawn in but made part of the feeling of home by the walls and the smoke and the fire. It was all a long way away from the wind in the tree on the hill.

Clare's younger sister Ruth and Margaret, their mum, came to stay around the oak for a few days; pitching their tents. It was good to have some old faces around. Meanwhile, I'd got wind of an Interfaith Service planned to be held around the oak that Sunday. There'd be Christians, Jews, Buddhists, Hindus, Muslims and Jains all celebrating the land and mourning the loss of life on the route. Which was great, only there was a distinct lack of any formal representatives of paganism, which was a bit strange to put it mildly. Apparently, it was all thanks to the Christians, who said they wouldn't come if the pagans did, the latter only being welcomed in an opening speech by the organiser. Pagans or not, it still sounded pretty laudable, only I was wary of the prospect of any further attention and escaped for the day to a re-enactors market with Clare and her mum. I bought a daft yellow waistcoat and Clare found an uncanny looking green cap. It was a good day off.

When we got back, all the women were wearing the first daffodils of spring. There was still a big crowd, with a gang of kids clambering over a swing that Balin had made out of old climbing rope. A new banner had appeared on the barricades that said 'The Wind Has No Sound But Each Leaf.' This took its place alongside a piss take of the local pro bypass lobby – 'Newbury Bypass – NOW'. The banner said 'Newbury Bypass – NOT' only I hadn't watched TV in ages and had read it out to the BBC filmcrew as "NOT the Newbury Bypass." I tried to be media tart, but not being exposed to TV, wasn't quite up to the job.

After that I'd occasionally escape and visit other camps. Just a change of scene broke the thread of continually waiting. Bagnor Lane was well populated by now with treehouses high up in the beeches. The very highest, right at the tip of one of these giants had been built and was lived in by Swampy. The straw bales looked a bit more dilapidated, though they were still as on the case as ever about washing up. On a notice board behind the firepit, someone had pinned up a huge rota.

Up in Bog Camp they were flat out preparing for the eviction. Ben, who'd been involved here since the start of the camp, had strung up an 'eviction plank'. This stood out horizontally from the trunk, held up at the end by a rope from above. It would only be strong enough to hold one person and he planned to sit on it unclipped. Getting him out of the tree ought to be a right pain in arse.

It was the second time a plank had played a prominent role in Newbury's history, the first being sometime in the Civil War, when two soldiers had seen a woman flying across the river Kennet on some kind of wooden board. Newbury was famous for it's witches at the time and when 'Restless John' had tried building a house on Cottingdon Hill , there were said to have been enough witches around to haul up a ton of stone, giving rise to the belief that his castle may have been built by magic.

As for the two men, they did what soldiers do too often when confronted with anything new. They tried shooting her first, but she displaced their lead musket balls with a laugh, only finally meeting her fate by one of their swords.

David Rendell – the local Liberal Democrat MP who had campaigned so vociferously for the road – probably deserves a mention here, talking of Newbury's history and planks. Though there are many better words.

Others at Bog Camp had spiked the trees with nails and wrapped them in wire to hamper the chainsaws. When Granny Ash was being evicted a tree surgeon, unconnected with the contractors, had come up to Middle Oak and advised me of the best way to spike a tree. He'd really done my head in. Like many others, I couldn't bring myself to drive nails into a still living tree. But it remained a contentious issue – some saw it as a perfectly valid tactic, almost a vital one if we were serious about slowing the work down. In anti logging campaigns overseas, given the sheer amount of territory to be defended, it was supposed to be a common practice.

There was a chance of injury to the chainsaw operator when his saw hit a nail, but everyone I met who advocated spiking was well aware of the need to signpost that it'd been done, so the chainsaw crews were aware. Any ceramic spikes needed to be specially signposted, if used, as they wouldn't show up on metal detectors and could cause chainsaw kickback just as easily. Most people who talked about spiking in my neck of the woods weren't popular and were usually fresh out from some city and still to sink into the undercurrents of life outdoors. Up in Snelsmore they'd 'quagged' the trees – covered their lower trunks with mud mixed with sand and strands of polyprop, which were meant to melt and clog up the chainsaw teeth.

A few days after my last visit, Bog Camp fell prey to the Under Sheriff of Berkshire, Nicholas Blandy. While the ancient title ought to have meant that Blandy's family had been evicting people with pride for generations, some said the original Under Sheriff had wanted nothing to do with our evictions and Blandy, his underling, had been only too willing to take up his place.

Ben's eviction plank was a success for a few hours, until a climber offered him a fag. When Ben reached over to grab it, he had his wrist handcuffed and that was that. He'd been proud of his plank, had Ben, and was gutted with himself for ages. It had all been going so well.

The refugees from Bog Camp made their way down to the swelling ranks of Rickety Bridge. There were always tatters from Rickety Bridge scurrying about in the mounds where Granny Ash had been, trying to salvage building materials. Tat meant stuff, often old, tatty but still potentially useful stuff, though strictly speaking any stuff at all was still tat. Tatting meant to grab it. Tatters were the people who tatted the tat. None of this had anything to do with potatoes.

The contractors had bulldozed all the remaining trees into huge mounds; fifteen foot, twenty foot high and set them on fire. The green wood not given to massive combustion, they burned with sickly, unsteady flames, that carried on for days if not weeks, giving out huge columns of smoke. At night you walked by and could see the flames clearly, like the woods had been reduced to furnaces, pointless furnaces, geared to make nothing but an empty testament to ignorance, to our capacity to scrub out everything beautiful left on this earth.

Rickety Bridge had two firepits now, joined hip to hip and whenever I went down, there was usually some kind of smoking or music session going on. It was good to visit, but seeing increasing drabs of the fresh faced, all smiles,

390

trooping down there, it was hard not to get a bit cynical. It was hard not to believe there were a lot of people down there now not really doing much work, just there for the crack and an easy life out of the wind. And I knew the feeling was shared by at least some of the people down there, among the many who were working flat out, in the full knowledge that their time was running out.

'Glastonbury Bridge' was what I dubbed it one evening, sat on a mound of wreckage at the remains of Granny Ash, a giddy pothead having just asked me the way, full of excitement, like this was all a big game still. Maybe I needed a proper long break but the same could have been said for at least half the people on route, and no one was thinking of leaving. Not while their tree was still standing.

Another camp had been set up down the way from us, in a little hollow at the other end of the field with three oaks. It had been set up with Pee G and his girlfriend Lucy, friends from town since the start and founders of Newbury Area Badger Watch. Pee G had been in the circus, still did his fair share of juggling and unicyling and had called the camp Quercus Circus. He'd wanted to turn the hollow into a bizarre and weird world of strangeness but so far this only consisted of a doorway roped upright with a plastic mouse nailed to the front. There was fake blood all down the door. "It's a doormouse" said Pee G, when people arrived. There were no drums there yet, though if you listened hard enough you could just about hear the drum roll on the wind, which was still north easterly, and coming down over from Donnington.

Down on the moors past Rickety Bridge, a new camp was being set up – Camelot, home of the Arthurian Warband and, inevitably, King Arthur himself. King Arthur was a funny old figure, fully believed in himself as the Pendragon and magical protector of Britain and walked around with a silver circlet on his head, wearing a full length, white, surcoat. He'd had his sword taken off him in the field at the Granny Ash eviction and had much later started to strip off in court when told he couldn't appear with it. To appear without his sword would be to effectively appear naked, he'd explained, so he might as well be properly naked. "Let him have his sword back" the judge said, exasperated and wanting to relieve the entire court room of the sight of a middle aged and hairy torso. I was just glad he was on our side, Pendragon or not, though he'd got here a bit late, all things considered.

A few people were drifting down there, to Camelot, largely for the crack they said but also to receive knighthoods and quests – like not to touch money for a year. A friend of mine had been knighted by him, outside a chip shop after some action in the West. He'd been fairly pleased about this until Arthur proceeded to knight someone's dog. Then he knighted the chip shop.

I went down to Camelot myself one evening and found a structure the size of a large yurt or communal, sat ragged but still stately on a small island, wood fringed, right in the middle of the damp moor. It looked like it'd been thrown together out of random bits of wood. Though, with that in mind, whoever had made it had done a good job, almost as though the sticks had risen up unaided, answering some spoken command. It was covered mostly with white plastic tarps, which let the last light in almost eerily, along with a lot of the cold.

Two lanky, pale faced, ginger headed lads were taking it in turns to stir a large pot full of watery stew, vapours rising up around their ears. I tried to make conversation but they practically waved it away and carried on stirring the stew. A crow croaked somewhere and I realised it was in my imagination. King Arthur was sat in an alcove of his own, his sword on his lap, bedecked in the regal light of a blue plastic tarp.

After we'd eaten and the fire had been banked up, at Arthur's behest, we all told a story or sang an old song. I managed to remember a poem about an old lady lived under a hill (and if she's not gone, she's living there still). Arthur's song was about shagging and engineer's balls. He made everyone join in. I was glad for the peace and dark of the moor when I left, not long after.

Late in the week that they evicted Bog Camp, they came in to finish off Snelsmore. Sarah and Ceri went up there with Simon where they sat in a treehouse, joined by the waist clips on their harnesses. When the climbers appeared, they told them they were joined by genital piercings. It took a long while before they were untangled, which involved the climbers sitting on Simon and Ceri's chests as they struggled to undo the carabinas.

Elsewhere in the eviction, a group of people in a net simultaneously developed a sudden condition where they couldn't think straight, where their minds seemed clouded to the point where they found it hard to move properly. There was no knowing what caused it, but the people who experienced it all had a sturdy head on their shoulders, were solid people and not given to conspiracy theories. And they afterwards reckoned they were the target of some kind of remote weapon. There was a popular theory that we might be getting bombarded with all kinds of secret and remote weaponry, some people putting metallic space blankets in the roofs of their benders as a means of protection, but this was the firmest thing I had heard that could prove it.

At the same time, they were evicting a camp called Gotan; just over the Wantage road from Snelsmore, near

393

the old orchard. Famous rock climbers had come down from Sheffield to help us out and this was where they made their stand. They knew some of the eviction climbers personally, had climbed beautiful places for years alongside them. Ben Moon evaded capture for hours, running rings around his contracted old mates. He got arrested for attempted kidnap after he tied some bailiffs to a tree, something we were laughing about up and down the route.

I'd heard the visiting Sheffield climbers had been putting up mini, steel cable aerial slides and training people up in belaying. This was where two people were hung counterbalanced on the same rope, giving at least one of them a wide range of movement. It had been used to great effect at the eviction of Whitecroft at Solsbury Hill, but had hardly been used since, which was a great shame. Like most people, I'd never tried it, and there were few enough people around who knew how to do it. When it came to the eviction, the Sheffield climbers were clipped on all the time; fully using their ropes rather that getting encumbered by them, which is how they were able to do such amazing stuff.

I started to think a bit more about my eviction strategy. Maybe with the new monster platform, the battle platform, we could hold them off collectively for a while, though they'd only bring the cherrypickers in. Maybe I'd climb up to the very top of the crown, where they'd probably have to use climbers to bring me down. I started climbing around on all the outlying branches to get used to them, and thought about putting up rope swings, that might help me keep out of their way a while longer.

Just thinking about it, feeling that old familiar buzz in my head, I knew that wrestling around with climbers, watching bits of the oak getting chainsawed, people screaming, the whole fucking carnage of an eviction, and then getting pigged on top of it, would very likely send me nuts again. But I tried not to think about that.

The day after Gotan, they came for the Kennet. People had flooded the nearest lock and dug trenches so the whole camp had become an island. There was no cherrypicker access either so people had been feeling pretty confident that this would be a hard eviction for Blandy. They came in around three in the morning, police in black and balaclavas, police frogmen nipping up and down the canal on a motorised dingy. The Mothership, which should have been such a stronghold, turned out to be reachable by ladder and bailiffs swarmed in from all sides.

The word was it was a rough eviction – they were meant to be a different breed, broadly speaking, south of the Kennet – more hardcore maybe, or more urbanised with less time for niceties. It wasn't something I particularly noticed, spending less and less time away from my neighbourhood, but there was meant to be a north/south divide in types and attitude, whether it was thanks to the tactics they adopted in the trees, or the calibre of abuse they hurled, or just because living in Penwood in the middle of all that just did things to your brain, it seemed to affect the treatment they got. But if you were good at what you did - delaying the eviction – however nice you were about it, you tended to piss them off and they tended to let you know about it. And anyway, in the Kennet eviction, the bailiffs or security on the ground had been using catapults in the dark, so it was hardly surprising if a few people kicked off.

The eviction lasted the whole day, and some of the next and then they went for Castle Wood where they left a bunch of people stranded up trees with all the branches below them cut off. They had to climb down last thing, after a whole day in the freezing cold, cramped from standing in one or two positions, hanging on just with their fingertips in the crook of cut branches.

They came for Reddings Copse the next week, though they were evicting camps somewhere or other all the time. A digger accidentally uprooted a big old oak, which spun round as it fell, landing on the cab of a cherrypicker and hospitalising one of the climbers with a blow to his head. They'd all seen the tree coming and made a run for it, though he hadn't quite made it. Blandy clocked it all and carried on eating his sandwiches. A crowd of people from the camp later went to the hospital to see how the climber was getting on and to offer their condolences. The cherrypicker had to be sent off to get fixed, which was good as there hadn't been a cherrypicker in the country big enough for the Pine and they'd only just shipped this one over specially from Holland.

Despite everyone's efforts, including Balin's scaling the whole Pine mid eviction with only a 'climbing stick', Reddings Copse was soon just a memory. They'd wanted to use the Pine as the main mast for a tall ship being built, but a bunch of people from the evicted camp burnt it instead. The mentality was that the tree was somehow ours, or at least a free standing being of its own and it would be an abuse of it's spirit to let it be used for a ship that in some roundabout way was seen as a part of the establishment. But to me, it seemed a pretty weird thing to do. It was the only tree on route taken down which they hadn't just driven into a pyre and set light to, and we went and burnt it anyway.

Everyone had been shocked about the climber, even though there'd been enough people come close to getting a tree on them in Penwood and even one bloke getting the walkway cut from underneath him. He'd managed to grab a branch on the way down. But the climber had been the first major cropper and was now critically ill.

Sometimes, however harshly, it felt as though nature herself was helping us out – like when the man who'd sold his lifetime's research of Newbury's bat population to the Highways Agency had been chased across the fields after disturbing a hornet's nest or like when the wild horses appeared.

The first day they'd started clearance work at Reddings Copse, two brown horses appeared out of nowhere, galloping around in front of the chainsaw workers, neighing and clearly distressed. Then they'd squared up to the police horses, sniffing their noses as if for signs of familiarity. Obviously not liking what they'd found, they rose up on their hind legs, boxing; indignant and unbroken in. The horses stopped the work, all the crowd of protestors shutting up for a while, all the slack shouldered, downtrodden security looking for once genuinely awestruck. Eventually they disappeared again back into the fields, still agitated, still angry and galloping side by side, shaking their necks, half mad with the sound of the saws and what they were doing to England.

"You'll Never Take Our Treedoon!"

Time wore on and there was a steady trickle of people back into Middle Oak. Sarah appeared, followed by a Scottish punk called Kirsten and a mate of hers, Laura. Kirsten and Laura were great to have around, having loads of fresh energy and doing everything with a cheerful enthusiasm. They could have been from another planet. Scottish Clare reappeared and another dreadlocked Jim rolled up, this one from Cornwall – a stocky bloke with a black beard and fat mohawk who I got on with at once. He was loud and friendly and good to have around. A friend known as Eric the Viking was around again too, as was John from Lincolnshire, a recorder playing town planner who'd camped under the tree for a few days in January. It was a gathering of old faces. As John chipped back to work on a Sunday we looked at each other as he left, both knowing the tree would be gone before he made it back.

The new battle platform underneath my treehouse was increasingly taking shape. Balin had been ambitious when laying it out, so it covered a good span of the middle of the hemisphere. This would be where everyone would flock to come the eviction, and hopefully help fend them off for a bit with sheer numbers. Scottish Clare was determined she was going to be up in the tree for it, even though she was scared of heights, and started to learn how to prussik. It didn't seem to help that, when climbing alongside to encourage her, I'd never be clipped on. Sometimes I'd just be sitting on my haunches on a branch near the top, at ease enough and on a fat enough limb not to feel the need to support myself with my hands. It hadn't occurred to me that I was doing it, though I was aware of my balance and aware of the branches nearby to grab onto if it looked like I needed to steady myself. All the same, it freaked Scottish Clare out to see me perched there like that. Being on a branch was now second nature, though standing around unclipped doesn't come recommended.

I went down to Rickety Bridge one night to see how things were. The population had obviously grown with all the other evictions, and they were anticipating the fight to start here anytime. A dozen watchfires were scattered around the wood now. Even though it was night, you could make out the lurking forms of treehouses everywhere you looked. Blandy was going to have a hard time here; the place was clearly saturated.

I approached one of the fires, answering "Police" when asked who it was. This was the current big joke. "That's alright then, we're all police too." We knew there had to be undercover police living on site, but had to be philosophical about it. Whoever they were, they'd be undercover because they were good at it and probably one of the last people anyone would suspect. It was all too easy to become suspicious of all but your closest friends and the worst thing you could do was initiate some kind of witchhunt against potential suspects. It was better to let it all go over your head and get on with it, rather than let them tacitly destroy the trust on a camp. The psychological effect of spying was potentially far greater than any information they might glean, and it was always best to belittle it.

The new platform in Middle Oak was finally finished, yellow painted pieces of chipboard laid down as flooring over the span of round beams. Work began on a lock-on next to the trunk. This was an old oil barrel with a wide metal tube shoved through the middle. A bar had been welded across the middle of the tube, which people could attach themselves to via carabina clips tied to their wrists with a piece of climbing tape. The rest of the barrel was filled with stones and cement – mixed on the ground and hoisted up in buckets. We'd put it by the trunk as this was the strongest point of the platform, bolstered from below by a beam driven into a fork a few feet beneath.

People had to be dug out of lock-ons, usually with hydraulic drills. It could take hours and was a full on experience to let yourself in for, though it remained one of the best ways of slowing down an eviction. It was wise to wrap up your forearm to stop the climbing tape being cut with a knife on a stick. As often as not, people in lock-ons would get tortured with pressure points or by having their arm driven up behind their back. Sometimes they just pulled at people until the joint in their arm or shoulder went. I just hoped I'd be carted away quick enough that I didn't have to hear my friends screaming.

People were doing more work on the trench and soon we had a two plank drawbridge to connect us to the outside world. Beyond this were two ranks of barbed wire. It was beginning to look like a real battlezone.

A friend called Heather, from Castle Wood, had made a Green Man banner and we stuck it around the trunk so the big, oak leafed face was the first thing you saw as you came in through the gate. This was half barred already and had to be climbed over. Before he allowed anyone in, Cornish Jim always made a big ceremony of asking them a riddle,
"Do you want to come in?" It was the little things that kept our heads together.

Simon had carried a green, reclining armchair back from town and we asked the Bartley's round for dinner so Mr B could sit among us in style. Sarah had cooked aubergine fritters and someone had got a bottle of wine. We all tried to be on our best behaviour. Mr B's elevated position meant he got more than his fair share of the smoke from the fire.

"Good God" he exclaimed, wiping his eyes, "how can you people live like this?" but he was obviously glad to be out here.

We speculated how long we had left, there were very few camps left now and we thought they'd have to come for us soon before our numbers swelled any more. We had a nightwatch set up, to ward off vigilantes and to give us warning if they did a dawn raid. I saw in many mornings drinking tea like this, an agony of waiting as the light seeped in and the traffic picked up. The birds by the A4 sang all night, swathed in sodium, which always seemed the most fucked up thing imaginable.

Finally, towards the end of March, the A4 and the smaller road filled up with police and security. Our time had come. The neon coats appeared from their vehicles and then disappeared down the track by Granny Ash - it was suddenly obvious they'd come for Rickety Bridge. There were about a hundred and fifty people in the trees to greet them.

With the eviction force so near to hand, we had to be on a constant state of alert. We hauled the reclining armchair up onto the battle platform. Someone was always up here now, ready to clip onto the telegraph line to protect the other tree. But they were bitterly cold days, a biting March wind coming up from the south and whoever was on duty had to be wrapped up in several blankets. Scottish Clare spent a lot of time up there as she didn't think she'd be able to get up in a hurry if they came for us suddenly. There was a foghorn to blow if it looked like they were coming. It took people a while to learn not to be trigger happy.

In the midst of the hecticness and confusion, the almost constant alarms and frenzied scuffling up and down the tree, Sarah and I gravitated towards one another for support. Before we knew it we were back together again. My spirits soared and suddenly I felt strong and ready for whatever was to come. Which was just as well.

A few days into the nearby eviction, Cornish Jim woke up and told us about a powerful dream he'd just had. He was almost rabid with excitement. A voice had told him;
"The tree's not coming down." Everyone looked wide eyed and suddenly hopeful. I didn't mention the dream I'd had.

Later in the day Mr Bartley came over to tell us he'd been going over the maps and it looked like Middle Oak wasn't on route after all, but on a small strip of land surrounded by cuttings for the interchange. He went down to Rickety Bridge later that day and was ushered in through the cordon to speak to Blandy. Blandy said he didn't want any trees to come down unnecessarily and if we left the tree he'd undertake that she wouldn't be felled.

Nearly everyone at Middle Oak was completely dubious about this. Why should we trust his word, and wouldn't it be making their lives very much easier if we simply walked away from the camp? But if we got him to say that the tree would stay in writing and in front of the cameras, what then? At least now the tree had a chance. And if we stayed to be evicted we'd almost certainly be writing that chance off. We agreed we'd leave the tree, but only if Blandy gave his word to the press beforehand.

It soon emerged there was a problem; the Highways Agency were furious that the subject had even been discussed with Mr Bartley. They were insisting that Middle Oak be felled. In the light of this, Blandy agreed to talk with the Highways Agency. We would have to wait another day to see if the tree would be saved.

The next morning I was sat round the firepit, cooking a late lunch with Sarah and Cornish Jim. Most of the others had gone to give support down at Rickety Bridge. Somebody looked up to see men in black running across the field towards us. The first was far ahead and as he got closer we realisesd he was a protestor. He ducked under the barbed wire and threw himself over the trench and the barricade. He made straight for the tree, climbing it faster than anyone I'd ever seen. Right behind him were a pair of policemen. They too got through the defences, one of them darting up the tree itself. All this had happened in seconds.

I went up the tree and persuaded the policeman to come down, telling him I'd talk to the treesitter, whose face was blackened with face paint. I told him as far as I was concerned he was welcome up the tree. He'd been arrested down at Rickety Bridge and brought up to a waiting meatwagon on the smaller road. They'd left him alone for just a moment, though that had been enough for him. Seeing Middle Oak, he'd made a break for it. The police threatened that if he didn't come down they'd bring up the cherrypickers from Rickety Bridge and evict the tree. But the escapee agreed that if it looked like cherrypickers were coming he'd leave of his own accord.

It should have been as simple as that but the camp was suddenly in turmoil, people arriving back to find out what had happened, everyone wanting an explanation at once. Some thought we should be doing more to help the man escape, others thought we should be booting him out as quickly as possible as he was jeopardising the oak's new chance of survival. Somebody was on the point of climbing up and bringing him down by force, but managed to be talked out of it. Evidence Gatherers were now filming the tree, as people intermingled with the runaway, swapping clothes and blackening their faces like his.

Then somebody else appeared from Rickety Bridge. The last time I'd seen him, a few weeks before, he was a trendily kitted cyclist type out from a city. Today he was dressed in black leggings and a small black poncho. Black face paint streamed down his cheeks with his tears, like crow's wings. He stopped on the drawbridge and collapsed on his knees. He looked every bit like a herald of death.
"Balin's fallen out of a tree!" He'd wailed the words, palms up and arms outstretched, his whole face cracked open.

Everyone stopped and looked at him. There was a sudden hush. Then everyone started up arguing about the man in the tree again. It was all too much, and we could only deal with one thing at a time. We got the man at the gate sat round with a cup of tea in his hands all the same. But there wasn't time to let the news sink in. A lot of people I'd never seen before had turned up in a heated mood and started, forcefully, to tell everyone what they thought we should do, without listening to what had already been said. The two policemen had stayed put by the tree to stop the man getting down.

The afternoon finally began to fall in on itself and the cherrypickers hadn't made their way up to us. The police drove off in their convoy, taking the two by the tree and the Evidence Gatherers with them, and the escapee came down, getting quickly bundled into the back of a van headed somewhere safe. He was more than grateful for the refuge, having had previous convictions from other protests that he would have been sent down for.

Only then did we find out that Balin was OK, that it'd been someone else who'd fallen and that whoever it was had been so pissed that he'd practically bounced off the ground.

It had been a hectic day, so I headed into town with Sarah, to try and forget about everything for a while. Down at the Clocktower pub, protestors were spilling out onto the streets, sitting around the old clocktower itself and ambling back and forth across the road. It had probably been much the same scene back in the 1640's. Though the Clocktower wasn't a whore house these days, the various punks ensured it was still a den of debauchery; sticking their tongues in everyone's ears. It was good to get off site for a while. It was good to get pissed.

By now the space inside the barricade was full of benders and tents. Kirsten and Laura had built a women's bender and a bunch of people down from Gotan had built a barn bender – complete with hay and a burner. It was a great place to go and get warm. Ceri's bender and the kitchen bender still stood. A few locals had dropped off their teenage daughters, who wanted to make a stand as much as anyone else. The site was full of people I barely knew. The Gotan crew had a working CB and were happy to use it. Everything seemed suddenly sorted and I began to feel pleasantly insignificant.

Then, the day after the trip to the clocktower and with Rickety's eviction still in full swing, a mass of security appeared over the ridge, making their way up the track with two cherrypickers. Everything seemed suddenly, coldly real. There'd still been no word back from Blandy about the future of the tree and, as the security crossed the A4, it looked like our number was up. We'd come close to saving her perhaps, but the world obviously wasn't to be cheated so easily. Everyone clambered up to the big platform, even Mr and Mrs B; stood together in one of the lower forks, indefatigable.

Kirsten and Laura planned to repeat the trick of clipping themselves together via their main carabinas. Only they'd also be wearing body armour made out of old shopping trolleys, wrapped up in a big, hefty chain. They started climbing into the armour up on the battle platform, half excited, half shitting themselves.

I took the time to try and finish off some climber proof fencing I'd been putting up around the edge of the platform – chicken wire stapled to the edges of the flooring at the bottom and held up with bits of rope and wire. It was better than just sitting there, watching them get closer.

The cherrypickers rolled across the field towards us; siege engines, dinosaur like, long necks bouncing along on their bodies. The security shuffled along beside them, forced to walk doubly slow, so they seemed all the closer to being undead; shoulders forward, hands in pockets, in thrall to the machines rising above their bowed heads. The cherrypickers looked alien, out of some film about monster machines, except they were only too real and were headed directly for us.

We started shouting, blew the foghorn and chorused "You'll never take our treedoon!" Braveheart had just come out on video and we'd been planning to get a cardboard cut out of Mel Gibson to stick by the armchair. I'd almost managed to get one, having asked nicely enough in a video shop in town with the required qualifications, only I walked out again meekly when the guy at the till point blank refused, when I really should have grabbed the cutout and run for it.

There'd also been a plan to get a tall, shaded lamp to go with the chair and maybe a row of flying wall ducks we could hang from above. None of these things had materialised though, and now it was all a bit late, so we had to make do with Mel's battlecry:

"YOU'LL *NEVER* TAKE OUR TREEDOON!!!"

We shouted it again as the cherrypickers began to roll past us. They were going past us. We watched them, stunned, as this sank in, the machines crawling over the ground, the flanking security dragging their heels alongside. They were heading for Seaview. Were they ever going to come for us? It was beginning to look like maybe, just maybe Blandy was pulling strings to have this tree saved. But I didn't dare let myself believe it. Now evictions were happening on both sides of us. More security made their way across to Seaview, sending us all up the tree again.

Soon they were burning felled trees down at Seaview and the thick smoke made its way over to us in the strong wind. It was bad enough for us, several hundred yards away, but it must have been that much worse for people still in the trees, right by the fires. It hadn't just been the trees at Granny Ash; they'd burned felled trees all along the route in a kind of scorched earth policy. Smoke drifted up from Rickety Bridge like an oversized funeral pyre. It Penwood it was nothing but smoke.

They finished evicting Seaview the same day they'd started, moving on to polish off Quercus Circus before they went home. Somehow Quercus Circus had never drawn the numbers it deserved. We ought to have directed people his way, but there had just been so much to think about, it had somehow kept slipping our minds. At any rate, when they came for Pee G he was alone, almost forgotten, and they plucked him off a walkway within minutes. But he had at least been there, facing the horde on his own, while the rest of us huddled like sheep in our separate camps.

I gathered spare building materials and carried them over to the tree by the A4. There were enough people to guard Middle Oak now, and this place needed better defending. Mr Bartley came over that night and thought I should leave it to someone else – my place was in Middle Oak, he said, now that I'd been here so long. It hadn't been an easy decision to move over the A4 and it didn't take much to talk me out of it.

Demelsa had re-appeared and was now the main negotiator – going down to Rickety Bridge again and again to try and talk to Blandy about Middle Oak. She came back up one afternoon, bearing the news that Blandy would say at the end of the week – in front of the cameras and in writing - that if we left the tree peacefully, it wouldn't be felled. But we wondered whether the tree wouldn't get felled later on, by contractors with nothing to do with Blandy. Eventually we agreed that it we stayed in the tree, they'd definitely evict and fell it. Evacuating the camp was the only chance the tree had. We'd have to put our trust in Blandy, strange as that seemed. But we wouldn't move an inch before he'd given his word in front of the press.

Despite the strength that pairing up with Sarah had given me, I'd still been around for too long without a break. It was beginning to tell – I spent most mornings sleeping now. I was woken one morning by shouts that the line to the other tree had been cut. Someone had come down from their guard duty and not been replaced. The security had obviously been watching and hadn't missed the chance. The rope had been cut with the knife on a stick they'd used at Stanworth, almost without anyone noticing, until it was too late.

People rushed over to try and climb the tree, but security had already surrounded it. We watched, dismayed, as they began to fell it. The building materials lay where I'd left them, now under the security's feet – no one had followed up my attempt to build a platform up there. The sound of chainsaws bought me back to my dream of the skeletal girl in the bath,

"They're going to get me anyway." I suddenly knew that that dream had been about the tree by the road, that that was where the sound of the chainsaws had come from, that Middle Oak hadn't come into it.

The tree by the road was the twin, in a way, of the one that Badger had made his last stand in. He'd shouted down to me, in his last night on route, about how it was amazing and strange to be building a treehouse right over the road. "There's the problem, Jim and we're building the solution."

Living like this, as gently as we could on the earth, was in so many ways the way forward if we were serious about our stewardship of the land. And these two trees almost arched over the A4 - though it could have been any road – the road that carried the problem, that was lit up with the wrong kind of light, that cut across the landscape. It would have been fitting to have been dragged out of that tree, mirroring Badger's, near to the middle of the route, our treehouses practically spanning the road, bridging the problem with an imprint of hope. I should have been up there. I was angry with myself.

Later in the week I made my way down to Rickety Bridge, planning to get up a tree. It was now Thursday, the eviction had started on Monday. It had been a very long week already. Twig had been seen at the very tops of the trees, swinging in them so they bent over and then grabbing hold of the next tree along. Plenty of others were just waiting in nets and treehouses for more run of the mill and predictably brutal encounters. I'd heard that Balin had climbed down from one tree, run across open ground and then scrambled up another that had just been cleared of protestors. I wondered if I couldn't manage something similar.

I approached the eviction site by the back of the woods, fearful of detection, wrapping my green, plaid blanket around me as camouflage. As was usual with this kind of skulking, I ended up accumulating a few others on the way and we made our way together, hopping on logs across boggy streams, hoping to get in unseen. When we reached the security line, we realised the caution was pretty unnecessary – a group of people were sat on a blanket as though having a picnic and all eyes, including the security's, were facing inwards and upwards – on the scuffles taking place above us. The security had only just confiscated a ladder that until now had been allowing unmolested access to the treetops. We'd got here just moments too late.

As I stared up, the eviction, the shouts, the trees just coming into leaf, the crashing through the branches, it all sent me back to Stanworth. It felt like a tide rushing to my head, as though I'd inhaled the whole scene. I had to sit down, feeling dizzy, glad now I hadn't got there in time to get up the ladder.

The next day I climbed down from Middle Oak to find Ralph had wrapped the trunk in corrugated iron, steel plates, tent poles and anything else he could get his hands on, all wrapped in reels of thick wire. In was funny, in a way, as all the poles had come from the Jimi Hendrix tent, which seemed to live on, despite the original structure having come down. He'd done a good job, but it was suddenly a bit inappropriate, all things considered, and I was worried he might have spiked the tree while he was at it. Fortunately, Cornish Jim had had the same fears and had made sure it hadn't happened. I scrawled a notice to put on the tree to indicate it hadn't been spiked.

Late in the afternoon, when Rickety Bridge had been finally cleared, an entourage of senior looking figures bundled their way across the field towards us, an array of different coloured hard hats bobbing amongst one another to denote their importance. Not knowing what to expect, we climbed up the platform. So when Blandy, a Highways Agency representative and the senior surveyors and engineers came into the compound, we were all peering over the edge of the platform, shouting and hooting like a bunch of kids. Which we pretty much were, just about.

It became obvious pretty quickly, with the bunch of snooker ball hard hats just staring up at us and Blandy trying to raise his voice above ours, that this was in no way an eviction and a few of us climbed down to hear what he had to say. There were television cameras and other journalists and Blandy launched on a rabbit that contained the confirmation that the tree would be saved. Cornish Jim's dream had been true. The past few months had all been worth it.

People were hooting and dancing around but I only felt a great tide of relief, and a deep gratitude that I wouldn't have to go through another eviction. A photographer took a photo of a group of us infront of the tree. We'd all had our faces painted, with oak leaves on our foreheads. I looked into the camera feeling jaded of photographers, tired of the whole circus raging around us, tired of everything now, but relieved. A local supporter, Isobel, gave us some money to celebrate and everything could have been worse.

The next day we got to work taking down the camp. I worked on my own, dismantling my treehouse with a crowbar, satisfied to feel the limbs of the tree spring free as I removed each beam. Of all the things I'd imagined about how this would end, this had never been one of them. The sun had come out. It was beginning to feel like the spring.

Rick from Fairmile appeared, the one who had spun me the story about the shoddy ladder. He'd been around for weeks at least, always with his camera, full of stories of close escapes with policemen.

Not long after, weirdly enough, Blandy appeared as well, unprotected by any entourage of security, entirely on his own, dumpy and squat in his big red coat. A few people went up to talk to him. Rick wanted to go up and deck him, in thanks for all the other trees he'd done for on route. It might have been satisfying, but it was just about the worst thing he could have done, which may have been why he wanted to do it. I managed to talk him out of it, almost physically holding him back with a barrage of argument. He reluctantly backed down, but said we both might regret it.

Later, the pair of us built a ramp at the edge of the platform, tying on two parallel beams as we hung underneath in our harnesses. This was to roll the lock-on off, so it would clear the lower branches. But night overtook us and we'd have to leave the lock-on for the next day.

By Sunday afternoon the camp had been dismantled, even the barricades had been pulled down, and all that remained was the lock-on and the platform it stood on. Big piles of tat sat outside the trench ready for transportation to a new camp up at Gotan. I went for a walk with Sarah and when we got back the lock on had been pushed off, leaving a foot-deep dent in the ground where it had landed.

The next day, after toppling Camelot, Blandy came to Middle Oak to formalise our vacation of the land. Protestors and news cameras gathered round him but I stayed at a safe distance with my dodgy friend, casting a sceptical eye over proceedings. Then everyone called me

412

over anyway, as Blandy wanted to speak to a representative of the camp and everyone thought it ought to be me.

I fixed my myopic eyes on an unfortunate newswoman's face as a way of not letting my head fall as I walked towards the crowd. People parted to let me in and suddenly I was face to face with Blandy himself. He blathered on at some length, saying how he hoped this would "herald a new era of cooperation between those who didn't want roads and those whose job is sometimes unpleasant to the environment." He seemed happy and at ease, almost carefree, despite months of overseeing destruction and displacememnt. There are certain breeds of men who never lose a night's sleep to their conscience.

For a long while after, I kept on thinking of things I could have said; about how we'd happily vacate every tree you promised not to cut down, Mr Blandy, or about how the fate of this tree shouldn't be used to gloss over that of the other ten thousand. Thinking of this, thinking of all the destruction that had happened and that was still to come, thinking of all my friends and brothers and sisters who had suffered in evictions at his hands, I only felt like hitting him. As it happened, when he asked me if he had formal possession of the land, I merely nodded, he said he'd take that as read and we shook hands. It was finally over.

A few minutes later, when Blandy and his entourage had left, I picked up the armchair and carried it outside the remains of the trench. Sitting in it, I got my baccy out and started to roll a fag. It was the most audacious gesture I could think of, though hardly anyone seemed to notice, as they were all so busy dancing around.

I took the flag down a few days later – some people thought it should stay up, as a symbol of defiance. One or two characters had even bowled up full of enthusiasm about how we should re-occupy the tree, as though it wouldn't be evicted within a few hours, and the tree taken

413

down with it. I made sure I put them straight, so some rogue tree squatting party didn't turn up in our absence.

As far as the flag went, it had never been discussed with the landowner, but Ralph had been looking at the tree and felt it would be good to see her again in her natural state, free from flags or banners or anything that suggested politics, just the tree in all her glory, untouched once again by humankind. This immediately struck a chord with most of us and this was the reason I took down the flag. The Bartley's could see Middle Oak from their house and gave me a big book on trees that said, inside the cover,
"Thanks for looking after it Jim."

I helped build a bender in the Boyles' woods along with Sarah, Clare, Mark from Seaview and Twig. It was huge and built under a rhododendron bush – hidden and out of the way. It was the darkest bender I'd ever known inside – pitch black even in daylight, but it was safe and quiet and there was a stream running nearby. It felt like peace.

After a day or two of lying around in the early spring sunshine, sheltered in the woods, we heard another Donga gathering was planned near Winchester. And then the Green Goddess appeared again, the truck from the early days of the office, manifesting out the blue on the side of the B road, just when we needed her most. A few of us piled in the back – she was going to Old Winchester Hill.

Later we heard that Blandy had appeared under Middle Oak to do a triumphalist end-of-evictions press conference, fully exploiting the fate of this one tree. Middle Oak was becoming a sop to the guilt of Blandy of others, a kind of happy ending which made the carnage that had led up to it almost worthwhile and excuseable. Blandy wanted to milk this for all it was worth, knowing how good it could help make him look. Though it had to be said, perhaps that was why he'd helped save it. But a better man might have had a sense of his own shame, his own sorry part in the shambles of a national tragedy, and kept a respectful distance.

Fortunately, a crowd of people had got wind of the conference and chased him away in front of the cameras, a Benny Hill mob running after his landrover, driving him off from the hill. It made the early evening news and in an all time classic of the entire campaign, the reporter rounded up:

"…and the Sheriff was literally run out of town."

Lights Above Snelsmore

It was good to get out of Newbury. Old Winchester Hill was full of old faces and after a night of fire and music I sat with the crew from Snelsmore, on the side of a chalk track, eating a slow breakfast as wave after wave of Yew pollen blew in the sun around us. Sarah and I went straight up to her folks' place in North Wales after that, after a quick stop at the bender in the woods to pick up tat. We saw an epic harp concert and went camping in Snowdonia, stumbling by accident onto the lake where the Welsh bard Taliesin was meant to have lived; Llyn Geirionydd, appearing below us in the morning as we emerged from a rough night in a mossy clump of oaks. Sarah wrote this;

At Llyn Geirionydd you can jet-ski
Or see on tourist notice-boards
A picture of Taliesin
Smiling stupidly.

Where sacred groves
Once graced these slopes
There lingers no whisper
Of the tylwyth teg[1].
All that remains
Are these dark ranks of spruce;
Footsoldiers of the Coedwigaeth[2].

Did we exchange the spirit of our land
For a D.I.Y. pine bunkbed

---

[1] Fairfolk fairies
[2] Forestry Commission

And a desk with drawers?
I'd like to plant a thousand oaks
For every year I live
To make up for belonging
To this race we call mankind.

I did a lot of reading. I shaved off my beard. We got back
to Newbury for the beginning of May, moving the bender
and its tat up to a new camp at Gotan. The new camp was
modelled as a Diggers community, after the movement at
the end of the first English Civil War, where Gerrard
Winstanley and his friends had squatted St George's Hill in
Surrey, growing vegetables and inviting all to come and
join them. It was a truly radical outcome of the turbulent
times of the mid 1600's where the old world of feudalism
and magic was becoming resolved with the changes that
had been set in motion with the renaissance and the
invention of the printing press. Had the Diggers movement
been allowed to continue, it might have gone a long way to
restoring us all to our true place on the land. As it was,
Cromwell and the merchants of London were well aware of
the dangers Winstanley's convictions represented to their
world and the community was brutally displaced with the
aid of the New Model Army. The parallels were more than
a little uncanny.

It felt good to be growing something on what was
otherwise a swathe of annihilation. The cut through the
trees was broad here, this being on top of a hill that was
itself due to be cut into. A line of churned, brown earth
stretched eerily down to the A34.

And on the other side of the Wantage road was
Snelsmore, or the place where Snelsmore had been. The
bulldozers were working here now. At night I had dreams
of running around here with a crew of close friends, trying
to stop massive oil tanker lorries, getting peeled off to be

417

dragged through the mud and arrested. Others had dreams of standing in front of huge machines that were swallowing the earth, larger than houses, so big you could run along their backs and not find the edge, where there was no cab, the brain of the machine being the thing itself, growing bigger the more it drew to itself.

With Aggravated Tresspass fully up and running, digger diving was a short cut to prison, even in the waking world. Scores of security would line the road when the diggers were working, begging me to do something, to get everyone else to do something, anything, to make their lives more interesting. But no one was going to get arrested, just to help pass the security's time. When I looked at the churned, bare mud where Snelsmore had been I expected to feel grief, or anger but was left only with a flat, barren sensation, as though I'd lost part of myself.

Lying on the watermeadows down the track from Granny Ash, surrounded by the sun and wild flowers, it suddenly felt as if the whole earth was crying out to me, fully alive and in anguish as it knew what was coming. The meadows, though off route here, were earmarked for gravel extraction and would soon be just holes in the ground. Up and down the route there were stirrings of contracts for industrial units and housing estates on the land between the road and the town. Diggers were already at work, clearing away trees and starting to level the hills, the access points swamped with long lines of bored security. More than anything else though, there was the sense of impermanence, like the land was holding its breath, knowing it sat on death row. And the place was still beautiful, despite the destruction, the landscape itself was still there, there was still the same soft Berkshire tranquillity, where buckets of diggers weren't scraping the ground.

I went nomadic between the new off route camps for a while. In most places, the arrival of the summer had taken the edge off the destruction – the fields and woods were green again and tiny trees were springing up all over the rough earth of the clearance zone. Potty Phil and Sarah spent a lot of time digging and potting them up. And Middle Oak was there still, in full leaf and proud on the hill. I'd sit under her whenever I passed by and offer my gratitude that she was still here, that no matter what happened now, she'd enjoy another summer in this place.

It was strange how things had worked out; the bypass effectively transferred the crossroads that Newbury lay on several miles west of the town centre. Newbury's importance had always lain with its location; the convergence of roads north and south for the crossing of the Kennet, the site of battles due to its strategic control of the crossroads. It prospered with the coaching trade, being an important stopping off point between London and Bristol. Later, with the coming of the canal, it became an important inland port. Transport, and the people and trade it bought with it had effectively determined the history of the town. Now the new road had removed the town from the picture. The only stopping off would be at the monolithic services on what once was Tot Hill. Travellers would glide through a landscape that had been altered beyond all recognition, immune from the elements, sanitised as their engines deposited oil in the waterways, unaware, for the most part, just what they were missing.

But at the centre of this, Middle Oak still stood, alone on the remains of the hill, a reminder of what had been lost and a sign of hope of what the future could still hold, with the right will in the world. It now stands at the middle of the A34/A4 interchange, at the heart of the crossroads. Things now being as they are, this has to be a good thing.

Much earlier, before the evictions, before even the swelling of numbers that came in November, a friend had taken mandrake on a quiet night at Snelsmore. Mandrake is a powerful herb, dangerous if not taken properly and is not to be messed with. While she was under its spell, she went for a walk to one of the older, quieter parts of the woods, where she experienced the sense that the older trees were constantly feeding information, the vast body of their inherited lore, to the trees growing up underneath them. In this way their knowledge remained unbroken, every oak holding far more than just centuries' worth of experience. So the loss at Snelsmore looked more profound than you might at first think.

Only, according to an article in the great eminence of the Newbury Weekly News itself, a local woman had been walking on a night shortly before the eviction and had seen a large, green luminescence, like a bright cloud in the sky above Snelsmore. I took heart on hearing this; it seemed as though the immense wealth that the trees at Snelmore held was now far from lost, that it had been taken into the arms of something older than the oaks themselves, something they were, in their spirit, comprised of.

But for me, the place wasn't the same. Everywhere I looked echoed lost pieces of my own memory. Bagnor Lane was a strangely prosaic opening onto the fields around it. Speenham Moor was scoured top and bottom, walking across it feeling just as wild, only desolate now and empty. I split up with Sarah. Somebody shaved off my dreads. Finally, after I was given a good pair of boots, I left altogether, walking up onto the North Downs, headed for Winchester. A woman I'd met had a house there where everyone was welcome and Winchester was meant to be good for busking. I'd live off busking for the summer. Walk somewhere else. Carry on walking 'til things began to make sense again.

I stopped to look back from Beacon Hill, feeling that somehow, this view would stay with me forever, that some part of me would always be looking out over this place. A few miles further on, past Watership Down where I slept in the crook of a beech tree, the track began to curve south. I looked back one last time in the direction of Newbury – now lost in a sea of woodland and greenery, as though, for a moment, nine miles wasn't such a long distance, as though there was still a lot more worth the fight. The path made its way over the ridge, curving round a hill of young corn. Behind me, everything dropped out sight. I was gone.

Later that summer I dreamt I was back in Newbury. There was a festival on and the streets were full of people and excitement. I realised I could go and see Snelsmore and Granny Ash, alive in their summer greenery, vivid in my imagination. And then the knowledge came crushing in that these places were gone, black holes in the countryside, never to be visited again. I wandered along disconsolate until I saw a woman singing, stood next to a group on the ground with drums and didges, all smiles. She was in Welsh national dress and eyed me knowingly, her face calm and full of quiet strength, her song in Welsh too and so beautiful and so full of hope that I could catch the meaning with my heart. Her smile as she sang and the smile of the group sat next to her was full of some secret, a secret they could only convey with their hearts and this song. "Hearts of Oak" went the chorus, Hearts of Oak, over and over again and it was like I could hear Granny Ash and Snelsmore now, hear them with the wind in the trees, as though all trees were carried in this noise, like the wind knew no boundaries of time and no matter what the future held, our strength always lay in the truth of our hearts.

The British anti-road campaigns of the mid nineteen nineties eventually proved highly successful. Public opinion swung strongly away from further road building and a large part of the government's road schemes were subsequently scrapped. Though this owed as much to their dwindling budget as to any great rethink in policy, the climate was set whereby such a move was made possible.

But in the absence of any comprehensive transport policy, and in a decade that saw the privatisation of Britain's railways, the spectre of further road building never went away.

The amount of roads being built, widened or under serious consideration of being built now looks dangerously close to the Tories' infamous road building scheme of the previous decade.

While the cost of rail and bus travel continues to rise, motoring grows effectively cheaper due to a continued freeze on petrol and diesel taxation.

Despite promises to cut carbon emissions, the Labour government are planning for a 40% rise in traffic growth by 2025. Road transport currently accounts for 18% of the UK's total carbon dioxide emissions.

Newbury's traffic levels have risen by 50% since the opening of the road – traffic levels nationally have risen 5% over the same period.

For more information, see:

www.roadblock.org.uk